Marc Kendel

Emanations

Emanations

*In-depth analysis
of the Jewish holidays through the
prism of rabbinic perspective*

Ari D. Kahn

TARGUM/FELDHEIM

First published 2002
Copyright © 2002 by Ari D. Kahn
ISBN 1-56871-209-X

Published by:
TARGUM PRESS, INC.
22700 W. Eleven Mile Rd.
Southfield, MI 48034
E-mail: targum@netvision.net.il
Fax: 888-298-9992
www.targum.com

Distributed by:
FELDHEIM PUBLISHERS
202 Airport Executive Park
Nanuet, NY 10954
www.feldheim.com

Printed in Israel

This book has been dedicated

in honor of

S. Daniel Abraham

שאול דוב בן שמחה הכהן

on the occasion of his birthday.

May we merit many more years in his company,
learning from him the traits he embodies:
kavod and *chesed*, honor, respect, and kindness.

May Hashem grant him many more years to celebrate the
holidays in good health, *ad meah v'esrim*.

With much love,
His children and grandchildren

In loving memory
of
David Miller

Merna Miller and family

To Naomi,
Matityahu, Hillel, Yishai,
Yosef, and Elisheva

In loving memory of my grandparents

Bella Machla and Avraham Aba Kahn
Mindel and Nechemia Meir Ribnick

Whose spirit and inspiration are present and whose
presence is missed every Shabbat and *yom tov.*

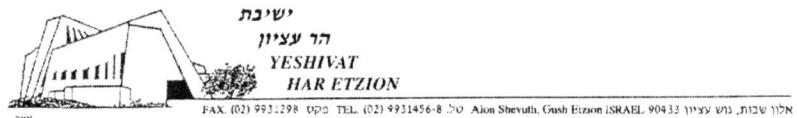

ישיבת
הר עציון
YESHIVAT
HAR ETZION

FAX. (02) 993.298 פקס   TEL. (02) 9931456-8 טל.   Alon Shevuth, Gush Etzion ISRAEL 90433 אלון שבות, גוש עציון

Rabbi Ari Kahn's *Emanations* focuses, structurally and thematically, upon a central aspect of Jewish experience: the annual cycle of months and special days — holy, festive, and other.

Drawing upon a variety of classical and modern sources, Rabbi Kahn elucidates his specific theme, on the one hand, and uses it as a vehicle for elaborating on more general topics, on the other.

The volume fuses information, interpretation, and insight. As such, it should be of interest and value to a wide range of readers, of varying backgrounds and emphases.

בברכת התורה והמצוה,

Aharon Lichtenstein

RABBI ZEV LEFF

Rabbi of Moshav Matityahu

Rosh Hayeshiva Yeshiva Gedola Matisyahu

d.n. modiin 71917 tel. 08-976-1138 fax. 08-976-5326

בס"ד

I have read a good portion of the manuscript *Emanations: In-depth Analysis of the Jewish Holidays through the Prism of Rabbinic Perspective* by Rabbi Ari Kahn. Rabbi Kahn presents novel insights into the themes and aspects of the various holidays. In developing his ideas he masterfully and ingeniously weaves together the various sources, finally presenting an intriguing tapestry that conveys fresh new perspectives on the topic.

I found Rabbi Kahn's essays interesting and exciting — gourmet food for thought and reflection. His presentation is scholarly and intellectual, supported by ample sources and enhanced with footnotes. The ideas presented, although at times not conventional explanations, are consistent with true Torah *hashkafah*.

I recommend this work to all those who wish to delve into the depths of the waters of Torah concerning our Holy Days and seasons — and with the aid of Rabbi Kahn discover a new world of ideas and insights.

May Hashem Yisbarach give Rabbi Kahn the ability to continue to provide works such as this and his previous work on the weekly *sedras*, to enhance and glorify the Torah by inspiring and illuminating those who thirst for its holy message.

Sincerely,

With Torah blessings,

Rabbi Zev Leff

Aish
HaTorah
AT THE WESTERN WALL

ב״סד

ירושלים ת״ו י״ט בטבת תשס״א

In our daily acknowledgment of the privilege of having been commanded to study Torah, we include the prayer והערב נא — May the words of Torah be made sweet to the taste — for ourselves — for our children — and for all of Israel. An emotional appreciation of the beauty of the Divine wisdom is an essential element both in facilitating an internalization of the truths of Torah as well as the fostering of an emotional relationship with the נותן התורה — Hashem Himself. (See Rambam, *Yesodei HaTorah* 2:2.)

In our sages' accounts of the most elevated moments of Torah study, we read of an intellectual dance from one area of Torah to another — to the point of a reenactment of the ecstasy experienced at the revelation at Sinai.

My friend and colleague Rabbi Ari Kahn is gifted with the natural ability to extract-combine-create Torah that provokes mind and heart to reach new levels of awe and appreciation of the beauty of the intertwining of the totality of Torah with itself.

May the author continue to inspire us all with his beautiful, creative works of Torah.

Yitzchak Berkovits

ב"ה ו' מנחם-אב תשס"ב

דברי ברכה

"שבת ויום טוב אינם צריכים אות" (עירובין צו ע"א) מסביר מרן הראי"ה
קוק זצ"ל בספרו חבש פאר (עמ' לח) משום שבהם צריך כל אדם מישראל להתעלות
מצד פנימיותו, עד שלא יהיה צריך סעד חיצוני לתומכו.

כי בבחינת הזמן, סדרה החכמה העליונה ענין הימים של חול ושל קודש
ובימי הקודש עצמם מדרגות, זו למעלה מזו כפי הנאות. והנה השבת מתנה
גדולה שנתן הקב"ה לישראל, להדרת שרצה שיהדר לו עם קודש, ואמנם גזרה
החכמה העליונה להוסיף לישראל קידוש וניתנה להם ימי קודש מלבד
השבת שבהם יקבלו ישראל מדרגות מדרגות הקידוש ויש ענינים פרטיים
מיוחדים לכל זמן מזמנים אלו, פי מדרגות קדושת הימים.

ושרש כולם הוא, מסביר הרמח"ל בדרך ה', סדר שסידרה החכמה העליונה,
שכל תיקון שנתקן ואור גדול שהאיר בזמן מן הזמנים, בשוב תקופת הזמן
ההוא, תחזרנה תולדות התיקון ההוא, ויאיר עלינו אור, מעין האור הראשון.
שהרי קדושת הזמן מתפשטת היא לכל אורך הזמן - "ברוך ה' רום יום" והולכים
קרני אורי הקודש ונמשכים בצורה מוסתרת, עד שהם באים לידי הבעה וגלוי
בזמנים המקודשים - בקדושת השבת שהיא תחילה למקראי קודש, בתור קדושה
מקררית המשפעת קדושה על העולם ועל ישראל, ובקדושת הימים הטובים, בתוך
מקבלי שפעת הקודש על ידי "ישראל דקדשינהו לזמנים".

אם היה בכוחנו להרגיש באותם הימים, את ההרגשה האדירה והנפלאה הזאת,
שהננו נמצאים אז בזמן שהוא שונה ונבדל מכל זמן, היינו מתרגשים ומתפעלים
ביותר לקיים בהם את המצוות עלינו, והיינו טועמים מנועם זיו קודשו כאותו
הנועם של העליונים שרפי קודש "מעין עולם הבא" - מעין הזמן של עולם הבא.

על כן, בואו ונחזיק טובה וברכה ליקר תפארת ורב פעלים לתורה ולהפצתה,
אציל הערוך רזך המחשבה, המשיב רבין מעורן הרב רבי ארי דוד קאהן
שליט"א על פעלו המבורך בחבור את ספרו היקר באנגלית על המועדים והזמנים
מלא יראת ד', כולו עשוי בטוב טעם ודעת, Emanations-Essays on Holidays עבור דברי השפה האנגלית מעשי ידי אומן
בספרו על פרשיות השבוע, שגליהם אמת לאמיתה של תורה הכל בשפה ברורה
ונעימה המשאירה את הקורא בהרגשה נכונה על התורה המועדים והזמנים - מתוך
אספקלריא של חכמינו זכרונם לברכה, השאובים מהתלמוד, המדרש ואף מן הזהר
הקדוש. לחזק את האמונה ואהבת השם יתברך מתוך תורת ארץ ישראל שעליה
נאמר "וזהב הארץ ההיא טוב מאוד" - (משל"ל כה, יא) אין תורה כתורת ארץ
ישראל - כתפרחי זהב במשכיות כסף, דבר דבור על אופניו.

הננו מברכים אותו מחזקים אותו ומעודדים אותו ולאמצו למען ימשיך
להגביר חילים לאורייתא יישר כחו וחילו לאורייתא, על פעליו המבורכים
הבאים להגדיל תורה ולהאדירה בישובנו גבעת זאב אשר בצפון יהודה יע"א
ובמקומות רבים אחרים בארץ ובחוץ לארץ, תוך עיסוק בזכוי הרבים ובקירוב
לבבות ישראל כולל אלה הדוברים עדינן בשפה אנגלית. אשרי חלקה של קהלתנו
גבעת זאב יע"א שזכתה שהמחבר יסתופף בצילה ועתה עמלתה ויגעתה רבעה רבה,
לערוך חיבור ערוך ומסודר על מועדי קודש בכדי לזכות את הרבים ולהביאם את
הרבים לידי הרגשת הרוממות של מועדי קודשי והזמנים המקודשים.

ויהי רצון שיהיו דבריו מקובלים ורצויים לפני אבינו שבשמים לעשות
נחת רוח ליוצרנו לעילא מן כל ברכתא. ה' ישלח עזרו מקודש, להמשיך לקרב
את ישראל בארץ ובתפוצות לאבהם שבשמים ולהמשיך בפעולותיו הכבירות לקרב
רחוקים וללמד קרובים תורה ויראת שמים.

בצפית ראיית הישועה השלימה על עמו ונחלתו.
הכו"ח לכבודה של תורה ולכבוד המחבר.

יוסף טולידאנו
הרב [חתימה] המקרמל
א

A Letter from the Author's Father

Rabbi Dr. Pinchas Kahn

The Jewish holidays, the *yamim tovim*, generate *simchah* — joy. They relate to agricultural events of harvest, to historical occurrences, as well as to celebrating God's role in history and the world. The experience of joy is manifested on an individual level, in the family, by the community, and in an encounter with God's presence.

Our son Rabbi Ari Kahn's teachings and writings, as seen in his previous book *Explorations,* on the weekly Torah readings, in his present book *Emanations*, on the Jewish holidays, as well as in numerous e-mail *shiurim* and lectures delivered orally, have demonstrated both creativity as well as authenticity. Especially impressive has been his analysis of Midrash and Kabbalistic writings and demonstrating their role in explaining text, narrative, and the rational world of halachah. Moreover, as an expression of a fundamental goal of weekly Torah readings as well as of the Jewish holidays, his writings have reached not only the overall community, but also a community in search of meaningful and authentic religious experience. And most of all, by his teachings of Torah, Reb Ari has enabled the reader to understand the words of God, thereby providing them with the opportunity to encounter His Presence.

As holidays generate joy on an individual and family basis as well, so has Reb Ari's work been a source of profound joy and pride for us, his parents. We are proud of him as we are proud of all his brothers and his sister, together with their respective spouses. This book honors the memory of his grandparents: Avraham Abba and Bella Kahn and Nechemia Meir and Mindel Ribnick, *a"h*. Though their lives were disrupted by World War I, the Great Depression, and World War II, they were nevertheless able to transmit their Jewish values and traditions under very difficult conditions. Their love and support for the emerging State of Israel was well known. Their involvement in their various communities included support for Jewish education as well as the neighborhood shul. Mention should also be made of Reb Ari's great-grandfather, HaRav Yair Chamudot *zt"l*, a Torah giant and patriarch of the family. He would have been so proud of all his great-grandchildren. For all of us, Reb Ari's book represents the true *yiddishe nachas* that all pray for.

It is our prayer that Reb Ari grow from strength to strength, that he, his wife Naomi, and their children be blessed by good health as well as finding God's presence in all their ways.

Pinchas and Rivka Kahn

Contents

Introduction xix

Rosh Chodesh

Rosh Chodesh
The Light of the Moon 3

Nissan

Shabbat HaGadol
The First Shabbat. 15

Pesach
The Wicked Son in the Pesach Haggadah 22
Pharaoh's Heart 31
The Firstborn 38
The Four Cups of Yosef. 49
The Matzah of Lot 60

Chol HaMoed Pesach
"These Bones Will Live!". 72

Iyar

The Omer
The Students of Rabbi Akiva 83

Lag BaOmer
Rabbi Shimon bar Yochai 97

The Twenty-eighth of Iyar
The Battle for Holiness 109

Sivan

Shavuot
The Word of God 119
Bikkurim: First Fruits 126
The Holiday of the Giving of the Torah 135

Av

Tishah B'Av
The Three Sins 147
To Climb the Mountain 156

Tu B'Av
Dancing in the Streets 168

Elul

Elul
"Return" 185
Pursuit of Righteousness 194

Tishrei

Rosh HaShanah
The Idea of Rosh HaShanah. 207
The *Akeidah*: Father and Son 212

The Ten Days of Repentance
The Three Books 222
Teshuvah from Love and Fear 235

Yom Kippur
The Inner Sanctum 249

Sukkot
A Universal Holiday? 259

Simchat Torah
"*Chazak*" 266

Kislev

Chanukah
"Bringing Down the *Shechinah*" 279
Catch the Bull by the Horn 288

Adar

Parashat Zachor
Amalek: A Question of Race? 301
Purim
The Heroism of Esther 308

Subject Index 317

Source Index 322

Introduction

Baruch shehecheyanu vekiyemanu vehigianu lazeman hazeh!

This book is the result of many years of research and teaching. Most of the essays were originally talks delivered in various Torah institutions, in Israel and around the world. There are, though, a few essays written specifically for this book. I hope and pray that the original ideas presented in this work are true, and may God protect me from error. To a large extent, this volume should be seen as a companion to my first book, *Explorations*; whereas that book followed the weekly portions, this one follows the holidays of the Jewish calendar.

The Jewish calendar is marked with days that are set aside, days that are different. These days are not simply holidays, they are — literally — holy days. In Judaism, holiness is not generic: each holiday possesses its own unique spirituality. In order to access the full holiness of the day, and thereby allow the days to elevate us and transform us, we must understand the unique aspects of each day. This is most likely the meaning of one of the most ancient "rabbinic *takanot*":

> "And Moshe declared to the children of Israel the festivals of God" (*Vayikra* 23:44). It is part of their observance that [the

section relating to] each one of them should be read in its season.

Our Rabbis taught: Moshe laid down a rule for the Israelites that they should enquire and give expositions concerning the subject of the day — the laws of Pesach on Pesach, the laws of Shavuot on Shavuot, and the laws of Sukkot on Sukkot.

(Megillah 32a)[1]

The Torah reading for each holiday, as well as the subject matter studied on that particular day, should reflect the specific holiday. This is what provides the spiritual compass that allows each Jew to fully appreciate the holiday and turn it into a holy day.

The purpose of these essays is to help elucidate the personality of our holy days, to attempt to identify the precious gift God has bestowed upon us with each unique celebration. If these essays help to elevate the reader's experience of the holidays, to bring more holiness into their lives, my efforts will have been well rewarded.

It is my hope that sensitive readers will recognize the enormous impact that the thought of Rav Yosef Dov Soloveitchik has had on this work. The Rav's ideas, which I heard either directly from the Rav or from my father, resonate in my mind and strongly impact the way I look at Torah in general, and *midrashim* in particular. His holistic approach of weaving together halachic and *hashkafic* material has been primary in my mind and, I believe, can be felt on every page.

Holidays and family are intertwined. Holidays have always been celebrated among the Jewish people in the extended-family setting, and it has been the holidays that have kept the Jewish people, and Jewish families, together. In that spirit, I would like once again to thank my family and friends, who have encouraged and helped me in so many ways. First and foremost, I thank my parents who taught me what Shabbat and *yom tov* are all about, both in terms of physical delicacies and spiritual nourishment. Our house was one

---

1   See Rambam, *Hilchot Tefillah* 13:8.

in which Shabbat was always felt, guests were always welcomed, and words of Torah always flowed at the table. Part of my motivation in publishing this book is to help those who may not have been privileged to celebrate the holidays as I was, who were not blessed with parents such as mine. May my mother and father, Rivka and Rav Pinchas Kahn, be blessed with many more productive years in health and happiness, and may they have *nachas* from all their children and grandchildren.

Our collective memories include the sounds, tastes, and textures of the holidays we celebrated in our youth, and it is at the holidays that we most miss those who are no longer with us. May the Torah written in this work serve as a source for the *ilui neshamot* of my grandparents, who are missed at every *yom tov*.

My sister, Rena, and her husband, Gershon Harris, have encouraged me from the first essay I had the audacity to write and send to others. Their continued love and encouragement are invaluable. My brother Rav Yair has been my sounding board for many of the ideas in this book; there are instances in which I don't know if the idea was his or mine, and I ask his forgiveness if I inadvertently neglected to cite him. I think he took as much pride in my first book as my parents did, and I am constantly aware of my good fortune in having a brother who combines sharp analytic skills and deep understanding. May he and his wife, Hadassah, continue to teach and inspire the larger community around them.

My brother Doni and his wife, Dina, and brothers- and sisters-in-law Josh and Helaine Linder, David and Cathy Linder, and Pini and Judith Balbin have all been great help, be it with a kind word, solving computer problems, or dealing with the complicated logistics involved in the distribution of this book. I thank them all for their friendship and love. The old adage says that one chooses friends and not relatives, but it is indeed wonderful to have relatives whom you would otherwise have chosen as friends.

I would like to thank my parents-in-law, Moshe and Bernice Linder, who have gently persuaded almost every person in Flatbush to read my first book. I wish them many years of health, and *nachas* from all their children and grandchildren.

I would also like to thank the many readers, both of my web *"shiur"* and *Explorations*; they have read, commented, and encouraged me to continue writing and publishing. I would also like to thank those who took the time to read this manuscript and give me the courage to publish it, especially *mori v'rabi* Rav Aharon Lichtenstein. Rav Zev Leff took time from his busy schedule to look through the manuscript and encouraged me with exaggerated praise, which was much appreciated. Rav Yitzchak Berkovits has been my friend and colleague for many years; his strong encouragement is one of the reasons this book was written.

Thanks also go once again to Rabbi Moshe Dombey, Chaya Baila Gavant, and D. Liff of Targum Press for producing, editing, and designing this book.

There are also a number of friends I would like to thank for their support: Alyssa Adler, Howie and Chaya Balter, Jerry Berlin, Howie and Susan Chusid, Ben Zion and Deena Fuchs, Barnet and Sarah Shona Goldberg, and Lenny and Gillian Solomon. I would especially like to thank Tammy Abraham, without whose support and encouragement this volume would never have come to fruition.

Again, as in the first book, it is my pleasure to thank my wife Naomi, who not only helped me with the writing and editing of this book, but who knows how to make Shabbat and *yom tov* in a way that merges the spiritual and physical. May the *zechut* of the Torah protect our children and may we merit celebrating the holidays with them and their children and our entire extended family in the rebuilt Beit HaMikdash in Yerushalayim.

Ari Kahn
Givat Ze'ev
Erev Shavuot 5762

Rosh Chodesh

Rosh Chodesh

The Light of the Moon

T oward the end of *Parashat Pinchas* we are told about the various offerings which will be brought in the Temple on the different holy days which mark the calendar.

> And God spoke to Moshe, saying: "Command the People of Israel, and say to them, 'My offering, the provision of My sacrifices made by fire, for a sweet savor to Me, shall you observe to offer Me in their due season.' "
>
> *(Bemidbar 28:1–2)*

The prescription of proper service of the Temple is set out for each day, beginning with daily service and proceeding with the Shabbat and festivals. On the various holidays a sin offering is included as part of the etiquette for the day.

> And in the beginnings of your months you shall offer.... And one goat kid for a sin offering to God shall be offered, besides the continual burnt offering and its drink offering.
>
> *(Ibid., 11, 15)*

> And on the fourteenth day of the first month is the Passover of God. And on the fifteenth day of this month is the feast; seven days shall unleavened bread be eaten.... And one goat for a sin offering, to atone for you.
>
> *(Ibid., 16–17, 22)*

Also on the day of the first fruits, when you bring a new meal offering to God, in your Feast of Weeks, you shall have a holy gathering; you shall do no labor.... And one goat kid to atone for you.

(Ibid., 26, 30)

And in the seventh month, on the first day of the month, you shall have an holy gathering; you shall do no labor; it is a day of blowing the horn for you.... And one goat kid for a sin offering, to atone for you.

(Ibid. 29:1, 5)

And on the tenth day of this seventh month you shall have a holy gathering; and you shall afflict your souls; you shall not do any work.... One goat kid for a sin offering, besides the sin offering of atonement.

(Ibid. 7, 11)

And on the fifteenth day of the seventh month you shall have a holy gathering; you shall do no labor, and you shall celebrate a festival for God for seven days.... And one goat kid for a sin offering....

(Ibid., 12, 16)

We find that each day requires a sin offering aside from the other offerings of the day. The choice of the goat as the vehicle to bring about forgiveness is significant. The Midrash draws a fascinating association which helps reveal the meaning of the goat.

"One goat kid for a sin offering" — this was to symbolize Yosef, in connection with whom it is written, "And they killed a goat" (*Bereishit* 37:31).

(Bemidbar Rabbah 14:5)[1]

The implication of this *midrash* is that each sin offering must

---

1   See *Rashi, Bemidbar* 7:22, and the comments of the Chizkuni to *Bemidbar* 28:15. The Rambam in *Moreh HaNevuchim* (3:46) is apparently quite enamored of this explanation: He cites this idea and advises us "not to take it lightly."

contain within it a measure of cleansing for the sin perpetrated against Yosef. The reference is to the goat in whose blood the brothers dipped the "coat of many colors." This coat was symbolic of the enmity of the brothers toward Yosef. This is the prototypical sin between man and his fellow man, our "model" of *sinat chinam* (groundless hatred). We may conclude, based on the usage of the goat in every instance, that this sin is constantly among us, and that more forgiveness and healing are in order.[1]

We may trace the origin of the problem between the brothers to Yosef's speech.[2] The Chafetz Chaim, based on this association, declares that *lashon hara* (gossip) and *sinat chinam* are identical — two sides of one coin.[3] According to the Sages, *lashon hara* is considered so severe that it is equal to the major sins in Judaism (*Arachin* 15b). Therefore, every holiday, when communal offerings where brought, the Jewish people were told to bring forth an offering which would heal the first breach in the community, the sale of Yosef.

This insight into the communal sin offering apparently breaks down when we read the command of the sin offering for the new month, which differs from all the other festive days. While on most days the Torah speaks of "And one goat kid for a sin offering to atone for you," on the new moon the form is changed, and instead the verse reads: "And one goat kid for a sin offering to God shall be offered." Here the verse speaks of a "sin offering to God." The language of the verse, however, is complex: The words read *l'chatat laHashem*, which could mean either a "sin offering to God" or a "sin offering for God." While man surely needs atonement for a host of offenses, past and present, what can the term possibly imply if, in fact, the sin offering is meant to brought "for God"?

The Talmud offers two interpretations of this verse and of the

---

1   The *Meshech Chochmah* (*Vayikra* 16:30) makes this observation and cites a *midrash* that says that the sin of the sale of Yosef remains unhealed and remains from generation to generation. The *Meshech Chochmah* cites *Midrash Mishlei siman* 1. I found this teaching in the *Yalkut Shimoni, Mishlei,* section 929.
2   See *Meshech Chochmah* on *Vayikra* 8:36
3   See the introduction to the book *Chafetz Chaim.*

shift in language from all the other sin offerings.

> What is Rabbi Yehudah's reason? Because the text says: "And one goat kid for a sin offering to God" — for a sin which is known only to God shall this goat atone. But this [superfluous word] we require for the deduction of Rabbi Shimon ben Lakish, for Rabbi Shimon ben Lakish said: "Why is the goat offered on the New Moon different in that [the phrase] 'to God' is used in connection with it? [Because] the Holy One, blessed be He, said, 'This goat shall be an atonement [for Me, as it were,] for making the moon smaller.' "
>
> *(Shevu'ot 9a)*

Rashi comments on the first interpretation offered in the Talmud that the purpose of the sin offering is to atone for the offenses committed by man unknowingly. All the sin offerings brought in conjunction with the *mussaf* (the special offering for a festival) were meant to atone for any inadvertent offense in the preparation of the offerings brought on that day. Here, Rashi explains, the words "for God" indicate that this offering is brought for offenses only God is aware of.

The second explanation is far more difficult. The Talmud insists that it is God who is in need of forgiveness! As stated above, the very suggestion that God requires forgiveness seems absurd, yet the Talmud insists that God atones for His abuse of the moon. This idea is expanded in a second passage:

> Rabbi Shimon ben Pazzi pointed out a contradiction [between passages]. The verse says: "And God made the two large lights" (*Bereishit* 1:16), and immediately after it says: "The large light...and the small light" (ibid.).
>
> The moon said to the Holy One, blessed be He, "Sovereign of the Universe! Is it possible for two kings to wear one crown?"
>
> He answered, "Go then and make yourself smaller."
>
> "Sovereign of the Universe," cried the moon, "because I

have suggested that which is proper must I then make myself smaller?"

He replied: "Go and you will rule by day and by night."

"But what is the value of this?" cried the moon. "Of what use is a lamp in broad daylight?"

He replied: "Go, Israel shall calculate the days and the years by you."

"But it is impossible," said the moon, "to do without the sun for the reckoning of the seasons, as it is written: 'And let them be for signs, and for seasons, and for days and years' (ibid., 14)."

"Go, the righteous shall be named after you, as we find, Yaakov the Small, Shmuel the Small, David the Small."

On seeing that it would not be consoled, the Holy One, blessed be He, said, "Bring an atonement for Me for making the moon smaller." This is what was meant by Rabbi Shimon ben Lakish when he declared, "Why is the goat offered on the New Moon different in that [the phrase] 'to God' is written concerning it? [Because] the Holy One, blessed be He, said, 'This goat shall be an atonement [for Me, as it were,] for making the moon smaller."

(Chullin 60b)[1]

The Talmud indeed concludes that God asks that an offering be brought for Him because of what happened to the moon.[2] According to Talmudic cosmology, there was a time when the moon and the sun enjoyed equal stature. This is understood by the verse:

And God made two great lights, the large light to rule the day, and the small light to rule the night; and He made the stars.

(Bereishit 1:16)

Because of the shift between the first part of the verse and the second, the Talmud concluded that at one time both the lights

---

1   Also see *Zohar, Bereishit, Hashmatot* (additional material) p. 252.
2   It is interesting that on Shabbat there is no sin offering. Shabbat is dependent solely on the sun; the moon is of no effect. See *Sha'arei Tzedek, Sha'ar Rishon.*

were of equal stature.[1] However, we must note that both of these lights are independent of the primordial lights, which are referred to on the first day of Creation:

> In the beginning the Lord created the heaven and the earth. And the earth was without form and void, and darkness was upon the face of the deep. And the spirit of the Lord hovered over the face of the waters. And the Lord said, "Let there be light"; and there was light. And the Lord saw the light, that it was good; and the Lord divided the light from the darkness. And the Lord called the light "day," and the darkness He called "night." And there was evening and there was morning, one day.
>
> *(Bereishit 1:1–5)*

The light that was created on the first day and which shone for the first three days is independent of the light of the sun or the moon, which do not make their appearance until the fourth day. This light which shone on the first day is not necessarily part of "creation." A careful reading of the verse in *Yeshayah* will provide insight:

> I am God, and there is no one else, there is no Lord beside Me. I girded you, though you have not known Me. That they may know from the rising of the sun, and from the west, that there is none beside Me. I am God, and there is no one else. I form the light and create darkness; I make peace and create evil; I, God, do all these things.
>
> *(Yeshayah 45:5–7)*

Light is described as "formed," while darkness is created. If light is formed, the implication is that it is formed from some type of metaphysical light; this light is refracted and shines at the moment of Creation. We have, then, this primordial light, in addition to the light of the first three days, as well as the light of the moon and sun in their original, equal status, and finally we have the light of the

---

1   It is unclear if the meaning is that each was an independent light, or that they were the same size even though the moon drew from the light of the sun as its source of light. See *Avodat HaKodesh* 4:8.

sun and the diminished moon. Each one of these stages provides its own mystery and meaning. Despite the obscurity of the ideas, this much we can say: the unfolding of Creation was not sudden. We can discern a process. As a finite world emerges from an infinite Creator, we witness a shift in light.

The moon may be seen as an example of a type of light which exists in darkness. Prior to Creation, all that existed was light, the radiant light of God. This is not the light of the sun or of other celestial bodies. It is the light of pure good. At the point of Creation, when God refracted this metaphysical light, something new was created — darkness. This is the result when God withdrew infinity in order to create the finite. This is the meaning of the verse that God says: "I form the light and create darkness." Something new now exists — darkness.

The verse continues, "I make peace and create evil." Evil is created. The natural result of God withdrawing from infinity in order to create coexistence is the possibility of evil. Now, in this new world there will be a possibility of pain and suffering. For this God asks man to bring a sin offering. On every month when the moon completes its cycle, we are reminded that the world goes through a similar cycle. There are times when God is more manifest, and there are times that God's presence is difficult to discern.[1] For this we are asked by God to bring a sin offering.[2]

1 The Vilna Gaon explained this idea by use of a verse in *Shir HaShirim*: "My beloved is like a gazelle or a young hart. Behold, he stands behind our wall, gazing in at the windows, looking through the lattice" (*Shir HaShirim* 2:9). There are times that we feel God looking through the window gazing at us, and on the other hand there are times which we barely feel God peeking through the cracks.

2 See *Zohar, Bereishit* 20b, where the sun and moon are associated with different Names of God: "Similarly, the two lights ascended together with the same dignity. The moon, however, was not at ease with the sun, and in fact each felt mortified by the other. The moon said, ' "Where do you pasture?" ' (*Shir HaShirim* 1:7). The sun said, ' "Where do you make your flock rest at noon?" (ibid.). How can a little candle shine at midday?' God thereupon said to her [the moon], 'Go and diminish yourself.' She felt humiliated and said, 'Why should I be as one that veils herself?' (ibid.). God then said, 'Go your way forth in the footsteps of the flock.' Thereupon she diminished herself so as to be head of the lower ranks. From that time she has had no light of her own, but derives her light from the sun.... The 'great light'

There is another level to understand the diminishment of the moon. When God attempted to console the moon for its new role and lost grandeur, He said, "Go, Israel shall calculate the days and the years by you." The moon is associated with the children of Israel. Just as the fortunes of Israel at times wane, there will come a time when Israel will shine bright.

The continuation of the dialogue elucidates this point: "Go, the righteous shall be named after you, as we find, Yaakov the Small, Shmuel the Small, David the Small." There are certain individuals in Israel who are known as "small" despite the capability of shining bright. Yaakov, the individual most associated with the collective entity known as the "Community of Israel"; Shmuel, the anointer of kings; and finally King David.

Israel in general is synonymous with the moon, and hence the moon is used by the Jews to anoint the seasons and months. But David more than any other individual is associated with the moon:

> Rabbi Chiya once saw the [old] moon in the heavens on the morning of the twenty-ninth day. He took a clod of earth and threw it at it, saying, "Tonight we want to sanctify you, and you are still here! Go and hide yourself."
>
> Rabbi thereupon said to Rabbi Chiya, "Go to Ein Tav and sanctify the month, and send me the watchword, 'David, King of Israel, is alive and in existence.' "
>
> *(Rosh HaShanah 25a)*

When intrigue did not allow a clear public declaration of the new moon, the phrase "David, King of Israel, is alive and in existence" was utilized, and all Jews understood the message. Just as the kingship of the Jews had unfortunately ebbed and fallen into disuse, the day would come when the grandeur of the Jews would return. If the world had become dark through exile of the *Shechinah*, we could still with confidence believe that the time would yet arrive when God would be fully manifest on this earth.

---

corresponds to Tetragrammaton, and the 'lesser light' to *Elokim*, which is the last of the degrees and the close of the Thought."

The *Zohar* expands on this idea:

"Create for me a pure heart, O Lord, and renew a steadfast spirit within me" (*Tehillim* 51:12): The term "a clean heart" he said, finds its parallel in the passage: "Give Your servant therefore an understanding heart" (*Melachim* I 3:9), and also in: "But he who is of merry heart has a continual feast" (*Mishlei* 15:15). This is assuredly the clean heart which David asked for. "And renew a steadfast spirit within me" indicates the spirit spoken of in the passage: "And the spirit of God hovered over the face of the waters," this being, as has been pointed out, the spirit of the Messiah. The same is alluded to in the promise: "And a new spirit will I put within you" (*Yechezkel* 36:26). David thus prayed for that steadfast spirit, since on the sinister side there is the unclean spirit called the spirit of perverseness that leads people astray, that unclean spirit referred to in the statement: "God has mingled within her a spirit of perverseness" (*Yeshayah* 19:14). David thus prayed: "And renew within me a spirit of steadfastness." The term "renew" also alludes to the renewal of the moon, a period which contains the assurance that David, King of Israel, is alive and in existence.

(Zohar, Bereishit 192b)

Creation of the world included a recoiling on God's part. Radiant Divine light that could fill the world is hidden. It is the mission and destiny of the Jewish people to bring back that light and have it fill the world with incredible luster and beauty. The individual who will spearhead this movement will be a descendant of David.

The passage cited a verse taken from the very beginning of Creation:

In the beginning the Lord created the heaven and the earth. And the earth was without form and void, and darkness was upon the face of the deep. And the spirit of the Lord hovered over the face of the waters.

"And the spirit of God hovered over the face of the waters," this being, as has been pointed out, the spirit of the Messiah.

Despite the cosmic metaphysical trauma of Creation, there was from the beginning an apparatus available to bring more light into the world: the spirit of the Messiah — the son of David.

Judaism knows of two messiahs, the son of David and the son of Yosef.[1] As we saw at the outset, the sin offering is associated with Yosef; it signifies the rejection of Yosef by the brothers. The complaint of the moon was that it is inappropriate for two kings to wear one crown. The brothers did not appreciate Yosef. They thought that he was trying to usurp the crown of Yehudah — the crown destined for David. They too thought that one crown can only adorn one king. They felt that greatness and grandeur was the realm of David; it was not meant for Yosef.

Ironically, in the period of the First Temple, the time came when the tribe of Yosef usurped the kingdom of Yehudah. From those days onward we have been saying, "David, King of Israel, is alive and in existence." We need to be able to usher in the age when both messiahs may shine bright. The key is the eradication of the hatred that caused the rejection of Yosef. When that is accomplished, both lights will be able to shine bright, and no sin offering will be necessary.

At the apex of history, a son of Yosef which usher in an age when a son of David will enter the world. They will teach us to bring more primordial light down. At that point pain and suffering will disappear, eclipsed forever. More and more light will shine. In that day the moon will return to its original size as the light of God caresses and fills the world. The people of Israel will be held in great esteem as they complete their mission. David will then be king. On that day we will no longer need to bring a "sin offering" for God. On that day the sun and the moon will shine bright, just as the people of Israel will radiate in the light of God and the light of a world perfected.

---

1   *Sukkah* 52.

Nissan

Shabbat HaGadol

The First Shabbat

The Shabbat prior to Pesach is called Shabbat HaGadol. The source of the term is unclear;[1] the term itself is not found in the Tanach or Talmudic literature.[2] In the Middle Ages, a number of authorities occupied themselves with explaining the origin of the term.

One approach sees the term as originating with the special haftarah, specifically the verse which refers to a day in the future which will be *gadol*, great:[3]

> Behold, I will send you Eliyahu the Prophet before the coming of the great and awesome day of God.
>
> *(Malachi 3:23)*

The prophet speaks of the day of redemption in the future. Pesach, which represents the day of redemption of antiquity, serves as the archetype of the future redemption.[4] Therefore, the Talmud teaches:

---

1 The *Machzor Vitri* (section 259) writes: "The people are accustomed to call the Shabbat pior to Pesach 'Shabbat HaGadol,' though they don't know why."
2 The term may be found in the *Zohar, Bereishit* 47b, II 204a, and *Tikunei Zohar* 40b.
3 Cited in the name of Rav Shlomo Luria, known as the Maharshal. See *Mateh Moshe*, section 542; Rav Ovadyah Yosef, *Yabia Omer* 4:39. Also see the Maharal in *Gevrurot Hashem*, ch. 39, and *Tiferet Yisrael*, ch. 44.
4 Rabbi Yosef Dov Soloveitchik pointed out that the term *geulah* is only used to describe two occurrences: the redemption from Egypt and the Messianic Age. Other times of salvation are called *purkan*, as in references to Chanukah and Purim.

In Nissan the world was created...the bondage of our ancestors ceased in Egypt; and in Nissan they will be redeemed in time to come.

(Rosh HaShanah 11a)

The tradition, which accords Eliyahu a primary role in the Messianic Age, calls upon us to read the portion of the prophet which alludes to that "great" day.

Other commentaries look back to the past for an explanation for the term. The Talmud teaches that the day the Jews left Egypt, the fifteenth of the month of Nissan, was a Thursday, and the tenth of the month was the previous Shabbat:

As to the Nissan in which the Israelites departed from Egypt, on the fourteenth they slaughtered their Passover sacrifices, on the fifteenth they went forth, and in the evening [of the fifteenth] the firstborn were smitten...and that day was a Thursday.

(Shabbat 87b)

The significance of the tenth of Nissan is mentioned in the Torah:

[God said to Moshe and Aharon:] "Speak to all the congregation of Israel, saying, 'In the tenth day of this month they shall take every man a lamb, according to the house of their fathers, a lamb for a house.' "

(Shemot 12:3)

Tosafot (commenting on *Shabbat* 87b) points out that by taking the lamb, the Jews piqued the interest, and the ire, of the firstborn of Egypt. They pleaded with Pharaoh to release the Jews. When he refused, the firstborn rebelled and attacked their own parents.[1]

---

1   See *Ancient Tanchuma Bo* 18 and *Midrash Tehillim* 136:6, commenting on the verse "To Him who struck Egypt with their firstborn" (*Tehillim* 136:10): "When God sent the plague of the firstborn...all the firstborn went to speak to their fathers and said, 'Everything which Moshe has said has come true. Don't you want us to live? Let us get the Hebrews out of our homes; otherwise we are dead.' They answered, 'Even if all of Egypt dies, they are not leaving.' All the firstborn gathered in front of Pharaoh

Therefore the day is considered great, due to the miracle of God which was manifest and the subsequent unraveling of Egyptian society. Furthermore, by slaughtering the object of Egyptians worship, the Jews liberated themselves from the chains of spiritual slavery.

"They shall take...a lamb" — Another interpretation: It is written: "Ashamed shall be all who serve graven images" (*Tehillim* 97:7). When the Holy One, blessed be He, told Moshe to slay the paschal lamb, Moshe answered, "Lord of the Universe! How can I possibly do this thing? Do You not know that the lamb is the Egyptian god?" As it says: "If we sacrifice the abomination of the Egyptians before their eyes, will they not stone us?" (*Shemot* 8:22).

God replied: "As you live, Israel will not depart from here before they slaughter the Egyptian gods before their very eyes, that I may teach them that their gods are really nothing at all."

This is what He actually did; for on that night He slew the Egyptian firstborn and on that night the Israelites slaughtered their paschal lamb and ate it. When the Egyptians beheld their firstborn slain and their gods slaughtered, they could do nothing; as it says: "While the Egyptians were burying those that the Lord had smitten among them, even all their firstborn; upon their gods also the Lord executed judgment" (*Bemidbar* 33:4).

(Shemot Rabbah 16:3)

God then said to Moshe: "As long as Israel worship Egyptian gods, they will not be redeemed; go and tell them to abandon their evil ways and to reject idolatry." This is what is meant by "Draw out and take for yourselves lambs" (*Shemot* 12:21). That is to say: Draw away your hands from idolatry and take lambs

and screamed, 'Please remove this nation. Because of them evil will befall us and you.' Pharaoh said to his servants, 'Remove them and break their knees.' What did they do? Each took a sword and killed his father. Thus, it says: 'To Him who struck Egypt with their firstborn.' "

See my essay on Pesach, "The Firstborn."

for yourselves, thereby slaying the gods of Egypt and preparing the Passover [sacrifice]; only through this will the Lord pass over you. This is the meaning of "In sitting still and rest shall you be saved" (*Yeshayah* 30:15).

(Shemot Rabbah 16:2)

The taking of the lambs was significant on another level as well. The Jews were now occupied with performance of a Divine decree; aside from the rejection of the Egyptian gods they were now actively fulfilling God's command.

All these explanations, though, seem to point to the significance of the tenth of Nissan,[1] rather than to the Shabbat which precedes Pesach.[2] While that tenth of the month in Egypt happened to fall on Shabbat, its significance has apparently no intrinsic connection with Shabbat. Our conclusion, based on the sources we have seen thus far, is that we should celebrate the tenth of Nissan as well as the fifteenth. But Shabbat HaGadol remains a mystery.[3]

In order to understand the idea we must first explore the relationship between Shabbat and the other holidays. Shabbat and the Jewish holidays should be seen as different orbits. Shabbat is a commemoration to Creation, while the holidays have a historical impetus. Moreover, Shabbat exists in a system established with, and as a result of, Creation. Every seventh day is Shabbat, independent of any other calendric input. The Divine precept which introduced

1   This question has been posed by many. See Taz, Magen Avraham, and other commentaries to section 430 of *Orach Chaim*.
2   There is some debate as to whether the special haftarah should be read on the Shabbat immediately preceding Pesach in the event that *erev Pesach* is Shabbat or if it should be pushed to the previous Shabbat.
3   Some have a custom of reading the Haggadah on Shabbat HaGadol. This is mentioned in the customs of the Maharil (*Hilchot Erev Pesach*, section 10), and was institutionalized by the Rama (*Orach Chaim* 430:1). The Vilna Gaon (*Biur HaGra* 430) looked askance at this custom, for the *Mechilta* and the Haggadah itself suggest that perhaps the commandment of telling the tale of the Exodus should be performed on the first of the month. However, this suggestion is turned down because the verse stresses, "And you shall tell your son *on that day*, saying, 'This is done because of that which the Lord did to me when I came forth from Egypt' " (*Shemot* 13:8). On that day you shall tell your son — and not on the Shabbat preceding Pesach.

the Passover holiday began with a command to keep time, to anoint time.

> And God spoke to Moshe and Aharon in the land of Egypt, saying: "This month shall be to you the beginning of months; it shall be the first month of the year to you. Speak to all the congregation of Israel, saying, 'In the tenth day of this month they shall take every man a lamb, according to the house of their fathers, a lamb for a house.' "
>
> *(Shemot 12:1–3)*

It is the responsibility of the Israelites to sanctify time. The court decides that the new month has arrived; then, and only then, are the holidays set up. It can be said that Shabbat comes from above, while the holidays come from below.[1] The Shabbat was holy due to God's creation and rest:

> For in six days God made the heavens and the earth, the sea, and all that is in them, and He rested the seventh day. Therefore God blessed the Shabbat day and made it holy.
>
> *(Shemot 20:11)*

Man dictates the calendar and the holidays:

> When the ministering angels assemble before God and ask, "When is Rosh HaShanah and when is Yom Kippur?" God says to them, "Why do you ask Me? You and I, let us all go to the Court on earth [and inquire of them]."
>
> *(Devarim Rabbah 2:14)*

While Shabbat existed from the time of Creation, only God was bound by this concept; Shabbat did not seem to have much to do with man. The description cited above of Shabbat being the result of Creation is absent the second time the Ten Commandments are written in the Torah. There, the verse illuminates a different aspect of Shabbat:

> And remember that you were a servant in the land of Egypt,

---

1   Rav Tzadok HaKohein from Lublin, *Pri Tzadik, Shabbat HaGadol* 3.

and that God, your Lord, brought you out from there with a mighty hand and with an outstretched arm. Therefore, God, your Lord, commanded you to keep the Shabbat day.

(Devarim 5:15)

Here we find a historical component to Shabbat. Our duty to observe Shabbat is not due exclusively to the theological concept of Creation and God's rest. Rather, the historical events of our slavery and redemption are the focus.

The Sefat Emet explains that the term *Shabbat HaGadol* results from the Shabbat taking on new significance. Only with the Jews' redemption from Egypt did Shabbat acquire the historical identity which intertwined with the theology. The Sefat Emet explains that Shabbat had now become "greater": Now the second aspect of Shabbat, articulated in the repetition of the Ten Commandments, would be realized.[1]

This Shabbat in Egypt was different from all other previous Shabbatot. Now man joined God in His holy day. Ironically, the mode of observance was not resting in the classic sense. Man was bidden to take his lamb, in what we have already noted was a strong polemical statement hurled at the polytheistic, lamb-worshiping Egyptians. The Sefat Emet states[2] that by taking the lamb the Jews observed Shabbat in Egypt. This was their first Shabbat as a people, a moment of passage in the national sense: They had reached the age of majority, became adults (*"gedolim"*), with responsibilities. This was Shabbat "HaGadol."[3]

The most basic teaching of Shabbat is the acknowledgement that God created the world in six days. By taking the lamb the Jews rejected idolatry and accepted God. This was not merely an action which took place on the tenth of Nissan. This was a watershed of Jewish history. Now the Jews joined God in a Shabbat.

The Talmud teaches that one who desecrates Shabbat is guilty of

---

1   *Sefat Emet, Shabbat HaGadol* 5637.
2   *Sefat Emet, Shabbat HaGadol* 5646.
3   *Sefat Emet, Shabbat HaGadol* 5674.

idolatry, for he has rejected the works of God. Now we see that those who rejected idolatry were viewed as "Shabbat observers." Moreover, in taking the lamb, they kept their only Shabbat commandment. This "perfect track record" made it a truly great Shabbat.[1]

Our Sages teach us that if all of Israel fully observe just two Shabbatot we will merit the coming of the Messiah:

> If Israel were to keep two Shabbatot according to its laws, they would be redeemed immediately.
>
> *(Shabbat 118b)*[2]

Interestingly, according to the mainstream Jewish approach the world was created in Nissan, which means that the Shabbat which takes place around the tenth of the month was the second Shabbat in the history of the world. Had those two Shabbatot been kept properly, the world would have been redeemed.

In the *Sifrei HaPardes*, Rav Yechiel Epstein writes that the two Shabbatot which must be observed are Shabbat HaGadol and Shabbat Shuvah. Each of these Shabbatot have a special power to them: One falls between Rosh HaShanah and Yom Kippur, and it is a Shabbat which teaches man how to return to God. The other Shabbat is the first Shabbat observed in Egypt. It is a Shabbat which contains within it the secret of redemption. If man could master these two Shabbatot, the Messiah would quickly arrive.

---

1 See *Chullin* 5a and the comments of Rashi there.
2 See *Explorations, Parashat Vayakhel*.

Pesach

The Wicked Son in the Pesach Haggadah

The story of the four sons, popularized by the Pesach Haggadah, has engaged centuries of readers. The questions of the
four sons may be found in various sources and varying
forms. The Haggadah version reads:

> The Torah refers to four sons, one wise, one wicked, one sim-
> ple, and one who does not know to ask.
>
> [The] wise [son], what does he say? "What are the testa-
> ments, the laws, and the judgments which God, our Lord,
> commanded you?" And you shall tell him of the laws of
> Pesach....
>
> [The] wicked [son], what does he say? "What is this service
> to you [or, of yours]?" To you and not to himself. And because
> he separated himself from the community, [he] rejects that
> which is essential [i.e., is guilty of heresy]. And you will blunt
> his teeth and say to him, "Because of this [i.e., in return for my
> offering the Pesach sacrifice] God acted for me [or, in my be-
> half] in my leaving Egypt." For you and not for him [the
> wicked son]; had he been there, he would not have been re-
> deemed.

[The] simple [son], what does he say? "What is this?" And you shall say to him, "With a strong hand did God take us out of Egypt from the house of bondage."

And for the son who knows not to ask, you shall open for him [i.e., prompt him], as it is said: "And you shall tell your son on that day, saying, 'Because of this God acted for me in taking me out of Egypt.' "

The questions posed by each of the first three sons are actually biblical verses which in the original are not associated with one another. The *midrash* related in the Haggadah brings these verses together and fashions "answers" out of other verses.

The Haggadah's sources for this passage are the *Yerushalmi* and the *Mechiltot* of Rabbi Yishmael and Rabbi Shimon bar Yochai (Rashbi). In the latter two sources, the *midrash* actually exists in two forms. It appears at one point in the form familiar to us from the Haggadah. At another point, only the wicked son is mentioned; no siblings are mentioned, nor are any other biblical verses cited. It is unclear, however, which of these two sources is the earlier one — which version of the four sons *midrash* came first.

In the more familiar version, the reader is presented with a wise son whose question is respected and even encouraged, and then a wicked son whose "teeth are blunted" because of the question he poses. Yet what distinguishes these two questions from one another? The careful reader will note that the wicked son, accused of separating himself from the community, refers to the People of Israel in the collective other: "to you" and not "to us" or even "to me." However, the wise son uses almost identical language in asking about the laws and testaments "which God, our Lord, commanded *you.*" Why is one son condemned while the other is praised?

The verse from *Devarim* attributed to the wise son seems to question all law and ritual as such: In its original context, the question relates to the relationship between God's rule over Israel and all of Mosaic law. Yet the verse attributed to the wicked son is far more circumscribed, relating, as it does, only to the isolated ritual of the Pesach sacrifice. The wise son uses the phrase "God, our Lord," and this alone may suffice to distinguish between the wise and wicked sons. But the distinction would have been sharper had the wise son said, "God, our Lord, commanded *us*."

Indeed, other versions of the *midrash* have attempted to alleviate the problem posed by the wise son's reference to "you" rather than "us." The *Yerushalmi*, *Mechilta*, and the Haggadah of the Rambam simply change the biblical verse attributed to the wise son to a more palatable form: "What are the testaments, the laws, and the judgments which God, our Lord, commanded us?"[1] In this case, the wise son is not citing the verse, he is paraphrasing it.[2]

Whether motivated by exegetical necessity or literary cohesiveness, the alteration of the biblical text placed in the mouth of the wise son is less important than the question which remains unanswered: What is it about the "wicked son" which so infuriates our Sages and the compilers of the Haggadah? The answer must lie deeper than the language used in the questions of the sons; otherwise, the "wise son" would either have been condemned as well, or the text of his question would have been uniformly altered. The answer must lie in the point of view each son represents, for in each case, the essence of each son's question, surprisingly enough, is overlooked.

The Haggadah responds not to the content of the questions but to the point of view from which they are posed. Our Sages, in either preserving or elaborating on this *midrash* and including it in the Haggadah, hoped to convey a very specific message. The four sons represent points of view or ideologies which are more meaningful than simply the terminology in which their ideas are couched.

This is clearly seen in the case of the wicked son. The verse from

---

1   See the comments of Rav Dovid Zvi Hoffman to *Devarim,* where the change from "you" to "us" is explained exegetically. Also see the discussion by Rav Menachem Kasher in *Haggadah Sheleimah.*

2   It is difficult to establish the authoritative version of these texts — see the discussion in *HaYerushalmi KiPhshuto* by Saul Liebermann, p. 520.

Shemot quoted by the wicked son is not, in its biblical context, seen as a negative query:

"And it shall come to pass, when your children shall say to you, 'What does this service mean to you?' you shall say, 'It is the sacrifice of God's Passover, who passed over the houses of the People of Israel in Egypt, when He struck the Egyptians and saved our houses.' " And the people bowed their heads and worshiped.

(Shemot 12:26–27)

The answer offered the child in *Shemot* is seen as a wonderful, educational response, with no hint of negativity. What made our Sages change the answer offered in the Torah and paint the questioner in the Haggadah as wicked? Why would our Sages overlook the answer to this same question offered in *Shemot* and replace it with an answer more appropriate for one so wicked? Clearly, it is not the words of the *rasha* which are problematic, rather the tone of voice which the Sages hear. The question, in and of itself, is one which would normally be encouraged; indeed, it is the goal of the parent at the seder to encourage the child to ask just such questions. The Sages, nonetheless, heard something insidious in this formulation, which led them to define the questioner as a "wicked son."

We may go so far as to say that the Sages had a specific typology of evil in mind when they formulated this *midrash*, someone who would have cited verses but would have twisted them to serve his own purpose.

We saw that it was the tone of voice of the *rasha* which represented his heresy. The biblical verse reads: "What is this service to you?" The *Mechilta's* response indicates the tone of the question:

רשע מה הוא אומר מה העבודה הזאת לכם. לכם ולא לו. ולפי שהוציא
את עצמו מן הכלל וכפר בעיקר אף אתה הקהה את שיניו ואמור לו בעבור
זה עשה ה׳ לי בצאתי ממצרים (שמות י״ג ח׳). לי ולא לך אלו היית שם לא
היית נגאל.

(מכילתא דרבי ישמעאל בא, מסי דפסחא בא, פרשה י״ח ד״ה ״והיה כי״)

"To you" and not to himself. And because he separated himself from the community and he rejects that which is essential [i.e., is guilty of heresy]....

Emphasis was clearly placed on the word *you*. The tone of voice in the *Mechilta* is quite different from the tone used by the *rasha* in the *Yerushalmi*, where the wicked son asks:

What is this service to you [or, of yours]? What is this toil with which we are burdened each and every year?

(Pesachim 10:4)

The *Yerushalmi* emphasizes the word *service*. This wicked son clearly has some problem with the content of Jewish ritual, whereas the wicked son presented in the *Mechilta* seems very different. In fact, the subtle difference in the answers to each version of the question are indicative of the different ways each question was perceived. The *Yerushalmi* addresses the content of the wicked son's question:

Because of this, because of my offering the Pesach sacrifice, God acted for me. For me, and not for that man; had that man been in Egypt he would not have been worthy of redemption from there for eternity.

(Ibid.)

In this case, our Sages impart some of the significance of the ritual which the wicked son questions. The wicked son of the *Yerushalmi* is condemned for questioning the efficacy or relevance of Jewish ritual, whereas the *Mechilta*'s wicked son is condemned for separating himself from the community. We may say, then, that the two sources represent two traditions; they portray two different wicked sons.

Interestingly, the *Mechilta* offers this teaching anonymously, while the *Yerushalmi* presents this teaching in the name of Rav Chiya. The version in the *Mechilta* is certainly the original source, as Rav Chiya in the *Yerushalmi* makes reference to it.

תני ר׳ חייה כנגד ארבעה בנים דיברה תורה בן חכם בן רשע בן טיפש בן
שאינו יודע לשאל... בן רשע מהו אומר מה העבודה הזאת לכם מה הטורח
הזה שאתם מטריחין עלינו בכל שנה ושנה (בכיי״ל שעה ושעה) מכיון
שהוציא את עצמו מן הכלל אף אתה אמור לו בעבור זה עשה ה׳ לי. לי
עשה לאותו האיש לא עשה אילו היה אותו האיש במצרים לא היה ראוי
להיגאל משם לעולם.

(תלמוד ירושלמי מסכת פסחים פרק י׳ דף ל״ז עמוד ד / ה״ד)

"What is this service to you [or, of yours]? What is this toil
with which we are burdened each and every year?"[1] Since he
separated himself from the community, you say to him....

Rav Chiya clearly utilizes the teaching in the *Mechilta*, as can be
seen from his second sentence, "Since he separated himself from
the community," a statement which does not relate to the efficacy
of "service" and is a clear reflection of the *Mechilta*'s understanding
of the wicked son's crime of separation. Thus, Rav Chiya created a
new teaching which compounded the rebellion of the *rasha*: Not
only is he guilty of separating himself from the community, but he
also questions the necessity of the paschal service.

The Sages who formulated the *Mechilta* had consciously created
their own teaching in a similar manner. They rejected the biblical
response to the son and insisted that such a question, such a questioner, is wicked, apparently reacting to the philosophical trends
which must have been current during the formation of the Midrash
and served as the model for this dialogue. There must have been
dissidents on the fringe of the Jewish community who articulated
their ideology in this manner.

We may attempt to identify each of these wicked sons histori-
cally with early Judeo-Christian sects who deviated from the Jewish
mainstream at the time that our sources were developed. Scholars
have traced the theological development of various distinct
streams of thought which later branched off from Judaism completely. Two of the major trends of thought espoused by these

---

1   See Lieden manuscript, which reads "each and every hour."

groups are voiced precisely by the wicked sons in each of our sources: One Judeo-Christian sect considered itself completely "Jewish," but would not take sides politically in the struggle against Rome. To this sect, our Sages may very well have said:

> "To you" and not to himself. And because he separated himself from the community and he rejects that which is essential [i.e., is guilty of heresy]....

The Sages condemn this political neutrality as incompatible with Jewish identity. One who separates himself from Jewish destiny also cuts himself off from Jewish history. He cannot remain in the religious community if he takes no part in the historical community and does not feel the historical continuity which begins with the Exodus and culminates in the final Messianic redemption. Such a Jew, the Sages of the *Mechilta* intimate, would not have been redeemed from Egypt; such a Jew would possibly have expressed sympathy for Egypt. He may even have refused to take part in the Exodus.

According to historians there were two occasions when the Judaic Christians separated themselves from the community. One was in the battle against Rome in 68 C.E., which culminated in the destruction of the Temple. The second occasion was during the Bar Kochva rebellion some sixty years later. We can clearly see why the Judaic Christians failed to rally around Bar Kochva, a man labeled "the King Messiah" by no less of an authority than the great Rabbi Akiva. The Christians felt that they already had their Messiah and had nothing at stake in this parochial battle between the Jews and Rome.[1] At just the time of these events, the *Mechilta* was formulated. It then comes as no surprise that the rifts in the Jewish community are reflected in the Midrash.

The Sages who later compiled the Haggadah created their own unique teaching by dropping off one letter which appears in the

---

1　See Gedalyahu Alon, *The Jews in Their Land in the Talmudic Age*, p. 295, note 28, and pp. 305–306.

Mechilta. The *Mechilta* version has an extra letter (in the Hebrew text; in the English it becomes an entire word) as compared to the version in the Haggadah. The Haggadah equates the wicked son's heresy with his separation from the community:

> "To you" and not to himself. And because he separated himself from the community, he rejects that which is essential [i.e., is guilty of heresy].

In the *Mechilta* the word *and* (in Hebrew, the letter *vav*) is added: he separates himself, in addition to already being guilty of heresy! First, this son accepted the Christian belief. Now, he separates himself from the community:

רשע מה הוא אומר מה העבודה הזאת לכם. לכם ולא לו. ולפי שהוציא את עצמו מן הכלל וכפר בעיקר אף אתה הקהה את שיניו ואמור לו בעבור זה עשה ה׳ לי בצאתי ממצרים (שמות י״ג ח׳). לי ולא לך אלו היית שם לא היית נגאל.
(מכילתא דרבי ישמעאל בא, מס׳ דפסחא בא, פרשה י״ח ד״ה "והיה כי")

> "To you" and not to himself. And because he separated himself from the community *and* he rejects that which is essential [i.e., is guilty of heresy]....

The Haggadah, in omitting the word *and*, subtly changes the message brought across by Rav Chiya in the *Yerushalmi*. The wicked son is now guilty solely of separating himself from the community; the issues of Christian belief are no longer the current problems which the Sages sought to battle.

The wicked son of the *Yerushalmi* has other historical parallels in Judeo-Christian theology. We know of the early Christians' objection to the entire practice of sacrifice and of the particular significance they credited to the Pesach sacrifice. It is not difficult for us to associate the Christian concept of the obsolescence of sacrifice after the Crucifixion with the point of view of the wicked son in the

Yerushalmi. In stressing the word *service*, he asks specifically why the sacrifice must continue to be offered year after year, implying that its utility is outdated. The new symbol of redemption, the "ultimate paschal lamb," has made continued sacrifice unnecessary according to this view. It is to this specific claim that the Sages in the *Yerushalmi* respond:

> God acted for me; for me and not for that man. Had that man been in Egypt he would not have been worthy of redemption from there for eternity.

"That man," *oto ha'ish,*[1] the Christian answer to paschal sacrifice, was not himself worthy of redemption; it would therefore be absurd to believe that his life or his death could redeem others. This is the theological answer to Judeo-Christian theology.

It is fascinating to trace Rav Chiya's adaptation of the earlier teaching to match the *rasha* of his own day. In a sense, this process of adaptation has been applied for generations. The *rasha* remains a dissident, either at the edge of or outside of the Jewish community. Mainly through artistic representations, we have clear evidence of how the face of the *rasha* has evolved, to match that which was considered askance in a particular place or time.

The *rasha* in the *Mechilta* won over his relative in the Yerushalmi, and serves as the direct source for the formulation incorporated in the Haggadah, most likely for a number of reasons: The *Mechilta* enjoyed a greater sphere of influence; it represents the original formulation; and its teaching seems somewhat broader. Nonetheless, we have noted the slight change which was made upon incorporation in the Haggadah, labeling the wicked son's separation as his heresy as opposed to being in addition to his heresy. Ostensibly, this change was made in order to fashion a generic *rasha* who could be used as an example of infamy at sedarim for millennia.

---

1   The term *oto ha'ish* in later Jewish writings is used in reference to Jesus. However, such an appellation, to the best of my knowledge, is not found in the Talmud. If my understanding is correct, then this would be the first usage of the term in reference to Jesus.

Pharaoh's Heart

O ne of the most intriguing elements of the Exodus story is the interplay between God and Pharaoh. Though they never actually speak directly, it is clear that they are the major players in the story. Moshe, for his part, finds himself running back and forth between God and Pharaoh, relaying messages and prophecies. God has the upper hand, and if not for Pharaoh's arrogance and delusions of grandeur, one could almost feel bad for him. Of course, the reader, observing from the outside, appreciates the absurdity of Pharaoh's position: He doesn't even know what he is up against, yet we see clearly from our vantage point that his hands are far too short to spar with God.

The cards are completely stacked against Pharaoh, for not only can God turn his beloved Nile into blood, but God can also play havoc with all of nature and the rules thereof. Pharaoh does not have a chance. The ultimate manipulation is where God controls Pharaoh's "heart." At this juncture we understand how futile a battle with the Almighty really is. Pharaoh is strung along like a marionette on a string, performing as dictated by God.

A simple, often-asked question presents itself[1]: How does God

---

1   Ramban writes about "the explanation of the question which everyone asks…" (*Ramban, Shemot* 7:3).

punish Pharaoh, if he was not even acting on his own volition? Furthermore, why did the divine plan need to include this violation of natural law — the suspension of Pharaoh's freedom of choice? As far as the second question goes, we appreciate that this can be posed regarding all of the plagues. There is a certain similarity between the plagues on the one hand and the limitation of Pharaoh's freedom of choice on the other. One is a violation of nature, the other a violation of the nature of man.

This question presupposes the centrality of freedom of choice in Jewish philosophy. This assumption, that we indeed possess such freedom, is the cornerstone of normative Jewish thought. According to Rambam, life without such freedom would be meaningless, a veritable theological nightmare. If man were simply programmed to perform various actions he would have no responsibility for those actions, and life itself would be futile at best, inane at worst.

The Midrash articulates this question, noting that it opens the door for heretical thoughts:

> "For I have hardened his heart" (*Shemot* 10:1) — Rabbi Yochanan said: "Does this not provide heretics with ground for arguing that he had no means of repenting, since it says: 'For I have hardened his heart?' "
>
> *(Shemot Rabbah 13:3)*

The Midrash does provide an answer:

> To which Rabbi Shimon ben Lakish replied: "Let the mouths of the heretics be stopped up. 'If it concerns the scorners, He scorns them' (*Mishlei* 3:34): when God warns a man once, twice, and even a third time, and he still does not repent, then God closes his heart against repentance so that He should exact vengeance from him for his sins. Thus it was with the wicked Pharaoh. Since God sent [Moshe] to him five times and he took no notice, God then said: 'You have stiffened your neck and hardened your heart; well, I will add to your unclean-

ness.' Hence, 'For I have hardened his heart.' "

(Ibid.)

According to this response, the hardening of the heart was itself the punishment, and not, as we assumed, merely the impetus for Pharaoh's actions for which he was ultimately punished. The punishment Pharaoh actually receives is quite exact, measure for measure: Just as Pharaoh had closed his heart and ignored God, now Pharaoh was punished by losing the sensitivity of his heart — which he had hardened himself.[1]

The Midrash speaks of five occasions when Pharaoh did not heed God. An analysis of the biblical text shows that God did not harden the heart of Pharaoh after any of the first five plagues. Quite the opposite: it is Pharaoh who hardens his own heart and ignores the unrivaled might of God.

Blood:
And the magicians of Egypt did likewise with their enchantments, and Pharaoh's heart was hardened and he did not listen to them, as God had said. And Pharaoh turned and went to his house, and he did not set his heart to this.

(Shemot 7:22–23)

Frogs:
But when Pharaoh saw that there was respite, he hardened his heart and did not listen to them, as God had said.

(Ibid. 8:11)

Lice:
Then the magicians said to Pharaoh, "This is the finger of God." And Pharaoh's heart was hardened, and he did not listen to them, as God had said.

(Ibid., 15)

---

1   The Midrash introduces a play on words with *kaved,* meaning both hard and "liver." See *Shemot Rabbah* 13:3: "For I have hardened [*hichbadti*] his heart' — What does '*hichbadti*' imply? That God made his heart like a liver [*kaved*] into which no juice enters even if boiled a second time. So also was the heart of Pharaoh made like a liver, and he did not receive the words of God. Hence 'For I have hardened his heart.' "

Wild Animals:[1]

And Pharaoh hardened his heart at this time also, and he did not let the nation go.

(Ibid., 28)

Cattle:

And Pharaoh sent, and, behold, not one of the cattle of the people of Israel was dead. And the heart of Pharaoh was hardened, and he did not let the nation go.

(Ibid. 9:7)

After the first five plagues, we note a subtle yet essential shift in language.

Boils:

And God hardened the heart of Pharaoh, and he did not listen to them, as God had spoken to Moshe.

(Ibid., 12)

Hail:

And Pharaoh sent and called for Moshe and Aharon, and he said to them, "I have sinned this time. God is righteous, and I and my people are wicked...." And when Pharaoh saw that the rain and the hail and the thunders had ceased, he sinned yet more and hardened his heart,[2] he and his servants. And the heart of Pharaoh was hardened, nor would he let the people of Israel go, as God had spoken through Moshe.

(Ibid., 27, 34–35)

And God said to Moshe, "Go to Pharaoh; for I have hardened his heart and the heart of his servants, that I might show these signs of Mine before him."

(Ibid. 10:1)

---

1 There is some contention regarding the identity of this plague. See *Shemot Rabbah* 11:3, where an opinion is expressed that the plague was swarms of hornets and gnats.

2 This reads as if Pharaoh had hardened his own heart, but in the next verse the reading shifts and it seems to have been the work of God. See the comments of the Chizkuni.

Locusts:
But God hardened Pharaoh's heart, and he would not let
the people of Israel go.

(Ibid., 20)

Darkness:
But God hardened Pharaoh's heart, and he would not let
them go.

(Ibid., 27)

Death of Firstborn:
"And I will harden Pharaoh's heart, and he shall chase after
them; and I will be honored over Pharaoh and over all his
army, so that the Egyptians may know that I am God." ...And
it was told the king of Egypt that the people fled; and the heart
of Pharaoh and of his servants was turned against the people,
and they said, "Why have we done this, that we have let Israel
go from serving us?"

(Ibid. 14:4–5)

Now it is God who is hardening the heart of Pharaoh. This observation of the shift in language was made by Reish Lakish. The
first five times Moshe approached him, Pharaoh ignored the display of God's power. At that point, Pharaoh lost the ability to repent. This is part and parcel of the punishment, this loss of the
ability to rectify his ways. The punishments he receives are for his
earlier deeds, not for the later rebellion. The "final solution" which
was plotted by Pharaoh at the outset of *Shemot* was sufficient reason
for the punishment. This, coupled with the harsh, bitter slavery to
which the Jews were subject, provides ample justification for the
torturous treatment of Pharaoh and his henchmen.

This idea is expressed more succinctly in a different *midrash*:

"But I will harden his heart" (*Shemot* 4:21) — to exact retribution from them.

(Shemot Rabbah 5:7)

Again, Pharaoh and the Egyptians are not punished for their

deeds subsequent to the hardening of their hearts. Rather, God's intervention here is designed to bring about the punishment for their earlier cruelty. There is, however, a subtle difference between these two approaches.[1]

In the explanation of Reish Lakish, the hardening of the heart is the punishment, measure for measure. Thus, the question of the lack of free will is avoided: Men may only be punished for actions done of their own free choice, and here Pharaoh is indeed punished for crimes committed against the Jewish people by choice. The punishment: God revokes Pharaoh's free choice. In this second *midrash*, God hardens Pharaoh's heart not as punishment, but in order to punish.

Had Pharaoh suffered through the various indignities of the plagues without God having manipulated his emotions and judgment, it is difficult for us to imagine Pharaoh not capitulating at some point to the awesome power of the Almighty. In fact, we can answer our previous question by turning the issue around: Surely it was the plagues which took away, or at least limited, the free choice of Pharaoh. Surely a beaten, abused Pharaoh does not have the freedom to make a rational, dispassionate decision regarding belief in God. In order to allow Pharaoh the freedom of choice to either accept or reject God, his heart had to be hardened, effectively restoring the equilibrium to Pharaoh's impaired, plague-ridden decision-making process.[2]

This idea may help us understand at least one specific event, as well as a general concept that held sway throughout the biblical period. The Jews who stood on Mount Sinai were also certainly extremely impressed by the theophany. It is difficult for us to imagine that any person who witnessed the Divine Revelation was not forever transformed by it. Hearing God declare "I am the Lord" and

---

1   See the comments of the *Ramban* (on *Shemot* 7:3) where he brings both explanations and declares that they are both true!

2   See the comments of the Seforno on *Shemot* 4:21 where this idea could be understood, though perhaps the thesis stated here goes beyond the Seforno's intention.

commanding "not to make graven images" must have had a lasting impact. Yet, a mere forty days later, we find the Jews worshiping a golden calf.

This nearly impossible juxtaposition becomes more understandable when viewed through the prism of the free-will dilemma we witness in the case of Pharaoh: After witnessing the Revelation, the Jews lost a certain element of free choice. They were no longer at liberty to accept or reject God in their lives; God's involvement in their lives was clear, immediate, palpable. This being so, their subsequent belief and performance of commandments would have been tainted, of lesser value, victims of Divine leverage. The very same Revelation that brings man toward God at the same time limits individual free will, making the actions of the individual, post-Revelation, meaningless. God reestablished the equilibrium in His relationship with man by imbedding in his nature the desire to rebel against the word of God. This is the key to the golden calf debacle.

In general, throughout the era of prophecy, the same dilemma existed: When man enjoys direct communication with God, his freedom is effectively curtailed. A generation which has a prophet in its midst will necessarily be affected. Therefore, throughout the age of prophecy there existed a powerful urge to worship idols. Only in the Second Temple period, when prophecy became a thing of the past, does the urge for idolatry disappear.[1] By then it was no longer needed; the relationship between man and God had changed and the need for individuals to choose belief and rejection of God was restored.

So many of us hope for revelation, craving the simple, nonintermediate relationship with God that such revelation would ensure. We forget that any revelation of this sort carries a heavy price tag, rendering subsequent belief almost meaningless unless accompanied by a counterbalancing temptation. Man believes that freedom of choice is an unalienable right. We forget that, at times, this right may be forfeited, as part of a punishment or as part of a larger scheme. The Torah reminds us of this with the lesson of Pharaoh.

---

1   See *Yoma* 69b and *Shir HaShirim Rabbah* 7:8.

Pesach

The Firstborn

Plague after plague befall the Egyptians; nonetheless, Pharaoh remains steadfast in his refusal to release the Israelites. Only the last plague, the death of the firstborn, beats Pharaoh into submission. This final plague was actually the first to be foretold to Moshe, before he sets out on his mission to Egypt:

> God said to Moshe, "When you go to return to Egypt, see that you do all those wonders before Pharaoh, which I have put in your hand; but I will harden his heart, so that he shall not let the nation go. And you shall say to Pharaoh, 'Thus said God, "Israel is My son, My firstborn. And I say to you, 'Let My son go, that he may serve Me. If you refuse to let him go, behold, I will slay your son, your firstborn.' " ' "
>
> *(Shemot 4:21–23)*

Thus, when the time finally comes, God does not even tell Moshe what the final plague will be, because Moshe already knows.[1]

> God said to Moshe, "I will bring one plague more upon Pharaoh and upon Egypt. Afterwards he will let you go from here.

---

1   See *Shemot Rabbah* 5:7: "God revealed to him [Moshe] that Pharaoh would not let Israel go free before the plague of the firstborn; hence there was no need to tell him of this plague later."

When he shall let you go, he shall certainly thrust you out
from here altogether."

(Ibid. 11:1)

And Moshe says to Pharaoh:

Moshe said: "Thus said God, 'About midnight I will go out into
the midst of Egypt, and all the firstborn in the land of Egypt
shall die, from the firstborn of Pharaoh that sits on his throne
to the firstborn of the maidservant who is behind the mill, and
all the firstborn of beasts. And there shall be a great cry
throughout all the land of Egypt — there was none like it, and
there shall be no more like it.' "

(Ibid., 4–6)

Tradition tells us that this plague was the most severe.[1] The fact
that this and no other plague is described to Moshe prior to his return to Egypt would indicate that the plague of the firstborn was, in
fact, one of the objectives of the Exodus.[2] The question is, why does
the punishment of the firstborn occupy such a central role?

If we return to *Bereishit* and analyze the promise that God gave
Avraham, the core of the Exodus story becomes more clear:

When the sun was going down, a deep sleep fell upon Avram;
and, behold, a fear of great darkness fell upon him. And [God]
said to Avram, "Know for a certainty that your seed shall be a
stranger in a land that is not theirs and shall serve them; and
they shall afflict them four hundred years. And also that nation whom they shall serve will I judge; and afterward they
shall come out with great wealth."

(Bereishit 15:12–14)

---

1   See the comments of Rashi to *Shemot* 4:23 and 9:14. There is a *midrash* which says
     that the plague of frogs was worst: "God brought the ten plagues upon them in
     accordance with the regular plan of campaign; and of these, the frogs were the most
     grievous, as it says: 'And frogs, which destroyed them' (Tehillim 68:45). They
     destroyed their bodies and emasculated them" (*Shemot Rabbah* 15:27).
2   In the opinion of Ibn Ezra, the killing of the firstborn was the main objective of the
     Exodus. See Ibn Ezra's comments on *Tehillim* 135:8. A slightly less sweeping
     statement can be found in his comments to *Shemot* 34:19.

The nation that afflicts the descendants of Avraham will be judged for their wrongdoing; the method of punishment is unclear. This verse is echoed in the revelation at the burning bush:

> I will stretch out My hand and strike Egypt with all My wonders which I will do in its midst; and after that he will let you go. I will give this people favor in the sight of the Egyptians, and it shall come to pass, that when you go you shall not go empty. Every woman shall borrow from her neighbor and from the one who sojourns in her house, vessels of silver and vessels of gold and garments; and you shall put them upon your sons, and upon your daughters, and you shall despoil the Egyptians.
>
> *(Shemot 3:20–22)*

Here both the "judgment" of the oppressing nation is recorded as well as the wealth the Jews would "inherit" from them on their departure. In *Bereishit*, only a judgment is mentioned. Ramban, in his comments to *Bereishit* (15:13), insists that the judgment would involve a determination whether the oppressing nation had followed the divine plan of enslaving the Jewish people, or if they had gone "beyond the call of duty." According to this opinion, ostensibly the Egyptians could have been judged and found innocent; the verses in *Bereishit* do not speak of any punishment per se. For the Jews to have left Egypt with great wealth, in payment for the sweat of their collective brows, would have sufficed as fulfillment of God's promise to Avraham.

But as we know, the Egyptians were not exonerated. They had assumed the role of oppressors with enthusiasm, with a vengeance. The promise to Avraham clearly described enslavement in a foreign land; genocide was never part of the promise. When Egyptians began casting the male Jewish children into the Nile, the plagues followed. The Midrash tells us that only when the Egyptians were found guilty of unnecessary cruelty, in the judgment promised to Avraham, was the plague of the firstborn initiated:

"This month shall be to you" (*Shemot* 12:2) — It is written: "And you shall say to Pharaoh: 'Thus said God, "Israel is My son, My firstborn. And I say to you, 'Let My son go, that he may serve Me. If you refuse to let him go, behold, I will slay your son, your firstborn.' " ' " Exalted be the name of the Holy One, blessed be He, who foretells the end at the beginning. In connection with Avraham, it says: "And also that nation whom they shall serve will I judge." What was the judgment? The slaying of the firstborn, which was called a plague, as it says: "One plague more." What is the meaning of "I will judge"? God said: "I will punish them with the slaying of the firstborn," for it says: "Behold, I will slay your son, your first-born."

(Shemot Rabbah 15:27)

The killing of the firstborn stands out from all the other plagues as Divine retribution directed toward Pharaoh and all of Egypt. Another *midrash* teaches that this was to be the only plague. The others were a reaction to Pharaoh's insolence:

When God first sought to bring the plagues upon Egypt, He intended to commence with the plague of the firstborn, for it says: 'Behold, I will slay your son, your firstborn." Pharaoh then retorted: "Who is God that I should hearken to His voice?" (*Shemot* 5:2). Then God said: "If I bring the plague of firstborn upon him at the outset, he will send them out at once. No, I will bring other plagues upon him first. By this means will I bring them all."

(Shemot Rabbah 18:5)

Again we see that the essential form of retribution was the striking of the firstborn. The other plagues were afterthoughts. What was it about the killing of the firstborn that was so severe? Needless to say, the death of any child is horrific. God's logic is clear: If you are callous to My children, I will wreak vengeance on your children. This, though, does not explain why specifically the firstborn are singled out. A number of *midrashim* explain the plague itself and shed light on this issue.

The *Mechilta* focuses on the immorality of Egypt:

> "The Egyptians urged the people, in order to send them out of the land in haste; for they said, 'We shall all be dead men' " (*Shemot* 12:33). They said, "This is not what Moshe had decreed. Moshe said only the firstborn of Egypt will die." They thought whoever had four or five children would only lose the first. They didn't know that their wives were suspected of sexual immorality, and each of their children were actually fathered by different young men. They had transgressed secretly, yet God caused it to become known.
>
> *(Mechilta D'Rabbi Yishmael Bo, Mesechta D'Pischa 13)*

Unbeknownst to the Egyptians, there were actually many "firstborn" in each family. The humiliation that they suffered must have been tremendous when the extent of infidelity and family breakdown became clear and undeniable. This *midrash* gives us further insight as to why Egyptian society had to be destroyed, yet does not completely satisfy as an explanation for the centrality of this plague: There may be a certain poetic justice in the eradication of a society which suffers such severe moral breakdown, but was this the point of the Exodus?[1]

In order to fully understand this plague we must appreciate the hierarchy within Egyptian civilization. It was a society ruled by primogeniture, a society based on power. The firstborn had absolute power within the family unit. Pharaoh was the firstborn of the firstborn of the firstborn, and it was from this birthright that he exercised his power. The attack against the firstborn was therefore a powerful polemic against the entire culture of Egypt, in which the eldest ruled the younger siblings and slavery was a cornerstone of the civilization. Without slaves, the lower classes had no one to

---

1   The moral breakdown of Egyptian culture is recorded and referred to in the Torah almost as an archetype or model of the immoral society: "Like the deeds of the land of Egypt, where you dwelt, you shall not do" (*Vayikra* 18:3).

control and dominate, leaving the hierarchy of power incomplete. Pharaoh controlled the firstborn — as firstborn of the firstborn; they, in turn, controlled the other Egyptians, and the "ordinary" Egyptians controlled the slaves.

The Netziv (Rabbi Naftali Tzvi Yehudah Berlin) in his commentary to *Shemot* elucidates this idea with a fascinating observation concerning the song that was sung after the splitting of the sea. The verses read:

> Then sang Moshe and the people of Israel this song to God, and they spoke, saying, "I will sing to God, for He has triumphed gloriously; the horse and his rider He has thrown into the sea...." And Miriam answered them, "Sing to God, for He has triumphed gloriously; the horse and his rider He has thrown into the sea."
>
> *(Shemot 15:1, 21)*

The main part of the song seems to be this idea of the "horse and the rider." The Netziv explains that this verse encapsulates the defeat of Egypt: It is the defeat of the philosophy of "the horse and the rider." As the rider rides on the subjugated horse, so must the rider listen to the officer, and that officer listen to the general, and that general listen to the commander in chief. According to the Netziv, this describes the horrors of Egyptian society as a series of horses and riders, where the Jewish slaves became the bottom of the proverbial totem pole, the lowest horse supporting the entire structure. The Egyptians' reluctance to free their slaves is understandable: the entire society would crumble without slaves at its base.

We now understand why the death of the firstborn was so essential to the Exodus, and why the splitting of the sea evoked such a powerful response. The "horse and rider" structure had sunk at sea; the lowly slaves were free. The death of the firstborn was the beginning this final chapter, of the liberation. The "riders," the most powerful, the elite, were to die.

This turning of the tables can be discerned in a *midrash* that changes our normative understanding of the plague.

"To Him who struck Egypt with their firstborn" (*Tehillim* 136:10): When God sent the plague of the firstborn...all the firstborn went to speak to their fathers and said, "Everything which Moshe has said has come true. Don't you want us to live? Let us get the Hebrews out of our homes; otherwise we are dead."

They answered, "Even if all of Egypt dies, they are not leaving."

All the firstborn gathered in front of Pharaoh and screamed, "Please remove this nation. Because of them evil will befall us and you."

Pharaoh said to his servants, "Remove them and break their knees."

What did they do? Each took a sword and killed his father. Thus, it says: "To Him who struck Egypt with their firstborn."

(Midrash Tehillim 136:6, Ancient Tanchuma Bo 18)

In this source one can feel the unraveling of Egyptian society: Children rebelled against their fathers;[1] the horses rebelled against their riders. The underpinnings of Egyptian society crumbled forever.[2]

We now understand that the death of the firstborn was not just

---

1 The *Zohar* describes the breakdown in a slightly different manner: "Mark the wondrous punishment that overtook the enemies of Israel. On the night of the Exodus there were three slayings in Egypt. First, the firstborn killed whomever they could lay hands on; then, the Holy One executed His judgement at midnight; and, lastly, Pharaoh, on seeing the havoc wrought upon his own household, himself arose and with bitterness and fury smote those princes and nobles who had advised him to persecute Israel. He rose up at midnight; at the hour and moment when the Holy One Himself began His judgement (*Shemot* 12:30). Pharaoh likewise rose up in wrath and killed his officers and nobles, just as a dog, if hit with a stone, goes and bites another dog. Having done this, Pharaoh roamed through the marketplaces crying, 'Rise up and go forth from among my people' (ibid., 31); and in fear he added, 'and bless me also' (ibid., 32), as if to say, 'Let me live.' Then, so eager was he to be rid of them that he himself accompanied them, as it says, 'He sent the people away' [*beshalach*, lit. escorted]" (*Zohar, Shemot* 45b).

2 One gets a sense of the plagues as attacks on Egyptian culture and beliefs from numerous sources. For example: "It is written: 'He sent Moshe His servant, and Aharon whom He had chosen' (*Tehillim* 55:26). As soon as God, as it were, entered,

another plague, another sign of Divine might. No, this plague struck at the very epicenter of Egyptian civilization and paved the way for spiritual and ideological liberation. The contrast with the role of the firstborn in Judaism is striking: Rav Soloveitchik explained the special role of the firstborn more as a reward for added responsibility than a privilege. As we have seen numerous times, all of *Bereishit* is a polemic against the automatic birthright of the older son.[1] Birth order does not guarantee position. The grandiose is not espoused as a Jewish ethic. A sage who is a *mamzer* will take precedence over a high priest who is ignorant; likewise, the Torah was given on the smallest mountain. Israel is called the first son, yet Esav was the eldest; the Midrash tells us that God Himself agreed, and indeed declared him firstborn.

What is the meaning? "Israel is My son, My firstborn"? It refers to Yaakov their ancestor, who purchased the birthright in order that he might serve God. [Hence], "And you shall say to him: 'Let My son go, that he may serve Me.' "

(Shemot Rabbah 5:7)

Here God Himself confirms that Yaakov's desire to serve God is what transformed him into a "firstborn." On the other hand, "real" firstborns lose their status:

"Instead of every firstborn that opens the womb among the children of Israel" (*Bemidbar* 3:12): Originally the Temple ser-

---

He smote their firstborn and their gods, for it says: 'And I plagued Egypt' (*Yehoshua* 24:5). Also among their gods did the Lord perform judgments" (*Shemot Rabbah* 15:15).

1   The mystical presentation of this idea is evident in the following passage from the *Zohar*: "When they begat children, the firstborn was the son of the [serpent's] slime. For two beings had intercourse with Chavah, and she conceived from both and bore two children. Each followed one of the male parents, and their spirits parted, one to this side and one to the other, and similarly their characters. On the side of Kayin are all the haunts of the evil species, from which come evil spirits and demons and necromancers. From the side of Hevel comes a more merciful class, yet not wholly beneficial — good wine mixed with bad. The right kind was not produced until Shet, who is the first ancestor of all the generations of the righteous, and from whom the world was propagated" (*Zohar, Bereishit* 36b).

vice devolved upon the firstborn, but when they committed the sin of the golden calf, the Levites, inasmuch as they had not erred in the matter of the calf, were privileged to enter in their stead.

(Bemidbar Rabbah 4:8)

Divine service utilizes the principle of "first come, first served":[1] The firstborn had the right and responsibility to serve God, but with the sin of the golden calf they forfeited this lofty responsibility. From the dawn of time there have been those willing to serve God, and others who have ignored or rejected such opportunities:

> Go back to the beginning of the creation of the world. Adam was the world's firstborn. When he offered his sacrifice, as it says: "And it pleased God better than a bullock that is horned and hooved" (*Tehillim* 69:32), he donned high priestly garments; as it says: "And God, the Lord, made for Adam and for his wife garments of skins and clothed them" (*Bereishit* 3:21). They were robes of honor which subsequent firstborn used.
>
> When Adam died he transmitted them to Shet. Shet transmitted them to Metushelach. When Metushelach died he transmitted them to Noach. Noach arose and offered a sacrifice, as it says: "And he took of every pure beast...and offered burnt offerings on the altar" (*Bereishit* 8:20).
>
> Noach died and transmitted them to Shem. But was Shem a firstborn? Yefet, surely, was the firstborn; as it says: "Shem...the brother of Yefet the elder" (*Bereishit* 10:21)! Why then did he hand them on to Shem? Because Noach foresaw that the line of the patriarchs would issue from him.
>
> There is proof that Shem offered sacrifices, since it says: "And Malkitzedek, king of Shalem, brought forth bread and

---

1 This is reflected by the protocol of Temple service, as can be seen in the *mishnayos* of *Tamid* and *Yoma*.

wine; and he was priest of the Lord, Most High" (*Bereishit* 14:18). Now was it to him that the priesthood was given? The priesthood, surely, was not given to any man until Aharon arose. What then is the meaning of the statement here, "and he was priest"? Because he offered sacrifices like priests.

Shem died and handed it on to Avraham. But was Avraham a firstborn? The fact is that because he was a righteous man the birthright was transferred to him, and he offered sacrifices; as it says: "And offered it up for a burnt offering in the place of his son" (*Bereishit* 22:13).

Avraham died and handed it on to Yitzchak. Yitzchak arose and handed it on to Yaakov. But was Yaakov a firstborn? No, but you find that Yaakov prudently took it [the birthright] from Esav. He said to him: "Sell me first your birthright" (*Bereishit* 25:31). Do you suppose perhaps that it was for no good reason that Yaakov asked Esav to sell him the birthright? No! Yaakov wished to offer sacrifices and could not, because he was not the firstborn.

(Bemidbar Rabbah 4:8)

The lineage of the Jewish people is the antithesis of Pharaoh. Rather than firstborn after firstborn after firstborn, the spiritual legacy we carry is of those who chose to serve God regardless of station, and at times despite modest ancestry. This is the significance of God's resounding declaration that we are His firstborn.

Others willing to serve in the future will likewise merit this status:

"Sanctify to Me all the firstborn" (*Shemot* 13:1). Rabbi Natan said: "The Holy One, blessed be He, told Moshe: 'Just as I have made Yaakov a firstborn, for it says: "Israel is My son, My firstborn" (ibid. 4:22), so will I make the King Messiah a firstborn, as it says: "I also will appoint him firstborn" (*Tehillim* 89:28).' "

(Shemot Rabbah 19:7)

One day the Messiah himself will merit to be called a firstborn. He will help teach the world that being a child of God transcends lineage, that being a firstborn of God is about how we lead our lives. It is the manifestation of the image of God within,[1] not a question of sequence of birth.

---

1   Rav Soloveitchik pointed out that by calling us His firstborn, God is clearly saying that He has other children as well. The rage directed against Egypt was partially due to the fact that as long as the Jews were subjugated, they could not receive the Torah and inspire the other "children" by being a "light unto the nations."

Pesach

The Four Cups of Yosef

On Pesach, one of the central aspects of the seder is the four cups of wine. Unlike the matzah or paschal offering, the wine is a Rabbinic obligation, whose source, according to the Talmud, is the four expressions of redemption in God's declaration to the children of Israel:

> Therefore say to the people of Israel, "I am God, and I will *bring* you out from under the burdens of the Egyptians, and I will *save* you from their slavery, and I will *redeem* you with an outstretched arm and with great judgments. And I will *take* you to Me for a people, and I will be to you a Lord. And you shall know that I am God, your Lord, who brings you out from under the burdens of the Egyptians.
>
> *(Shemot 6:6–7)*[1]

However, when one consults the *Yerushalmi* we find other traditions concerning the symbolism of the four cups (*Yerushalmi, Pesachim* 10:1, 37b–c).The Talmud notes that the word *cup* is mentioned four times in the narrative of Yosef and the wine steward.

1   The next verse has a fifth expression, "And I will bring you into the Land." This may be the source for the fifth cup, which is on the table and not drunk: the cup of Eliyahu. See *Haggadah Sheleimah* by Rav M. Kasher for a full discussion. Also see the discussion in *Chokrei HaZemanim* , vol. 2 , by Rav Alter Hilovitz, where he claims to have written about this idea prior to the publication of Rav Kasher's book.

While this is indeed the case, the association seems obscure at first glance. On the other hand, we should consider that Yosef's descent to Egypt marked the beginning of the exile of the children of Yaakov, or, if you will, the antithesis of redemption. However, the association runs deeper: Yosef, who languishes in the pit of the Egyptian legal system, puts his faith in the wine steward, who will one day mention the name and talents of this Jewish boy to the king, Pharaoh. On that very day, Yosef undergoes an incredible metamorphosis: One day a slave, the next a king.

This prototype is also embedded in the story the Exodus: the story of the slave who became king, the story of God's salvation which takes place in the blink of an eye. The Jews' exodus is as stunning as Yosef's metamorphosis. One day they are slaves, and the next day they are free. The downtrodden rise above their oppressors, acquire all the wealth of Egypt, and change the Egyptian Empire forever.

When Yosef and his brothers meet after years of separation and Yosef's metamorphosis is complete, the tension of the preceding chapters finally reaches its crescendo. Yosef is unable to contain himself, and with a few words he startles and frightens his brothers.

> Then Yosef could not restrain himself before all those who stood by him, and he cried, "Remove every man from before me." And no man stood with him when Yosef made himself known to his brothers. He wept aloud, and the Egyptians and the house of Pharaoh heard. And Yosef said to his brothers, "I am Yosef. Does my father still live?" His brothers could not answer him, for they were panic-stricken by his presence.
>
> *(Bereishit 45:1–3)*

While his brothers stand in shock, Yosef continues his soliloquy:

> And Yosef said to his brothers, "Come near me, I beg you." And they came near. And he said, "I am Yosef, your brother, whom you sold into Egypt. Now be not grieved, nor angry with your-

selves, that you sold me here, for God sent me before you to preserve life. For these two years the famine has been in the land, and there will be yet another five years without plowing or harvest. God sent me before you to preserve you a posterity in the earth and to save your lives by a great deliverance. So now it was not you who sent me here, but God; and He has made me an advisor [literally, father] to Pharaoh, and lord of all his house, and a ruler throughout all the land of Egypt.

"Hurry back to my father, and say to him, 'Thus said your son Yosef, "God has made me lord of all Egypt. Come down to me, do not delay. And you shall live in the land of Goshen, and you shall be near me — you, your children, your grand-children, your flocks, your herds, and all that you have. And I will sustain you there, for there are another five years of famine; lest you, and your household, and all that you have come to poverty." '

"And behold your eyes see, and the eyes of my brother Binyamin, that it is my mouth that speaks to you. Tell my father of all my glory in Egypt and of all that you have seen. Hurry and bring down my father here."

(Ibid., 4–13)

While the initial burst of speech — the incredible disclosure — seems to be an explosion of emotion,[1] the second part of Yosef's talk sounds more measured, perhaps rehearsed. Here Yosef speaks, not merely in practical, human, or personal terms.[2] Yosef speaks again, using the words of the visionary that he is. Yosef shares his theological perspective of recent history with his brothers.

And Yosef said to his brothers, "Come near me...for *God* sent me before you to preserve life. For these two years the famine

---

1 The question "Is my father alive" seems illogical. If Yaakov were dead, why would Yehudah risk his neck to save Binyamin?

2 Yosef speaks twice without response. It sounds as if the repetition of the phrase, "And Yosef said" indicates a change in tone. Similarly, in *Bereishit* 20:9–10 Avimelech speaks, and speaks again. The shift in that case may be attributed to a change in tone, from cynicism to curiosity.

has been in the land, and there will be yet another five years without plowing or harvest. And *God* sent me before you to preserve you a posterity in the earth and to save your lives by a great deliverance. So now it was not you who sent me here, but *God*; and He has made me an advisor to Pharaoh, and lord of his entire house, and a ruler throughout all the land of Egypt. Hurry back to my father, and say to him, 'Thus said your son Yosef, *God* has made me lord of all Egypt. Come down to me, do not delay....' "

Yosef's words are peppered with references to God. While his first words inform his brothers that he, Yosef, still lives, the second message conveyed is that Yosef is still spiritually intact. This is one cause of the brothers' shock: Perhaps Yosef, with great resilience and ingenuity, could have remained alive, but he could not possibly have survived the depravity of Egypt and emerged unscathed. Part of the brothers' problem vis-à-vis Yosef was their constant and continued underestimation of him. They never thought they would bow down to him, nor did they think that anyone else would prostrate himself before Yosef. Yosef as lord of Egypt was an idea beyond their wildest dreams. But if there was a more bizarre suggestion, it was that Yosef would survive spiritually.

The path toward the highest echelon in any society is fraught with spiritual landmines, all the more so in ancient Egypt. If Yosef survived, and indeed flourished, the brothers surmised that his soul would have been bought and sold numerous times, retaining no sanctity. Yosef would surely be a corrupt shell of his former self, whom the brothers did not particularly respect in the first place.

Now we understand Yosef's numerous references to God. He speaks in theological terms, indicating that he has, indeed, survived. The brothers need not fear: Yosef continues to speak the language of his youth. The boy who sat on Yitzchak's knee, the boy who was closest to their saintly father Yaakov, yet lives. It is Yosef who lives, not some Egyptian despot. From his words we see that Yosef has not only survived, he has thrived.

Such references to God were not always a part of Yosef's speech. In Yosef's first dream, and indeed, in his first words in the Torah, we find his vision, but no Divine perspective.

> And Yosef dreamed a dream, and he told it to his brothers. And they hated him even more. And he said to them, "Listen, I beg you, to this dream which I have dreamed. Behold, we were binding sheaves in the field, and, lo, my sheaf arose, and stood upright; and, behold, your sheaves stood around, and bowed to my sheaf."
>
> And his brothers said to him, "Shall you indeed reign over us, or shall you indeed have dominion over us?" And they hated him even more for his dreams and for his words.
>
> And he dreamed yet another dream, and he told it to his brothers, and he said, "Behold, I have again dreamed a dream; and, behold, the sun and the moon and the eleven stars bowed to me."
>
> *(Ibid. 37:5–9)*

Yosef tells of his dreams, but we do not know if God plays a part in his worldview. When the wife of Potifar makes her advances, Yosef does speak of God:

> And it came to pass after these things, that his master's wife cast her eyes upon Yosef, and she said, "Lie with me."
>
> But he refused, and said to his master's wife, "Behold, my master does not know what is with me in the house, and he has committed all that he has to my hand. There is none greater in this house than I, nor has he kept back anything from me but you, because you are his wife. How then can I do this great wickedness, and sin against *God*?"
>
> *(Ibid. 39:7–9)*

While Yosef's consciousness of God certainly aided him in his battle against his desires, it does not seem to impress this wanton woman.

The next time we see Yosef is in his prison cell, where he again makes references to God, but again his listeners do not hear:

And they said to him, "We have dreamed a dream, and there is no interpreter of it."

And Yosef said to them, "Do interpretations not belong to *God*? Tell them to me, I beg you."

And the chief butler told his dream to Yosef, and said to him, "In my dream, behold, a vine was before me...."

And Yosef said to him, "This is the interpretation of it: The three branches are three days.... Think of me when it shall be well with you, and show kindness, I beg you, to me, and make mention of me to Pharaoh, and bring me out of this house. For indeed I was stolen away from the land of the Hebrews, and here also have I done nothing that they should put me in the pit...."

Yet the chief butler did not remember Yosef, and forgot him.

(Ibid. 40:8–23)

The Rabbis perceived within this dialogue a sin on the part of Yosef:

"Happy is the man who has made God his trust" (*Tehillim* 40:5) alludes to Yosef. "And has not turned to the arrogant nor to such as fall away treacherously" (ibid.): Because he said to the chief butler, "Think of me...and make mention of me," two years were added to his sufferings.

(Bereishit Rabbah 89:3)

Yosef, who speaks of God's dominion over all things, including dreams, has sinned in the eyes of the Sages, by not trusting sufficiently in God.

Indeed, when the butler recalls the conversation and remembers Yosef's power to interpret dreams, God is not in his vocabulary.

And there was there with us a young man, a Hebrew, servant to the captain of the guard. And we told him, and he interpreted to us our dreams; to each man according to his dream he did interpret. And it came to pass, as he interpreted to us, so it was; me he [Pharaoh] restored to my office, and him [the baker] he [Pharaoh] hanged.

(Bereishit 41:12–13)

Over the next few years we discern a change in Yosef. The ideas of which he spoke earlier now become solidified. When Pharaoh approaches, it is no longer Yosef's personal God of whom he speaks, nor does he give God only a passing reference. Now Yosef succeeds in affecting others with his belief.

Then Pharaoh sent and called Yosef, and they brought him hastily out of the dungeon. And he shaved himself, and changed his garment, and came in to Pharaoh. And Pharaoh said to Yosef, "I have dreamed a dream, and there is none who can interpret it. I have heard say of you that you can understand a dream to interpret it."

And Yosef answered Pharaoh, saying, "It is not in me; *God* shall give Pharaoh a favorable answer...."

And Yosef said to Pharaoh, "The dream of Pharaoh is one; *God* has revealed to Pharaoh what he is about to do.... This is the matter which I have spoken to Pharaoh; what *God* is about to do He is showing to Pharaoh.... And for that the dream was doubled to Pharaoh twice, it is because the matter is established by *God*, and *God* will shortly bring it to pass...."

And Pharaoh said to his servants, "Can we find such a one as this is, a man in whom is the spirit of *God?*" And Pharaoh said to Yosef, "For as much as *God* has shown you all this, there is none so discreet and wise as you are."

(Ibid., 14–39)

The impossible seems to have transpired: Not only does Yosef speak of God, but his belief is infectious. The corrupt, self-made deity, Pharaoh, speaks of God. Yosef was not changed by Egypt, Egypt was changed by Yosef. This idea is critical in understanding a later chapter in the Torah.

When the time for the Exodus had arrived, Moshe was instructed to ask Pharaoh for permission to leave for three days:

> Go and gather the elders of Israel together and say to them,
> "God, the Lord of your fathers, the God of Avraham, of
> Yitzchak, and of Yaakov, appeared to me, saying, 'I have surely
> visited you and seen that which is done to you in Egypt. And I
> have said, "I will bring you out of the affliction of Egypt to the
> land of the Canaanites and the Hittites and the Emorites and
> the Perizzites and the Hivites and the Jebusites, to a land flow-
> ing with milk and honey." ' " They will heed your voice, and
> you shall come, you and the elders of Israel, to the king of
> Egypt, and you shall say to him, "God, the Lord of the He-
> brews, has met with us. Now let us go, we beseech you, three
> days' journey into the wilderness, that we may sacrifice to
> God, our Lord." And I am sure that the king of Egypt will not
> let you go, except by a mighty hand.
>
> *(Shemot 3:16–19)*

> And afterward Moshe and Aharon went in, and told Pharaoh,
> "Thus said God, the Lord of Israel, 'Let my people go, that they
> may hold a feast for Me in the wilderness.' "
>
> And Pharaoh said, "Who is God, that I should obey His
> voice to let Israel go? I do not know God, and I will not let Is-
> rael go."
>
> And they said, "The God of the Hebrews has met with us.
> Let us go, we pray you, three days' journey into the desert, and
> sacrifice to God, our Lord, lest He fall upon us with pestilence
> or with the sword."
>
> *(Shemot 5:1–4)*

I once heard Rav Yosef Dov Soloveitchik pose an intriguing
question regarding these passages: What would have happened
had Pharaoh allowed the Jews to leave for three days? Would they
have returned afterward? Would the promise of the land of milk
and honey have gone unfulfilled? Would they really have returned
to Egypt? Of course, the question is a tautology: God had already

stated that Pharaoh would not acquiesce. Why, then, ask for three days' leave, especially when the object of the Exodus is complete, permanent liberation?

The purpose of the three-day sojourn would have been to receive the Torah. After receiving the Torah, the Jewish people would have returned to Egypt. After teaching the Egyptians and impacting, even revolutionizing, Egyptian society, they would have continued their march toward destiny, to the Land of Israel. Such a march would have been qualitatively different from the circuitous path they eventually took.

Had the Egyptians, the greatest nation in antiquity, been sufficiently theologically mature to encourage the Jews to worship God, the path to the Messianic Age would have been inestimably shorter. But how could the Egyptians possibly have reached such spiritual heights? The answer is that the prototype for influencing the local population was Yosef. Just as the name of God reverberates from Pharaoh's lips after one meeting with Yosef, the entire nation should have been spiritually invigorated after interfacing with the Jewish nation over a period of hundreds of years.

This is part of the reason for the exile to have been specifically in Egypt. This corrupt, twisted society would have to be either healed or obliterated in order for a Messianic Age to flourish. Our tradition has no illusions about Egypt.[1]

> Do not do the actions of the land of Egypt, where you dwelt, and do not do the actions of the land of Canaan, where I am bringing you; and do not walk in their ordinances.
>
> *(Vayikra 18:3)*

> Similarly, when Israel were in Egypt the Egyptians practiced whoring, as it says, "Whose flesh is as the flesh of donkeys" *(Yechezkel 23:20)*. When they entered the land of Canaan the Canaanites practiced whoring and witchcraft, as it says, "Be-

---

1   See *Sifra, Acharei Mot* 8 (cited in Rambam's *Hilchot Issurei Bi'ah* 21:8), where a number of the offenses of the Egyptians are enumerated, including lesbianism and other sexual rebellions and peccadilloes.

cause of the multitude of the harlotries of the well-favored har-
lot, the mistress of witchcraft" (*Nachum* 3:4). The Holy One,
blessed be He, said to them: "My children, be careful that you
do not act either in accordance with the practice of these or in
accordance with the practice of those." Hence it is written,
"Do not do the actions of the land of Egypt, where you dwelt,
and do not do the actions of the land of Canaan, where I am
bringing you; and do not walk in their ordinances."

(Vayikra Rabbah 23:7)

We have learned that these ten species of wisdom came down
to this world, and all were concentrated in Egypt, save one
which spread through the rest of the world. They are all species
of sorcery, and through them the Egyptians were more skilled
in sorcery than all other men.

(Zohar, Vayikra 70a)

If Egyptian society could be spiritually healed, the entire world
would surely follow suit. Egypt was the epicenter of the ancient
world. Unfortunately, the Jews as a people did not rise to the challenge. They were not successful in reaching out to the surrounding
culture in any meaningful way and did not reach the spiritual
stratosphere, which was Yosef's domain. After Yosef's death, a new
king arises who knows neither Yosef nor the God of Yosef:

And Yosef died, and all his brothers, and all that generation....
And there arose a new king over Egypt who did not know
Yosef.

(Shemot 1:6, 8)

And Pharaoh said, "Who is God, that I should obey His voice
to let Israel go? I do not know God, and I will not let Israel go."

(Ibid. 5:2)

With Yosef gone, the possibility of influencing the Egyptians
seems to evaporate. By telling the Jews that they are to ask for three
days, they are being told that this is the way it should have been: A
three-day journey, following the two-hundred-year exile, should

have been enough to revolutionize Egypt.

If this seems impossible, they, and we, should remember that Yosef changed Pharaoh's outlook in but one conversation. The crux of the matter is never to underestimate the power of the idea of God or, for that matter, never to underestimate the power of the Jewish people to convey that idea. The power contained therein is sufficient to change the world, and Yosef's greatness lay in his awareness and use of this power.

When we drink from the four cups of wine we must recall the sudden transformation from slavery to freedom, how Yosef metamorphosed from slave to king. When we drink the wine we should taste the possibility of our own transformation, and always recall that the salvation of God is in the blink of an eye. That is the secret of redemption.

The Matzah of Lot

L ot, the nephew of Avraham, is a strange, tragic figure. His uncle was the greatest man of the age, yet Lot was unable to get along with him. We are taught that after Lot's father passed away, Avraham adopted him and took him under his tutelage. The childless Avraham must have had a special place in his heart and home for his orphaned nephew, yet Lot was unable or unwilling to work on this relationship. Even after Lot and Avraham part ways, Avraham remains concerned and leaps into action when Lot gets into trouble and is kidnapped.

The most famous and tragic story of Lot is his part in the destruction of Sedom. Lot escapes, though not unscathed, as his adopted city crumbles behind him. His behavior in Sedom and the manner in which he takes leave of the city draw our attention. Viewing this episode in its chronological context may afford us insight to its inner meaning.

Rabbinic tradition tells us that Yitzchak was born on Pesach (*Rosh HaShanah* 11a), which may be borne out by the language used in the verses: When the angels visit Avraham and Sarah with the promise of Yitzchak's birth the following year, they are served "cakes." While we know that cakes are not necessarily kosher for Pesach, there is at least a linguistic similarity between the food prepared by Sarah, and the food prescribed for Passover — both are called *ugot* (cakes).

> And Avraham hurried to the tent to Sarah, and said, "Quickly make ready three measures of fine meal, knead it, and make cakes [*ugot*]."
>
> *(Bereishit 18:6)*

> And they [the Jewish people] baked unleavened cakes [*ugot matzot*] of the dough which they brought forth out of Egypt, for it was not leavened; because they were thrust out of Egypt and could not remain, and they had not prepared for themselves any provision.
>
> *(Shemot 12:39)*

Interestingly, when Lot is visited in Sedom by the same angels who visited Avraham, we find that he serves the guests actual matzah:

> And he [Lot] pressed upon them [his visitors] greatly. And they turned in to him and entered into his house. And he made them a feast and baked matzot, and they ate.
>
> *(Bereishit 19:3)*

If Lot was serving matzah, and Avraham was serving *ugot*, it must have been Pesach. There is only one problem with this theory: it sounds absurd. How can Avraham (and Lot!) be observing Pesach long before the Jews were enslaved — and certainly before they left Egypt?

We may explain Avraham and Sarah's behavior in one of two ways. On the one hand, we can say that, as spiritually sensitive people, they kept the Torah even prior to its being given.[1] On the other hand, one could make the argument that Avraham had a special affinity for Pesach. God had told Avraham that his children would be enslaved and eventually liberated, and Avraham celebrated this event, or at least the promise itself.[2] This, then, is what lies behind

---

1   *Yoma* 28b and *Kiddushin* 82a. There are sources that see the reverse — the Jews received the mitzvah because Sarah prepared *ugot*. See *Shemot Rabbah* 15:12.

the Midrashic identification of Avraham's *ugot* with a Pesach feast. Avraham was celebrating the Exodus from Egypt, the realization of God's promise to him, an event which he anticipated with great joy and celebration.

Lot's practice would be more difficult to explain. We could say that as a follower of Avraham he simply mimicked Avraham's lofty deeds. Let us return to the text:

> And the two angels came to Sedom at evening, and Lot sat in the gate of Sedom. And Lot saw them and rose up to meet them, and he bowed himself with his face to the ground. And he said, "Behold now, my lords, turn in, I beseech you, to your servant's house and remain all night and wash your feet, and you shall rise up early and go on your way."
>
> And they said, "No, we will stay in the street all night."
>
> And he pressed upon them greatly, and they turned in to him, and entered into his house. And he made them a feast and baked matzot, and they ate.
>
> *(Ibid., 1–3)*

Lot's behavior requires analysis: First of all, he sits at the gate of the city. This is reminiscent of Avraham sitting in the opening of his tent. As Avraham waits for guests to serve, so does Lot. The main difference is that Avraham lives alone, while Lot lives in a most inhospitable city. A second connotation of the gate of the city is the place of judgment, or the locale of the judges, as we see in several places in Chumash.[1] In fact, later on in the narrative Lot is attacked by his neighbors for placing himself as judge upon them.

---

2   *Bereishit* 15:13–14: "And He said to Avram, 'Know for a certainty that your seed shall be a stranger in a land that is not theirs and shall serve them; and they shall afflict them four hundred years. And also that nation whom they shall serve will I judge; and afterward they shall come out with great wealth.'"

1   For example, see *Devarim* 22:24 and *Bereishit* 34:20. The second example is of particular interest, since the Rambam rules that the reason Shimon and Levi were justified in killing the city of Shechem was that the city did not keep one of the Noachide laws, namely to maintain a just society. Apparently Rambam holds all the inhabitants of the city responsible for the outrage because they failed to mete out justice to Shechem (*Hilchot Melachim* 9:14).

And they said again, "This one fellow came in to sojourn, and he wants to be a judge? Now we will deal worse with you than with them."

(Ibid., 9)

Here we have the first clue to the tragedy of Lot. Rather than be second to Avraham, Lot strikes out on his own. He craves "top billing" as a leader in Sedom, and not just leader but judge. While it is true that to be a judge is an honorable position, judge of Sedom does seem to be an unfortunate career choice, at best. It must not have been easy to be constantly and totally overshadowed by his illustrious uncle; Lot decided to make it on his own, and while he tries to be like his uncle, he always seems to fall short.

With guests entering his (empty?) courtroom, Lot has an opportunity to be like Avraham. Here is a chance to extend hospitality and kindness. There is only one problem: the people of Sedom will not tolerate this type of behavior, and Lot knows it. Time is of the essence. We hear it in his words; he welcomes his guests, and he discusses their departure before they even agree to stay.

And he said, "Behold now, my lords, turn in, I beseech you, to your servant's house and remain all night and wash your feet, and you shall rise up early and go on your way."

Lot wants to do the right thing; he wishes to perform *chesed*. The text indicates that these visitors were angelic.[1] He knows what he has to do, but he sounds scared. He wants them to leave before they step in the door. This is why he makes them matzah — it is the fastest type of bread! Unleavened bread — doesn't even have time to rise. Based on the narrative, that would seem to be the sad reason that Lot gives his guests matzah: Not because he is celebrating the seder, but because he is scared and he wants them out as quickly as possible.[2]

---

1   When the visitors came to Avraham they were described as people; when they came to Lot they are described as angels. Perhaps Avraham treated all guests as if they were angels, but Lot needed some extra motivation, so God sent him angels.

On the other hand, Lot did rise to the occasion. He convinced them to stay; he made a feast. Soon enough, there was knocking on the door.

> But before they lay down, the men of the city, the men of Sedom, surrounded the house, both old and young, all the people from every quarter. And they called to Lot and said to him, "Where are the men who came in to you tonight? Bring them out to us, that we may know them."
>
> *(Ibid., 4–5)*

Maybe taking them home was not the best idea; not in Sedom, not even for the judge. Make no mistake: the mob outside was not the "*chesed* committee" welcoming guests. This was a group of Sedomites, looking for a "good time." They wanted to get to "know" them better (keep in mind that this is the Bible, making it superfluous to say that they wanted to know them in the biblical sense). Lot was now in trouble. His celestial guests were about to be abused in his front yard. He probably wondered what Avraham would do in a situation like this.

Lot acts heroically yet tragically; he offers the men a better deal:

> And Lot went out the door to them and closed the door after him, and said, "I beg you, my brothers, do not do so wickedly. Behold now, I have two daughters who have not known man. Let me, I beg you, bring them out to you, and do to them as is good in your eyes. Only to these men do nothing, seeing that they have come under the shadow of my roof."
>
> *(Ibid., 6–8)*

Lot's interpretation of *chesed* took a remarkable wrong turn: Rather than endanger his guests, he offers his virginal daughters to the mob. "Do what you wish," he tells them. "Just don't harm my

---

2   There is an earlier Midrashic reference to matzah: When Lot was kidnapped someone came to inform Avram of Lot's situation. According to the Midrash (*Bereishit Rabbah* 42:8) the person was Og, who found Avram preparing matzah because it was the fourteenth of Nissan. Significantly, the text records that the battle to free Lot is waged at midnight.

guests." Something seems terribly wrong. This is not what *chesed* is supposed to be about. Lot's behavior is morally outrageous. Then again, Lot was never more than a pretender[1] to Avraham's greatness. He paled in comparison to Avraham, which was why he came to Sedom in the first place. Now, the judge of Sedom makes a most injudicious decision that sets the stage for an exodus.

While at face value this entire episode has nothing to do with leaving Egypt, textual analysis reveals some surprising lines of comparison.

In retrospect, the feast that takes place the night before Lot's departure from Sedom does remind us of the first Pesach seder which took place in Egypt. However, in Egypt the Jewish people knew they would be leaving in the morning. In Sedom, at the time of the feast, Lot has no idea of what is in store.

Second, Lot's confrontation with the people of Sedom took place at the door of his home:

> And Lot went out the door to them, and closed the door after him.... And they said, "Stand back." And they said, "This one fellow came in to sojourn, and he wants to be a judge? Now we will deal worse with you than with them." And they pressed hard upon the man, Lot, and came near to break the door. But the men [the angels] put forth their hand, and pulled Lot into the house to them, and closed the door.
>
> *(Ibid., 6–10)*

In Egypt the Israelites were instructed to mark their doorposts with blood.

> And they shall take of the blood and put it on the two side posts and on the upper doorpost of the houses, in which they shall eat it [the paschal offering].
>
> *(Shemot 12:7)*

A third point of which we should take note: When the mob continued their assault they were blinded, echoing the plague of dark-

---

1   Lot even bore a physical resemblance with Avraham (see *Bereishit Rabah* 41:6).

ness that would afflict the Egyptians.

> And they [the angels] struck the men who were at the door of the house with blindness, both small and great; so that they wearied themselves to find the door.
>
> *(Bereishit 19:11)*

There are other elements of the narrative that remind us of the Exodus, although they seem somehow inverted. In Sedom, the perpetrators were young and old, while in Egypt young and old were the victims, the liberated:

> ...surrounded the house, both old and young, all the people from every quarter.
>
> *(Ibid., 4)*

> And Moshe said, "We will go with our young and with our old, with our sons and with our daughters, with our flocks and with our herds will we go; for we must hold a feast for God."
>
> *(Shemot 10:9)*

The angels lead Lot out of Sedom, while the Haggadah stresses that God Himself led the Jewish people out, not an angel nor a messenger.

Leaving Egypt, negotiations take place between Pharaoh and Moshe, with Moshe pleading for the Israelites to be allowed to leave. In Sedom, the angels try to convince Lot to leave. In the end they must literally grab him, for he tarries.

> And he lingered, and the men laid hold of his hand and the hand of his wife and the hand of his two daughters.
>
> *(Bereishit 19:16)*

The term used here is "lingered" (*vayitmahmah*), the same term used to explain the origins of matzah: "For they left so quickly they had no time to linger" (*Shemot* 12:39).[1]

---

1   Other connections include the term *vayashkef* in *Bereishit* 19:28, and the same word used in *Shemot* 14:24 (two of the three appearances of the word in the Torah). The description of the crying out and the suffering has similarities, verse 13, and *Shemot* 2:23–25

By now we clearly discern a connection between these two events, but what is the nature or meaning of the connection? Lot was not a great man. He may not have been wicked,[1] but greatness eluded him. Why was he saved from Sedom? Was he a "tzaddik"? Or was it that he was related to Avraham? (Rashi, for one, says that Lot was saved only on Avraham's merit [*Rashi* on *Bereishit* 19:17].) The only memorable action performed by Lot is serving his guests.[2] Why would his leaving Sedom serve as a prototype for the great Exodus from Egypt?

Perhaps in his failures, in his imperfections as a man, we have the perfect prototype for the eventual salvation. Our Sages tell us that the children of Israel in Egypt had slipped through the forty-nine levels of impurity. Egypt was a corrupt land, and the Israelites had become acculturated. Why were they saved? Perhaps simply because they were related to Avraham, and God had promised that they would to be saved — even though they may not have merited liberation.

The one thing the children of Israel had was confidence that they would be saved. This confidence gave them the courage to perform the paschal ceremony in Egypt, to slaughter a symbol of the Egyptian gods, to smear the blood on the doorpost, to sit and eat their matzah, and to know that they would leave in the morning. What gave them this confidence? Perhaps the answer lies in the matzah. When they were ordered to eat the matzah they knew they were really leaving. After all, in their collective memory they knew that matzah symbolized the imperfect act of *chesed* performed by Lot immediately before he was saved. And, they reasoned, if Lot

---

1   Actually, Rashi on *Bereishit* 13:14 calls him wicked — but that was when he left Avraham and he didn't keep his shepherds in line. Perhaps his behavior in trying to save the angels would allow him to lose the appellation of "wicked."

2   The only other positive actions Lot does is accompany Avraham and keep silent about Sarah's true identity. See *Bereishit Rabbah* 51:6: " 'And it came to pass when God destroyed the cities of the plain, that God remembered Avraham and sent Lot out of the midst of the turmoil' (*Bereishit* 19:29). What recollection was brought up in his favor? The silence which he maintained for Avraham when the latter passed Sarah off as his sister. He knew of this, yet was silent."

was saved from Sedom despite his peccadilloes, they would be saved as well. God's plan is beyond human comprehension; in both cases, human judgment would find the subjects undeserving of God's salvation, but God Himself thought otherwise.

The exodus of Lot, then, is the first exodus and serves as the prototype for the future salvation in Egypt, just as the exodus from Egypt is the prototype for the future, final messianic salvation.

The aftermath of Lot's liberation is particularly sordid and tragic:

> And Lot went up out of Tzo'ar, and lived in the mountain, and his two daughters with him, for he was afraid to live in Tzo'ar. And he lived in a cave, he and his two daughters. And the firstborn said to the younger, "Our father is old, and there is not a man on earth to come to us after the manner of all the earth. Come, let us make our father drink wine, and we will lie with him, that we may preserve seed from our father."
>
> And they made their father drink wine that night, and the firstborn went in and lay with her father. And he did not perceive when she lay down, nor when she arose.
>
> And it was on the next day and the firstborn said to the younger, "Behold, I lay last night with my father. Let us make him drink wine this night also, and you go in and lie with him, that we may preserve seed from our father."
>
> And they made their father drink wine that night also, and the younger arose and lay with him. And he did not perceive when she lay down, nor when she arose.
>
> And both the daughters of Lot became pregnant by their father. And the firstborn bore a son, and she called his name Moav. He is the father of the Moavites to this day. And the younger, she also bore a son, and she called his name Ben Ami. The same is the father of the Amonites to this day.
>
> *(Bereishit 19:30–38)*

The connection of this episode to the exodus from Sedom is not immediately clear. Are we being given insight into the lasting

moral effects of life in a corrupt society upon the younger generation? Lot is anything but an impressive character: He drinks himself into a stupor and commits incest (though unaware, which is
not a glowing testimonial, either!). Are the children solely to
blame? Perhaps Lot himself was not fully aware of the repercus-
sions his choice of neighborhood would have on his family and
eventually on the history of nations. Here, then, is a completely different type of plague of the firstborn. Yet the rabbis have an incredible insight into this episode.

"Arise, take your wife and your two daughter that are found"
(ibid., 15) — Rabbi Tobiah ben Rabbi Yitzchak said: "Two
'finds' [would spring from them], Rut the Moavitess and
Naamah the Amonitess." Rabbi Yitzchak commented: " 'I
have found David My servant' (Tehillim 89:21): where did I
find him? In Sedom."

(Bereishit Rabbah 50:11)

One eventual result of this incident is the birth of David: King
David, the chosen, progenitor of the Messiah, who descended from
Rut the Moavitess. Long before the enslavement in Egypt, God pre-
pared the building blocks for the messianic redemption.[1]

The primary trait of Avraham is *chesed*. Lot is an imposter; his
chesed is misguided. He commits incest with his daughters, which,
remarkably, is described in the Torah as *chesed* (see *Vayikra* 20:17,
which speaks of sibling incest, and Rashi's comments).

Many years later the Moavites, the descendants of Lot and his
older daughter, send their daughters down to Israel's camp and try
to corrupt the morals of Avraham's descendents rather than welcoming the Israelites from their travels in the desert — as Avraham
would have done[2] (*Bemidbar*, ch. 25). When God condemns Moav,
it is specifically for their lack of *chesed* that they are chastised:

---

1   For a similar teaching see *Bereishit Rabbah* 85:1: "Before the last who shall enslave
    [Israel] was born, the first redeemer was born."
2   The numerical value of Moav is 49 — indicating the forty-ninth level of depravity,
    the level the Jewish people sunk to in Egypt.

An Amonite or Moavite shall not enter into the congregation of God; to their tenth generation they shall not enter into the congregation of God forever, because they did not meet you with bread and with water on the way, when you came out of Egypt, and because they hired against you Bilam ben Beor of Petor of Aram Naharayim to curse you.

(Devarim 23:4–5)

The Israelites are elsewhere instructed to avoid conflict with the descendants of Lot, apparently to keep the deal Avraham made all those years ago with Lot (*Bereishit*, ch. 13):

And God said to me, "Distress not the Moavites, and do not contend with them in battle, for I will not give you of their land for a possession, because I have given Ar to the sons of Lot for a possession."

(Devarim 2:9)

Because Moav has its roots in Avraham's tent they are expected, even many generations later, to adhere to a higher moral standard. They are expected to perform *chesed*, and when they do not they are excluded from joining the Jewish people. Only when Moavites internalize the true teaching of *chesed* can they once again join the community of Israel.[1] This occurs only generations later, when a young woman from Moav did know how to perform *chesed*: Instead of "getting on with her life" after her husband passed away, she cared for her mother-in-law. The woman's name was Rut the Moavite. She is the great-grandmother of David. David's kingdom, then, begins in Sedom — or, more precisely, in the exodus from Sedom.

We see then that the first exodus from Sedom, the Exodus from Egypt, and the final salvation spearheaded by a descendant of David are all remarkably related. The matzah served by Lot is the key to deciphering the inner message of the story. When we eat matzah

---

1   The justification of Rut converting was that only the males of Moav were excluded by the Torah's ban, not the women. See *Yevamot* 76b and *Vayikra Rabbah* 14:1.

on Pesach we say that it is *lechem oni* — often translated as "poor man's bread." The Talmud makes a second suggestion for the etymology of the word *oni* from the word "to answer" or "respond."

> The fact that we read it *oni* [is explained] as Shmuel's [dictum]. For Shmuel said: "Bread of *oni* [means] "bread over which many words are recited ['*onin*']."
>
> *(Pesachim 36a)*

Apparently matzah is more multifaceted than we ever would have imagined. It represents a mitzvah performed quickly and imperfectly. How amazing that this meal could have so inspired the oppressed slaves in Egypt, and that as a result of this hasty meal the Messiah will one day arrive.

Chol HaMoed Pesach

"These Bones Will Live!"

The Talmud in *Megillah* teaches:

Rav Huna said in the name of Rav Sheishet: "On the Sabbath of Chol HaMoed, on both Pesach and Sukkot, we read from Scripture '*Re'eh Atah*' (*Shemot* 33). The haftarah on Pesach, 'The Dry Bones' (*Yechezkel* 37), and on Sukkot 'The Day of the Arrival of Gog' (*Yechezkel* 38)."

(Megillah 31a)

The passage in the Talmud discusses the appropriate readings for the various festivals. Generally the text which is read has an intrinsic connection with the day, but in this case no connection is apparent. Over a thousand years ago, this question was asked of Rav Hai Gaon, the leading scholar of his generation. He responded that he was not aware of any intrinsic connection between the scripture read in the haftarah and these holidays, but continued:

I have a tradition from the Sages that Resurrection will take place in Nissan, and victory over Gog and Magog will take place in Tishrei. Therefore in Nissan we read of the Dry Bones [which will be resurrected] in the haftarah, and in Tishrei we read of the battle of Gog.

(Tur, Orach Chaim 490; see Otzar HaGaonim, Megillah, p. 64)

This tradition, that Resurrection is to take place in Nissan, is the key to a number of passages in the Talmud.

> Rabbi Eliezer said: "In Tishrei the world was created, in Tishrei the *avot* were born, in Tishrei the *avot* perished, on Pesach Yitzchak was born, on Rosh HaShanah Sarah, Rachel, and Chanah were answered. On Rosh HaShanah Yosef left prison, on Rosh HaShanah the slavery came to an end in Egypt. In Nissan we were redeemed, in Tishrei we will be redeemed in the future." Rav Yehoshua said: "In Nissan the world was created, in Nissan the *avot* were born, in Nissan the *avot* perished, on Pesach Yitzchak was born.... In Nissan we were redeemed, in Nissan we will be redeemed."
>
> *(Rosh HaShanah 10b–11a)*

In this passage we find that two of the great *tannaim*, Rabbis Eliezer and Yehoshua, argue not only about biblical chronology but also about eschatology. At the root of this disagreement is the intricate relationship of history and destiny in the view of these great Sages. Days have a personality or a charisma of their own, just as people do; therefore the understanding of the past allows us to better understand the future. Rabbi Eliezer and Rabbi Yehoshua have a fundamental argument regarding when the world came into being, and their differences are interrelated with the question of how the End of Days will shape up.

Tishrei is a month of judgment, while Nissan is a month of miracles, as is indicated by its very name ("Nissan" is perhaps from the root *nes*, miracle). In this context, Rabbi Eliezer and Rabbi Yehoshua differ over the very nature of existence: Is our life defined primarily by justice or mercy? Tosafot, in their comments to the passage in *Masechet Rosh HaShanah*, point out that actually both aspects are accurate representations of our existence: Rabbi Eliezer focuses on the thought of creation which came into existence in Tishrei, while Rabbi Yehoshua focuses on the actual creation which took place in Nissan. It is interesting to note that Jewish law reflects the opinion of Rabbi Yehoshua, as is evidenced by a relatively obscure law: *Birkat hachamah*, a blessing on the sun which may be made every twenty-eight years when the sun is in the exact alignment it was at the moment of creation, is pronounced in Nissan (see *Shulchan Aruch* 229:2, *Mishnah Berurah* 7).

If Creation indeed took place in Nissan, thereby establishing the law in accordance with Rabbi Yehoshua, then we may conclude that Redemption will also take place in Nissan, as per Rabbi Yehoshua. This is interesting in and of itself, but does not seem connected with our original question regarding Resurrection. The connection is only brought out by an additional passage:

> Rabbi Eliezer said, "If Israel repent they will be redeemed. If not they will not be redeemed."
>
> Rabbi Yehoshua said to him, "If they don't repent they won't be redeemed? Rather, the Holy One, blessed be He, will bring a king whose decrees are as difficult as Haman, and the Jews will repent and rectify their ways."
>
> Another [*beraita*] taught: Rabbi Eliezer said: "If Israel repent, they will be redeemed, as it is written, 'Return, you backsliding children, and I will heal your backslidings' (*Yirmiyah* 3:22)."
>
> Rabbi Yehoshua said to him, "But is it not written, 'You have sold yourselves for naught, and you shall be redeemed without money' (*Yeshayah* 52:3)? You have sold yourselves for naught — for idolatry; and you shall be redeemed without money — without repentance and good deeds."
>
> Rabbi Eliezer retorted to Rabbi Yehoshua, "But is it not written, 'Return to Me, and I will return to you' (*Malachi* 3:7)?"
>
> Rabbi Yehoshua rejoined, "But is it not written, 'For I am master over you, and I will take you one of a city, and two of a family, and I will bring you to Zion' (*Yirmiyah* 3:14)?"
>
> Rabbi Eliezer replied, "But it is written, 'In returning and rest shall you be saved' (*Yeshayah* 30:15)."
>
> Rabbi Yehoshua replied, "But is it not written, 'Thus says the Lord, the Redeemer of Israel, and his Holy One, to him whom man despises, to him whom the nations abhor, to a ser-

vant of rulers, "Kings shall see and arise, princes also shall worship" ' (ibid. 49:7)?"

Rabbi Eliezer countered, "But is it not written, ' "If you will return, O Israel," says God, "return to Me" ' (*Yirmiyah* 4:1)?"

Rabbi Yehoshua answered, "But it is elsewhere written, 'And I heard the man clothed in linen, which was upon the waters of the river, when he held up his right hand and his left hand to heaven, and swore by Him that lives forever that it shall be for a time, times, and a half; and when He shall have accomplished to scatter the power of the holy people, all these things shall be finished' (*Daniel* 12:7)."

At this Rabbi Eliezer remained silent.

(Sanhedrin 97b–98a)

Again, Rabbi Eliezer's view of the world is based on merit, on judgment and justice. Redemption is possible only if the Jews deserve it, if they repent. In its conclusion, the Talmud teaches that according to Rabbi Yehoshua, Redemption is unconditional; his statement that God would bring a wicked tyrant to persecute us was Rabbi Yehoshua's understanding of Rabbi Eliezer's opinion. (The *Yerushalmi* [*Ta'anit* 1:1] reports that it was Rabbi Eliezer's opinion, and not Rabbi Yehoshua's, that God would bring a wicked tyrant on the Jews if they do not repent on their own.)

In the end of the passage Rabbi Eliezer is silenced by the arguments of Rabbi Yehoshua. Apparently both agree that Redemption will come sooner or later, but Redemption will inevitably come.[1]

Juxtaposing these two Talmudic teachings allows us to draw conclusions regarding the Sages' debate: In *Masechet Rosh HaShanah*, Rabbi Eliezer and Rabbi Yehoshua argue as to when Creation took place and when the final Redemption will come. If these two arguments are connected, the passage in *Sanhedrin* is highly instructive. The argument regarding Redemption ends with the ac-

---

1 The Ramban clearly states that in conclusion Rabbi Eliezer concedes to Rabbi Yehoshua, as is indicated by his silence. See *Sefer HaGeulah, Kitvei Ramban*, vol. 1, p. 277.

quiescence of Rabbi Eliezer, which is consistent with our understanding of the passage in _Rosh HaShanah,_ where the law is also established in accordance with the view of Rabbi Yehoshua. Tosafot's teaching, which reconciles the two positions by identifying each with a "different" Creation, may be applied to both passages equally: There is no fundamental argument; rather, one passage refers to the idea of Creation, while the other refers to the actual Creation.

In other words, do we consider the beginning of the process, or are we concerned with the end result? Rabbi Eliezer focused on the beginning of the process of Creation; therefore he speaks of Tishrei, which is the time of Creation in thought, long before anything existed in reality. Similarly, Rabbi Eliezer, when considering Redemption, spoke of the upheaval which will lead to spiritual renaissance. This is the beginning of the process of Redemption. On the other hand, Rabbi Yehoshua focused on the end of the process, the actual Creation. The tradition referred to by Rav Hai Gaon, that Resurrection will take place in Nissan, refers to the end of the process of Redemption, Resurrection.

Rabbi Eliezer's opinion finds its own expression in the Talmud. The Talmud only uses the phrase _"atchalta d'geulah"_ (beginning of the Redemption) in one place:

War is also considered the beginning of the Redemption.

(Megillah 17b)

Rabbi Eliezer, who looked at the beginning of the process of Creation, considered the beginning of the redemptive process as well: The haftarah for Chol HaMoed Sukkot describes the apocalyptic battle between Gog and Magog, the beginning of the process of Redemption. This epic battle, which Israel is destined to be swept into if they do not repent in due course, is to take place in Tishrei, the month in which Sukkot is celebrated. Here, then, is the link with the haftarah which we sought. It is the link between Tishrei and the _atchalta d'geulah_ which Rabbi Eliezer illuminated.

The association of Resurrection with Nissan has a number of expressions and implications. One of the teachings which both Rabbis agreed on was the birth of Yitzchak on Pesach. Yitzchak is the first biblical figure who is linked with resurrection. One *midrash* describes the connection in the following terms:

> [When Yitzchak was tied down to the altar at the *akeidah*] the angels began to cry and their tears fell on the blade. The knife rose up to the neck of Yitzchak, for he [Avraham] could not control it. His [Yitzchak's] soul departed from him. God called [the angel] Michael and said, "Why are you standing there? Do not allow him to slaughter him."
> Immediately, Michael called out, "Avraham, Avraham...."
> He let go [of the knife] and his soul returned. He [Yitzchak] stood on his feet and pronounced the blessing, "Blessed is He who restores life to the dead."
> *(Otzar Midrashim, p. 146)*

According to this *midrash*, the first one to utter the blessing on restoration of life was Yitzchak, when his own life was restored. This idea is also consistent with a second teaching. We are taught that the first three blessings of the *Amidah* are called *"Avot."* While the other elements of the *Amidah* vary depending on the day, these three blessings are constants. The first of these blessings, which speaks of God's *chesed*, is *"Magen Avraham,"* associated with Avraham and the spiritual realm so inseparably associated with him. The second blessing is *"Mechayei HaMeitim,"* and is related to Yitzchak. This blessing starts with *"Atah gibor,"* *gevurah* being the spiritual attribute associated with Yitzchak and the one which is preserved and expressed three times a day by Jews for millennia. The second blessing of the *Amidah* is instructive in other ways:

> You are eternally mighty, my Lord, the resuscitator of the dead are You; abundantly able to save....

In the winter, the phrase which follows is: "He makes the wind blow and the rain descend; He sustains the living with kindness." In Israel, in the summer months the subsequent phrase reads: "He brings down the dew. He sustains the living with kindness."

The difference between these two phrases seems obvious, the distinction being in the object of our prayer, either rain or dew. There is, however, a more subtle difference. The prayer said in the winter is "He makes the wind blow and the rain [*geshem*] descend; He sustains the living with kindness." There are some who have a custom of saying *gashem* (with a *kamatz*, instead of a *segol*). The significance of the punctuation goes way beyond the grammatical: "*Geshem*" is the form of the word which would appear in the middle of a sentence, whereas "*gashem*" indicates the end of the sentence. The alternative readings would indicate whether the second half of the blessing modifies the first or stands alone. *Geshem*, rather than *gashem*, would indicate that the kindness which is bestowed is the rain itself. The phrase used in the summer is "*morid hatal*," the word *tal* (dew) punctuated with a *kamatz*. "Dew" is the end of the sentence, as opposed to a later appearance in the weekday *Amidah* where the word *tal* with a *patach* is used in the middle of the sentence.

If the term "He brings down the dew" is the end of the sentence, then it must modify what immediately preceded it: "You are eternally mighty, my Lord, the resuscitator of the dead are You; abundantly able to save: He brings down the dew!" Dew is directly connected with resurrection. But what is the nature of this connection? In numerous places in Talmud, Midrash, and *Zohar*, we see that dew is the catalyst which brings about the Resurrection!

> Dew will be used in the future by the Holy One, Blessed be He, to bring about Resurrection.
>
> *(Chagigah 12b)*

> After each of the ten commandments [the people died when God spoke] so [God] brought dew on them which will be used in the future to resurrect man, and they came back to life.
>
> *(Shabbat 88b)*

How do we know that Resurrection will only take place via dew?...

(Yerushalmi, Berachot 5:2)

The dead [bones] which Yechezkel brought back to life — dew from heaven descended upon them.

(Pirkei D'Rabbi Eliezer 33)

Dew is a symbol of resurrection.

(Tanchuma, Toldot 19)

By means of that dew all will rise from the dust, as it says, "For Your dew is as the dew of lights" (*Yeshayah* 26:19), these being the supernal lights through which the Almighty will in future pour forth life upon the world.

(Zohar, Bereshit 130b)

Rabbi Chiya said: "And what is more, from the words, 'Your dead ones will live' (*Yeshayah* 26:19), it is evident that not only will there be a new creation, but that the very bodies which were dead will rise, for one bone in the body remains intact, not decaying in the earth, and on the Resurrection Day the Holy One will soften it and make it like leaven in dough, and it will rise and expand on all sides, and the whole body and all its members will be formed from it, and then the Holy One will put spirit into it." Said Rabbi Eliezer: "Assuredly so. And the bone will be softened by the dew, as it says: 'Your dead ones shall live...for Your dew is as the dew of lights' (ibid.)."

(Zohar, Shemot 28b)

We would expect that the second blessing of the *Amidah*, the one connected with Yitzchak, the blessing which concludes, "Blessed is God who brings the dead to life," would naturally make reference to the final Resurrection. If so, when we say "He brings down the dew!" our intention should be "Bring the Resurrection!"

The prayer for rain is said only in the winter. On Pesach, we begin to ask for dew. At the time of our redemption from Egypt, the time of the birth of Yitzchak, we say this blessing with anticipation of the complete Redemption, the end of the Redemption: Resurrection. This is the full circle of the second blessing of the *Amidah* and the link between the month of Nissan, the birth of Yitzchak, the Exodus, and the result of the Redemption which Rabbi Yehoshua sought to draw in the passage in *Rosh HaShanah*.

When the Jews left Egypt they had three goals: 1) to leave Egypt, 2) to receive the Torah, and 3) to build the Temple. In the Ramban's introduction to *Sefer Shemot* he explains that *Shemot* is the book of redemption, but the book cannot end after the Exodus nor after the receiving of the Torah. The book does not end until the Mishkan is built.

Pesach marks the celebration of leaving Egypt, but it cannot be seen in a vacuum. On Pesach we immediately begin counting the days until the Torah is given at Sinai. But receiving the Torah is not an end in and of itself. Receiving the Torah means living the Torah, following its statutes, taking the ideals described in the Torah and turning them into a wonderful reality. The reality of living the Torah necessarily leads to the Messianic Age and culminates in the end of this Age — Resurrection. For this reason, on the Shabbat of Chol Hamoed we read the description of how dry bones shall live, for the bones coming to life are the culmination of the Redemption begun on Pesach.

> You are eternally mighty, my Lord, the resuscitator of the dead are You; abundantly able to save: Bring the Resurrection!

Iyar

The Omer

The Students of Rabbi Akiva

The days between Pesach and Shavuot are known as the Omer. These days are counted as we anxiously await the holiday of Shavuot, the day commemorating the giving of the Torah. It is interesting to note that the Torah itself does not explicitly state that Shavuot is the day on which the Torah was given. From the biblical perspective, the counting is directed toward a date of agricultural significance, as the new fruits would be brought to Yerushalayim on Shavuot. On the other hand, the understanding that this is indeed the day of Revelation is based on simple mathematics, implicit in the narrative.[1]

The Torah successfully merges pedestrian, mundane activity with deep theological constructs. While from man's perspective the harvest may be the impetus for joy, the Torah stresses that these first fruits must be brought within a religious context. We can readily understand how agricultural man would have been overjoyed when the literal fruits of his labor came to fruition. The Torah's order places this very human, natural joy within a religious context. Moreover, linking this agricultural festival with the very day on which the holy Torah itself was revealed surely elevated the

---

1   The actual date on which the Torah was given is a subject which is debated in the Talmud. See *Shabbat* 86b and the essay on Shavuot, "The Holiday of the Giving of the Torah."

joy from the mundane to the sacred. Thus, the counting in Temple times between Pesach and Shavuot had a dual component, sacred and mundane, each independently a reason to rejoice.

Be that as it may, in the contemporary religious collective experience, these are days of mourning. No weddings or other public expressions of joy are celebrated. The accepted explanation for this transformation of a joyful period into a time of mourning is the demise of the students of Rabbi Akiva:

> The practice is not to get married between Pesach and Shavuot — until Lag Ba'Omer — because during this time the students of Rabbi Akiva perished.
>
> *(Shulchan Aruch 493:1)*

The reference of the *Shulchan Aruch*, and therefore the source of the well-established custom, is the tragic story of Rabbi Akiva's students who died during this time of the year:

> It was said that Rabbi Akiva had twelve thousand pairs of disciples, from Givata to Antipatris; and all of them died at the same time because they did not treat each other with respect. The world remained desolate until Rabbi Akiva came to our masters in the South and taught the Torah to them. These were Rabbi Meir, Rabbi Yehudah, Rabbi Yosei, Rabbi Shimon, and Rabbi Elazar ben Shamua; and it was they who revived the Torah at that time. A *tanna* taught: All of them died between Pesach and Shavuot. Rabbi Chama bar Abba or, it might be said, Rabbi Chiya ben Abin said: "All of them died a cruel death. What was it?" Rabbi Nachman replied: "Croup."
>
> *(Yevamot 62b)*[1]

The Talmud speaks of twelve thousand "pairs" of students and not of twenty-four thousand, ostensibly in order to stress the lack of unity of which they were guilty. The Talmud does not mention that their deaths are commemorated with the yearly mourning pe-

---

1   See *Bereishit Rabbah* 61:3, *Kohelet Rabbah* 11, and *Yalkut Shimoni, Kohelet* 989, for parallel sources. Also see *Tanna D'Vei Eliyahu Zuta* 22.

riod of the Omer. And so, while the authority of switching a biblically happy time into a time of mourning is said to be based on a
passage in the Talmud, the Talmud tells a sad tale but does not draw
this all-important conclusion. There are those who have claimed
that the custom of mourning was instituted during the Talmudic
period;[1] there is, however, no Talmudic statement which supports
this opinion and consequently there are those who opine that the
custom is, in fact, of later origin.[2]

Of particular interest is the formulation of Rav Yechiel Michel
Epstein in his classic *Aruch HaShulchan*. The tragedy of the students
of Rabbi Akiva is connected with the Crusades, pogroms, and blood
libels suffered over the course of Jewish history. These attacks were
often rooted in a twisted Christian perspective of the Pesach ceremony, and the days after Pesach became a time of peril for Jews in
Christendom. Rav Epstein describes these days as well-established
days of "judgment."[3]

According to this approach, the rabbis in the Middle Ages felt
that the nature of this period was harsh, despite the Torah's perspective that this was a time of joy. The Talmudic passage concerning Rabbi Akiva's students served as an anchor for turning a happy
period into a time of mourning. The logic was that if the students of
Rabbi Akiva died specifically during these days, their nature is not
as straightforward as we might have thought. In other words, the
reason that the Omer has become a time of mourning is the death
of the students of Rabbi Akiva, but the specific impetus for institut-
ing customs of mourning was the blood libels of the Middle Ages.[4]

1 See *Otzar HaGeonim* on *Yevamot* 62b (p. 141) and sources cited. Rav Ovadyah Yosef,
   Yabia Omer, vol. 5, *Orach Chaim* 38.
2 See *Birkei Yosef* 493:10, which cites a number of opinions that the custom not to
   wed during this period is late and spurious.
3 *Aruch HaShulchan* 493:1. Rav Epstein also cites the *Chok Yaakov* (493:3) and
   mentions the opinion of Rav Yochanan ben Nuri, that the maximum hell to which
   a soul may be sentenced is the length of the period between Pesach and Shavuot
   (*Mishnah Eduyot* 2:9), which further points to the "judgment" aspect of this period.
4 The *Aruch HaShulchan* specifically states that the custom began in the time of the
   geonim. This may also explain why specifically Sefardic *poskim* found the custom
   difficult.

The story of the deaths of the students of Rabbi Akiva may be part of a much larger issue. An analysis of a later parallel source may provide the clue necessary to unravel the mystery. Rav Sherira Gaon, commenting on the original passage, uses a very telling expression to describe the death of the students:

> Rabbi Akiva raised many students, [but] there was a religious persecution [*shmadah*] on the students of Rabbi Akiva.
> *(Iggeret Rav Sherira Gaon, Sefardic recencion, p. 13)*

The Talmud spoke of a plague striking the students, yet Rav Sherira speaks of religious persecution! The change is subtle yet the implication drastic. The Talmudic tradition seemed quite clear: these students treated one another without respect, and therefore died of a plague. What caused Rav Sherira to introduce religious persecution as the cause of the students' demise? A careful reading leads us to the conclusion that Rav Sherira does not disagree with the Talmud. Surely, in the tradition of thousands of commentaries before and after his time Rav Sherira saw his task as interpreting the Talmudic passage, and not disagreeing with the Talmud.

Apparently Rav Sherira had a tradition that the students died during a religious conflict. The book that this information is found in is primarily a book with an historical agenda. The work *Iggeret Rav Sherira Gaon* contains singular traditions of the Talmudic period. This book — or "letter," as it is called — is the major source for information about the Talmudic age. If we posit that Rav Sherira saw his role as the telling of history, while the role of the Talmud is to share theological perspectives, the question dissipates: Rav Sherira tells us how the students died, while the Talmud tells us why they died.

The Talmud, the unparalleled work of Rabbinic Judaism, had no need to retell well-known historical episodes. Its task was to illuminate and explain God's hand in history — to explain why things, especially specific tragedies, befell our people. Ironically, in this instance, the Talmud became our primary source for what were well-known events. Though the Talmud was not interested in telling us what happened, rather why it happened, uninitiated readers were deluded into thinking they knew what happened as well. Rav Sherira wished to set the record straight. Therefore he tells us what happened: The students died due to religious persecution. The question that emerges is which religious persecution is referred to? We know that Rabbi Akiva was himself eventually murdered as part of the Hadrianic executions. We also know that Rabbi Akiva was an enthusiastic supporter of Bar Kochva.[1] Therefore the association between Rabbi Akiva's "students" and the followers of Bar Kochva is likely.[2]

---

1   The Talmud says that the students died from the croup, which is the English word for *askara*, a term which denotes choking. The association with Bar Kochva may explain this term, as Bar Kochva's death is described as taking place when a snake (a symbol of his sins) choked him (*Yerushalmi Ta'anit* 4:5, *Eichah Rabbah* 2:4).
"Forthwith the sins caused Beitar to be captured. Bar Koziba was slain and his head taken to Hadrian. 'Who killed him?' asked Hadrian. A Goth said to him, 'I killed him.' 'Bring his body to me,' he ordered. He went and found a snake encircling its neck; so [Hadrian, when told of this] exclaimed, 'If his God had not slain him who could have overcome him?' "
However, the *Bavli* describes the death of Bar Kochva as taking place at the hands of the Sages (*Sanhedrin* 93b). "Bar Koziba reigned two and a half years, and then said to the Rabbis, 'I am the Messiah.' They answered, 'Of Messiah it is written that he smells and judges: let us see whether he [Bar Koziba] can do so.' When they saw that he was unable to judge by the scent, they slew him."
Most likely, the intention that the Sages wished to convey was that once the rabbis withdrew their support, Bar Kochva was defeated. The motivation for this response may be seen from another source, which shows that Bar Kochva was unable to discern the greatness of one of the rabbis, whom he suspected of treason, and had him killed (*Midrash Eichah* and *Yerushalmi, Ta'anit* 4:5). The *Talmud Yerushalmi* adds that Bar Kochva was a great warrior, and he said to God, "Do not help nor hinder us and we will be successful." The Rambam and Ra'avad reflect these two traditions; see *Hilchot Melachim* 11:3, where the Rambam most likely understands that the sources complement one another as I described above, because it is unlikely that he would reject the *Talmud Bavli* in favor of another tradition.
2   This would explain the incredible number of "students" who perished. There have been historians who have made this association. On the other hand, a number of sources speak of students of Rabbi Akiva not behaving properly.
"Did it not once happen that one of Rabbi Akiva's disciples fell sick, and the Sages did not visit him? So Rabbi Akiva himself entered [his house] to visit him, and because they swept and sprinkled the ground before him, he recovered. 'My master,' said he, 'you have revived me!' [Straightway] Rabbi Akiva went forth and

The Rambam describes Rabbi Akiva as an "arms bearer" of Bar Koziba.[1] The source of the Rambam's assertion is a passage in the *Talmud Yerushalmi*:

Rabbi Shimon ben Yochai taught: "Akiva my master would expound the verse 'A star will come from Yaakov' as 'Koziba will come from Yaakov.' When Rabbi Akiva would see Bar Koziba he would say, 'There is the King Messiah.' " Rav Yochanan ben Torta said: "Akiva, grass will grow from your cheeks and still the son of David will not come."

(Ta'anit 4:5)

The verse in question is in the prophecy of Bilam, Israel's wouldbe anathema who instead blessed the Jewish people:

I shall see him, but not now; I shall behold him, but not near. A

---

lectured: He who does not visit the sick is like a shedder of blood" (*Nedarim* 40a).

"Rabbi Tarfon was sitting and asked this question: 'What [is the reason for the difference in law] between [what is offered] before the Omer and [what is offered] before the two loaves?' Said Yehudah ben Nechemyah before him, 'No; you can say [that what is offered] before the Omer [is invalid], for the prohibition [of the new corn] does not admit of any exception to the private individual, but can you say so [of what is offered] before the two loaves, seeing that the prohibition does admit of an exception to the private individual?' Rabbi Tarfon remained silent, and at once the face of Yehudah ben Nechemyah brightened with joy. Thereupon Rabbi Akiva said to him, 'Yehudah, your face has brightened with joy because you have refuted the Sage; I wonder whether you will live long.' Said Rabbi Yehudah bar Ila'i, 'This happened a fortnight before Pesach, and when I came up for the Atzeret I inquired after Yehudah ben Nechemyah and was told that he had passed away' " (*Menachot* 68b).

This second source is particularly impressive as the death clearly takes place between Pesach and Shavuot, and, ironically, the topic of discussion was the Omer! One would have to posit that this type of behavior was exhibited by twenty-four thousand individual students in order to take the first passage at face value. There is, however, another source, which speaks of a "mere" three hundred students who perished. See *Midrash Tanchuma, Chayei Sarah* 8, and *Responsa Minchat Yitzchak*, vol. 3, section 38, who surprisingly reads the number three hundred into our passage in the Talmud.

1   The real name of the supposed messiah was Bar Kosba (see below). After his failure, he was known as Bar Koziba, and this is how the Rambam refers to him in *Hilchot Melachim* 11:3. The name Bar Kochva as such is not found in Talmudic literature, cf. Buber edition of *Eichah Rabbah*.

star will come from Yaakov, and a scepter shall rise from Yisrael, and shall strike the corners of Moav and destroy all the sons of Shet.

(Bemidbar 24:17)

Bilam's clairvoyance allowed him to see a star who would yet emerge and lead the Jewish people. Rabbi Akiva declared that the fulfillment of this verse was in the person of Bar Kochva (literally, "son of a star"). In fact, his name was not actually Bar Kochva: Based on recent archeological finds, we know that his actual name was Bar Kosba (with the Hebrew letter *samech*). The appellation Bar Kochva was part of the messianic identification made by Rabbi Akiva, by applying this verse from Bilam's prophecy to Shimon bar Kosba. After the rebellion was quashed, he was called Bar Koziba, "son of deceit" or "son of disappointment."

Rabbi Yochanan said: "Rebbe used to expound, 'A star will come from Yaakov' thus: Read not *kochav* but *kazav* [lie]."

(Eichah Rabbah 2:4)

The aftermath of the painful defeat caused Bar Kochva to receive a new moniker, which recorded the profound failure for posterity.

While Rabbi Akiva afforded messianic status to the rebellion in general, and to Bar Kochva in particular, there was another voice which spoke out in opposition:[1]

Rabbi Yochanan ben Torta said: "Akiva, grass will grow from your cheeks and still the son of David will not come."

The phrase is enigmatic.[2] What is the inference of grass growing from the cheeks of Akiva? If it means "Akiva, you will be in the grave before the Messiah arrives," the passage should have read

---

1   Although the Rambam (*Hilchot Melachim* 11:3) makes it sound as if the entire generation was in agreement with Rabbi Akiva, the language "all the sages of the generation" must mean "most," unless this represents a later view, after the revolt began to unravel.

2   Rabbi Soloveitchik once suggested that the idiom referred to Rabbi Akiva's eloquence.

"Akiva, grass will grow from your cheeks and then the son of David will come."[1] It sounds as if Rabbi Yochanan ben Torta rejects the Messianic Age completely.[2] This position is untenable for we know that Rabbi Yochanan ben Torta believed in the coming of the Messianic Age:

> Rabbi Yochanan ben Torta said, "...But [regarding] the last Temple [the third] — may it be rebuilt in our lives, in our days — it is written, 'And it shall come to pass in the last days, that the mountain of God's house shall be established on the top of the mountains and exalted above the hills, and all nations shall flow to it. And many people shall go and say: "Come, and let us go up to the mountain of God, to the house of the Lord of Yaakov; and he will teach us of his ways, and we will walk in his paths; for from Zion shall go forth Torah, and the word of God from Yerushalayim" ' (*Yeshayah* 2:2–3). And it says, 'For there shall be a day when the watchmen[3] upon Mount Efrayim shall cry, "Arise, and let us go up to Zion to God, our Lord" (*Yirmiyah* 31:5).' "
>
> *(Tosefta Menachot 13:23)*

If Rabbi Yochanan ben Torta indeed believes in an impending Messianic Age, what is the nature of his attack on Rabbi Akiva? If we listen to his words carefully it seems that there are two problems:

> Rabbi Yochanan ben Torta said: "Akiva, grass will grow from your cheeks and still the son of David will not come."

---

1   There is another teaching of Rabbi Yochanan ben Torta (*Shir HaShirim Rabbah* 7:16) which relates to the grave: "Rabbi Yochanan ben Torta said: 'Even when one is dead, his lips quiver in the grave. How do we know? Because it says, "Causing the sleepers' lips to murmur" (*Shir HaShirim* 7:10).' "

2   The Talmud does record one opinion of a certain Rabbi Hillel that the Messianic Age was exhausted in the days of Chizkiyahu, but this opinion is considered antinomian. See *Sanhedrin* 99a.

3   The Hebrew word for "watchmen," *notzrim*, may be a play on words hinting to Christians — not, of course, in the Biblical text, but in the particular usage by Rabbi Yochanan ben Torta.

Even if this elusive grass were to grow from Rabbi Akiva's cheeks, there may be a second impediment. If we were to look at the previous paragraph of the *tosefta* cited above, this becomes clear:

> Rabbi Yochanan ben Torta said, "Why was Shilo destroyed? Because of the desecration of the sacred things thereof. Yerushalayim? The first Temple, why was it destroyed? Because of idolatry, sexual licentiousness, and the spilling of blood within. But this previous Temple [the second Temple] we knew [the people of that era]. They were diligent in Torah study and careful with tithes. Why were they exiled? Because they loved their money and man hated his neighbor."
>
> *(Ibid., 22)*

Rabbi Yochanan ben Torta is the author of the well-accepted view that the cause of the destruction of the Second Temple was groundless hatred;[1] if this is the case, we have now come full circle. We saw at the outset that the students of Rabbi Akiva died because they did not treat one another with respect. Therefore, Rabbi Yochanan, who indeed believes the Messiah will come, is adamant that the cause for the destruction of the Second Temple must be repaired before one can speak of a new messianic movement.

What then is the reference to the "grass growing" from Rabbi Akiva's cheeks? An analysis of the passage of the Rambam will provide explanation.

> You should not think that the Messiah must perform miracles or wonders, or create new realities, or bring back the dead,[2] or other similar things; the matter is not so. For Rabbi Akiva was the greatest sage of the age of the Mishnah, and he was an arms

---

1 This teaching is also found in *Yoma* 9a, but the Talmudic discussion clouds the authorship of Rav Yochanan ben Torta. A careful reading of that source will yield the same conclusion.

2 It should be noted that Rabbi Menachem M. Shneerson, in his commentary on this passage, concludes that the Messianic Age — the coming of the Messiah — will predate the epoch of the Resurrection. See *Chokrei HaZemanim* by Alter Hilovitz, Mosad HaRav Kook, vol. 2, p. 19–35, for the Rebbe's treatise on this passage.

bearer of Bar Koziba the King, and he said concerning him, "He is the King Messiah," until he was killed due to his sins. Once he was killed it became apparent to them that he was not [the Messiah]. And the sages did not ask of him neither sign nor wonder....

(Rambam, Hilchot Melachim 11:3)

The Rambam explains that life in the Messianic Age will be no different from current times in terms of the miraculous.[1] What is the Rambam's source? Rabbi Akiva, in our passage in the *Yerushalmi*. If Rabbi Akiva concludes that the Messiah need not perform miracles, and Rabbi Yochanan ben Torta disagrees with Rabbi Akiva, then we may deduce that Rav Yochanan ben Torta believed that the Messiah must perform miracles. Now we understand why he says, "Akiva, grass will grow from your cheeks and still the Messiah will not come."[2] He seems to be saying, "As far as I am concerned the Messiah must perform miracles, but even if a miracle worker appears, I do not believe that the Messianic Age can begin prior to rectifying the cause of the destruction of the previous Temple."

The core of this argument between Rabbi Akiva and Rabbi Yochanan ben Torta may be based on a similarity between these two great individuals. Both began their careers as outsiders, and joined the sages at a later point in life. Rabbi Akiva was an adult be-

---

1   As seen in the previous footnote, we must stress that there are various epochs described as being part of the Jewish eschatological vision. According to the Rambam, the Messianic Age is the first part. While this epoch requires no change of nature, subsequent epochs must include basic changes. For example, the Rambam clearly believes in Resurrection, as is evidenced by his including lack of belief in Reurrection as tantamount to heresy in his *Hilchot Teshuvah*. Therefore we may conclude that Resurrection is part of a later epoch. See article cited in previous note.

2   This comment would be more caustic if Rabbi Akiva was in fact bald, as is implied by at least one Talmudic source and is the understanding of a number of medieval authorities. "Ben Azzai says: 'All the Sages of Israel in comparison with myself are as thin as the husk of garlic, except that bald head' " (*Bechorot* 58a). Rashi identifies the "bald head" as Rabbi Akiva. Hence Rabbi Yehoshua ben Korcha is the son of Rabbi Akiva. See *Tosafot* s.v. "*Chutz*," *Tosafot* on *Bava Batra* 113a, *Rashbam* and *Tosafot* on *Pesachim* 112a, and *Machzor Vitri* 424.

fore he began to study Torah, a fact preserved in numerous sources. Of particular relevance is the description offered in *Avot D'Rabbi Natan*:

"Drink thirstily their words" (*Avot* 1:4) — this is Rabbi Akiva. What were the origins of Rabbi Akiva? It was said that he was forty years old and had not learned anything. One time he was standing near a well and asked, "Who made a hole in this stone?"

It was said to him, "The water which constantly falls every day. Akiva, don't you know the verse 'Water erodes stones' (*Iyov* 14:19)?

Rabbi Akiva immediately inferred the teaching regarding himself, and said, "If that which is soft can engrave that which is hard, then the words of Torah which are like steel can certainly penetrate my heart which is but flesh and blood." He immediately returned to study Torah.

(Avot D'Rabbi Natan 6)

Here we are privy to the moment of enlightenment which begins Rabbi Akiva's spiritual odyssey from ignorant shepherd to legendary scholar.[1] The process was a natural one, just as one drop at a time can add up to an ocean of water with incredible kinetic power.

The transformation of Rabbi Yochanan ben Torta is not as well known. The source is the *Pesikta* which describes the incredible spiritually redemptive power of the *parah adumah* (red heifer):

Our Rabbis taught: There was once a story of a Jew who owned a cow, with which he used to plow. He fell on hard times, so he sold his cow to one particular non-Jew. The non-Jew took it out and plowed with it for six days of the week. On Shabbat he took it out to plow and placed it under the yoke. He walked and beat the animal, but it would not budge from its place.

When he saw this he went to the Jew who sold him the cow and told him, "Take your cow. It must be injured, for no mat-

---

1   See *Pesachim* 49b for an example of Rabbi Akiva's attitude from his days as an *am haaretz*. See the article "Pursuit of Righteousness" for more on Rabbi Akiva's origins.

ter how much I beat it, it will not move from its place."

The Jew understood that it must be because of Shabbat, since the cow was accustomed to rest on the Shabbat. He said, "Come and I will get the cow moving."

When they got there he went over to the cow and said in its ear, "Cow, cow, you know that when I owned you, you plowed during the week, and rested on Shabbat. Now due to my sins [I lost my money and had to sell you. Now] you are owned by a non-Jew. Please, I ask you, get up and plow."

The cow immediately arose and plowed.

The non-Jew said, "I ask of you, please take your cow. Until now I have been moving myself trying to get the cow up. Moreover, I am not releasing you until you tell me what you said in that cow's ear. I exhausted myself and beat the animal and it would not get up."

The Jew tried to placate the non-Jew, and said, "It was not magic and the cow is not possessed, but this is what I said in its ear..., and as a result it got up and plowed."

The non-Jew immediately became frightened. He said, "If a cow which cannot speak and has no human intelligence can recognize its Creator, while I, whom my Creator created in His image and endowed me with human intelligence — I don't recognize that I have a Creator?!"

He immediately came and converted. He studied and merited [great success in] Torah. They called him Yochanan ben Torta [literally, "son of the ox"], and until this very day the Rabbis teach laws in his name. And if you are astounded by how a cow brought a person under the wings of the *Shechinah*, by virtue of a cow is the purity of the entire community of Israel.

(Pesikta Rabbati 14)

In this amazing passage we find that Rabbi Yochanan ben Torta was born a non-Jew. Only upon witnessing a miracle was he shocked into seeking his Maker. His very name "Ben Torta" — "son of the cow" — is testimony to his metamorphosis.

Rabbi Akiva, who saw a natural process, extended his individual experience to the entire community of Israel. He postulated that just as he found his Maker as a natural process, as the result of a natural process all of Israel would find themselves and join God in the partnership which He offered them all those years ago. Rav Yochanan ben Torta, on the other hand, felt that in order for the entire world to recognize God as Creator and Sustainer of the Universe, nothing less than an open miracle would be effective.

The Rambam tells us that the law is according to Rabbi Akiva: the messianic process is a natural one. Though Rabbi Yochanan ben Torta is credited for pointing out the reason for the various destructions, Rabbi Akiva was correct about the theory of redemption.

The passage which tells us about the death of Rabbi Akiva's students seems to vindicate at least part of Rabbi Yochanan ben Torta's observation: A generation which is no better than the generation which suffered the destruction cannot expect to witness the rebuilding of the Temple. Rabbi Akiva was surely aware of this; however, Rabbi Akiva was perhaps the greatest optimist our people has ever had.[1] He thought that once the process begins the idea of redemption would spread like wildfire, and the people would reach the levels of greatness of which they were capable. If he accomplished his incredible learning despite his advanced age and abject poverty, certainly his illustrious people could bring about the Messianic Age. Unfortunately, the people failed; the students and followers did not rise to the occasion, and instead of redemption, further destruction ensued.

The days between Pesach and Shavuot mark the redemption that did not happen. We mourn that failure. On Pesach, when we celebrate the Redemption from Egypt, we also try to discern the art of redemption in order to make it a reality in our own days. While ultimately Rabbi Akiva and his generation failed, we must recognize that Rabbi Akiva was completely correct in his understanding

---

1 See *Explorations, Parashat Bo.*

of the process and his understanding of the capability of man. Too many Jews are followers of Rabbi Yochanan Ben Torta, awaiting the miraculous as a prerequisite for redemption. These naysayers wait passively for the sign from heaven that the time for redemption has come. We must follow Rabbi Akiva and take proactive steps, accepting our partnership with the Almighty. Drop after drop after drop adds up to a tidal wave of activity. When we succeed, the days between Pesach and Shavuot will reacquire their original identity and become a time of joy.

> Rabbi Yochanan ben Torta said, "...But [regarding] the last Temple [the third] — may it be rebuilt in our lives, in our days — it is written, "And it shall come to pass in the last days, that the mountain of God's house shall be established on the top of the mountains and exalted above the hills, and all nations shall flow to it. And many people shall go and say: "Come, and let us go up to the mountain of God, to the house of the Lord of Yaakov; and he will teach us of his ways, and we will walk in his paths; for from Zion shall go forth Torah, and the word of God from Yerushalayim." ' "

Lag BaOmer

Rabbi Shimon bar Yochai

Lag BaOmer is a day associated with Rabbi Shimon bar Yochai (sometimes referred to by the acronym of his name, "Rashbi"). According to tradition this is the day which commemorates his death. While the Omer represents a sad period of the Jewish year, the thirty-third day is a day celebrated. This celebration needs to be explained, especially in light of the tradition that the sadness is associated with the death of the students of Rabbi Akiva. After all, the Rashbi was a student of Rabbi Akiva — perhaps his greatest student. Why should his death be cause for celebration? Technically, the question is imprecise, for the death of Rashbi was in a subsequent generation, and not at the same time as those of the twenty-four thousand students. He was one of the later students.[1] Nonetheless, we still need to explain why his death is celebrated.

Rashbi was considered to be one of the greatest men of his generation, if not the greatest. We are told that in his generation a rainbow — that ancient sign of God's benevolence — never needed to be utilized. In order to understand this and a bit more about Rashbi

---

1   See *Yevamot* 62b: "The world remained desolate until Rabbi Akiva came to our masters in the South and taught Torah to them. These were Rabbi Meir, Rabbi Yehudah, Rabbi Yosei, Rabbi Shimon, and Rabbi Elazar ben Shamua; and it was they who revived Torah at that time."

we need to investigate the rainbow and its origin.

After the deluge Noach emerges from his craft. The world had been punished by the wrath of God; now God speaks:

> And God spoke to Noach and to his sons with him, saying, "And I, behold, I establish My covenant with you and with your seed after you, and with every living creature that is with you, of the bird, of the cattle, and of every beast of the earth with you; from all that go out of the ark, to every beast of the earth. And I will establish My covenant with you; and never again shall all flesh be cut off by the waters of a flood, nor shall there ever be another flood to destroy the earth."
>
> And God said, "This is the sign of the covenant which I make between Me and you and every living creature that is with you, for everlasting generations. I set My bow in the cloud, and it shall be for a sign of a covenant between Me and the earth. And it shall come to pass, when I bring a cloud over the earth, that the bow shall be seen in the cloud. And I will remember My covenant, which is between Me and you and every living creature of all flesh; and the waters shall no more become a flood to destroy all flesh. And the bow shall be in the cloud; and I will look upon it, that I may remember the everlasting covenant between God and every living creature of all flesh that is upon the earth."
>
> And God said to Noach, "This is the sign of the covenant, which I have established between Me and all flesh that is upon the earth."
>
> *(Bereishit 9:8–17)*

Man is given the rainbow, a breathtaking display of nature, as a sign that God will never again ravage the earth by water as a punishment for man's sins.

The Midrash notes that the world *dorot*, "generations," is written defectively (twice omitting the letter *vav*). The explanation offered is that certain generations will need this sign, while others will not.

"And God said, 'This is the sign of the covenant...for everlasting generations [*ledorot*].' " Rabbi Yudan said: "This is written '*ledorot*' (lacking the two *vav*s), which thus excludes two generations, the generation of Chizkyahu and that of the Great Assembly." Rabbi Chizkiyah omitted the generation of the Men of the Great Assembly and substituted that of Rabbi Shimon bar Yochai.

(Bereishit Rabbah 35:2)

These two generations are superior, righteous, or blessed with righteous men, thus rendering the symbol of God controlling His wrath superfluous. Among the generations singled out are the generation of Rashbi. Subsequent *midrashim* elaborate on the righteousness of Rashbi:

Eliyahu, of blessed memory, and Rabbi Yehoshua ben Levi were sitting and studying together when they came to a ruling of Rabbi Shimon bar Yochai. Said one: "Here is the author of the ruling; let us go and question him about it." So Eliyahu, of blessed memory, went to him.

"Who is with you?" he [Rashbi] asked.

"The greatest of his generation, Rabbi Yehoshua ben Levi," he [Eliyahu] answered.

"Has the rainbow appeared in his days?" he [Rashbi] inquired. "If it has, he is not worthy of being received by me."

Rabbi Chizkiyah related in Rabbi Yirmiyah's name: "Rabbi Shimon bar Yochai had but to say, 'O field, O field, be filled with gold dinars,' and it was filled.... Thus did Rabbi Shimon bar Yochai say: 'If Avraham is willing, he can effectively intercede for [all generations] from his days until mine, while I can intercede for [all generations] from my time until the advent of Messiah. While if he is not willing, let Achiyah the Shilonite unite with me, and we can intercede for all from the days of Avraham until those of Messiah.'...

"Thus did Rabbi Shimon bar Yochai say: 'The world

possesses not less than thirty men as righteous as Avraham. If there are thirty, my son and I are two of them; if ten, my son and I are two of them; if five, my son and I are two of them; if two, they are my son and I; if there is but one, it is I.' "[1]

(Bereishit Rabbah 35:2)[2]

Despite the perhaps unparalleled greatness of Rashbi, we are somewhat taken aback by his declarations of his own piety and greatness. This statement is not an isolated "slip of the tongue"; the Talmud contains many similar statements by Rashbi.

Chizkiyahu further stated in the name of Rabbi Yirmiyahu who said it in the name of Rabbi Shimon bar Yochai: "I am able to exempt the whole world from judgment from the day that I was born until now, and were Eliezer, my son, to be with me [we could exempt it] from the day of the creation of the world to the present time, and were Yotam ben Uziyah with us, [we could exempt it] from the creation of the world to its final end."

Chizkiyahu further stated in the name of Rabbi Yirmiyahu who said in the name of Rabbi Shimon bar Yochai: "I have seen the sons of heaven and they are but few. If there be a thousand, I and my son are among them; if a hundred, I and my son are among them; and if only two, they are I and my son."

(Sukkah 45b)

Again, we find supreme self-confidence, bordering on arrogance. It seems strange that the merit of such a man would obviate the appearance of the rainbow in his generation. This idiosyncratic statement may also be found in one of the most famous passages regarding Rashbi, the story of the cave. An understanding of that passage holds the key to the entire topic.

---

1   There are various opinions in Talmud and Midrash regarding the minimum number of righteous men needed in each generation to justify the world's continued survival. See *Sukkah* 45b, *Sanhedrin* 97b (36), *Chullin* 92a (45), *Bemidbar Rabbah* 3:1 (3), and *Tikunei Zohar* (71).

2   The Talmud likewise tells how Rashbi judged other righteous men, who allowed the rainbow in their days. See *Ketubot* 77b.

For Rabbi Yehudah, Rabbi Yosei, and Rabbi Shimon were sitting, and Yehudah, a son of proselytes, was sitting near them. Rabbi Yehudah commenced [the discussion] by observing, "How fine are the works of this people [the Romans]! They have made streets, they have built bridges, they have erected baths."

Rabbi Yosei was silent. Rabbi Shimon ben Yochai answered and said, "All that they made they made for themselves; they built marketplaces, to set harlots in them; baths, to rejuvenate themselves; bridges, to levy tolls for them."

Now, Yehudah the son of proselytes went and related their talk, which reached the government. They decreed: "Yehudah, who exalted [us], shall be exalted; Yosei, who was silent, shall be exiled to Tzippori; Shimon, who censured, let him be executed."

(Shabbat 33b)

The passage introduces us to the deep-seated enmity which Rashbi held for the Romans. In the wake of the Hadrianic persecutions, this is certainly understandable. Though this approach would seem valid on a personal level, surely the response of Rashbi transcends personal feelings and calculations.

The Talmud recounts how the other Sages had made their peace with the Roman occupation, and had even come to appreciate the Roman contribution to the physical infrastructure of Judea. Rashbi, on the other hand, refuses to be seduced by the beauty of the Roman edifice.

He and his son went and hid themselves in the *beit hamidrash*, [and] his wife brought him bread and a mug of water and they dined. [But] when the decree became more severe he said to his son, "Women are of unstable temperament: she may be put to the torture and expose us." So they went and hid in a cave. A miracle occurred and a carob tree and a water well were created for them. They would strip their garments and sit up to their necks in sand. The whole day they studied; when it was time for prayers they robed, covered themselves, prayed, and then took off their garments again, so that they should not wear out. Thus they dwelt twelve years in the cave.

Now, in the face of the Roman threat, Rashbi retreats to a cave, together with his son Rebbi Eliezer. The two study day and night for twelve years, in a manner reminiscent of Gan Eden: the tree, the stream, the nakedness are all symbols of the purity and beauty of man at his apex, prior to that first act of infamy. The two studied and ascended from level to level in knowledge and fear of God.

After some time, Eliyahu stands at the door of the cave and invites them to leave:

> Then Eliyahu came and stood at the entrance to the cave and exclaimed, "Who will inform the son of Yochai that the emperor is dead and his decree annulled?" So they emerged.
>
> Seeing a man plowing and sowing, they exclaimed, "They forsake life eternal and engage in life temporal!" Whatever they cast their eyes upon was immediately burnt up.[1]

Coming down from their "ivory tower," or leaving their cave, as the case may be, proved quite difficult for Rashbi and Rabbi Eliezer. Obviously, seeing people not completely righteous, not totally immersed in Torah, was traumatic for Rashbi and, consequently, for the entire world.

> Thereupon a Heavenly Echo came forth and cried out, "Have you emerged to destroy My world? Return to your cave!"

God wished to protect the world from this great man. Upon contemplation, the decision to return them to the cave seems strange: The years in the cave are apparently what caused this distorted worldview. Perhaps it would have been more appropriate to send them anywhere *but* back to the cave. However, upon leaving the cave for the second time one year later, something interesting

---

1   This position is certainly related to Rashbi's opinion articulated in *Berachot* 35b.

happened: Rashbi is indeed healed, while his son Rabbi Eliezer continues to hurl fire. Only at the end is the son healed as well.

So they returned and dwelt there twelve months, saying, "The punishment of the wicked in Gehinnom is [limited to] twelve months."

A Heavenly Echo then came forth and said, "Go forth from your cave!" Thus they exited: wherever Rabbi Eliezer wounded, Rabbi Shimon healed. Said he to him, "My son! You and I are sufficient for the world."

On the eve of the Shabbat before sunset they saw an old man holding two bundles of myrtle and running at twilight. "What are these for?" they asked him.

"They are in honor of the Shabbat," he replied.

"But one should suffice you?"

"One is for 'Remember' and one for 'Observe.'"

Said he to his son, "See how precious are the commandments to Israel." His mind was tranquilized.

Obviously, returning to the cave did have some type of cathartic affect, as it served as the impetus of Rashbi's "rehabilitation." In retrospect, we must conclude that the initial problem was not the years spent in the cave, but that Rashbi was not in the cave long enough. In order to understand this idea we need to see another passage, which tells us about the students of Hillel.

Our Rabbis have taught: Hillel the Elder had eighty disciples, thirty of whom were worthy of the Divine Spirit resting upon them as [it did upon] Moshe our Master, thirty of whom were worthy that the sun should stand still for them as [it did for] Yehoshua the son of Nun, [and the remaining] twenty were ordinary. The greatest of them was Yonatan ben Uziel, the smallest of them was Yochanan ben Zakkai. They said of Rabbi Yochanan ben Zakkai that he did not leave [unstudied] Scripture, Mishnah, Gemara, Halachah, Aggadah, details of the Torah, details of the Scribes, inferences a minori ad majus, analogies, calendrical computations, *gematrias*, the speech of the ministering angels, the speech of spirits, and the speech of palm trees, fullers' parables, fox fables, great matters, or small matters. "Great matters" means the *ma'aseh merkavah*, "small matters" the discussions of Abayei and Rava; in order to fulfill what is said, "That I may cause those that love Me to inherit substance, and that I may fill their treasuries" (*Mishlei* 8:21).

And if the smallest of them was so great, how much more so was the greatest? They said of Yonatan ben Uziel that when he used to sit and occupy himself with the study of the Torah, every bird that flew above him was immediately burnt.

(Sukkah 28a)

The least of Hillel's students possessed a dazzling array of knowledge, the scope of which is difficult to imagine. After describing Rabbi Yochanan ben Zakkai's intellectual prowess and knowledge, we can only wonder about the exalted level of his superior colleague, Rabbi Yonatan ben Uziel, the intensity of whose Torah personality caused passing birds to be consumed by fire.

This passage has an interesting postscript, told in chassidic circles:[1] Once a chassidic Rebbe was learning the above passage with his son. The son had one question: If the least of the students (chassidim) possesses superior knowledge, and the greatest student (chassid) has combustible passion, what is the exalted level of the master (the rebbe)? The son was probing his father, attempting to discern the essence of being a Rebbe.

The Rebbe answered that Hillel the Elder was on such an exalted level that when a bird would fly above nothing would happen; it would remain unscathed. This is the sublime secret of being a teacher. Students are often filled with passion. The secret of teaching is the ability to harness the passion, to control the fire.

When Rashbi leaves the cave the first time, he is still a student — full of passion, but still a student. In his eyes, the world is black

---

1   Generally the story is attributed to the Kotzker Rebbe. See *Torah Sheleimah*, addendum to *Ki Tisa*, p. 182, where the story is cited in the name of the Sefat Emet (*Likutei Yehudah*) and the Kotzker (*Siach Siftei Kodesh*, vol. 1).

and white: Anyone not directly, constantly involved in Torah is wasting his life and is unable to justify his existence. The voice from heaven declares that Rashbi must learn more. He must undergo the metamorphosis from student to teacher, from secretive mystic[1] to tzaddik who will take responsibility for the world and be prepared to do all to save the world. He must learn how to harness the power. He must become like Hillel — when birds fly over his head, they will remain unharmed.

This metamorphosis is discernable in an amazing passage in the *Zohar*:

Once Rabbi Shimon went out and saw that the world was dark and cloudy and all the lights had been sealed. He said to his son Rabbi Eliezer, "Let us go and see what God has planned for the world."

They went and came to one angel that looked like a large mountain,[2] with thirty large torches of fire in its mouth. Rabbi Shimon said, "What are you planning to do?"

He said, "I came to destroy the world, because there are not thirty righteous people in this generation, for God had [thus] decreed to Avraham...."

Rabbi Shimon said to him, "I order you — go in front of God and say to Him, 'Bar Yochai is in the world.' "

The angel went in front of God and said: "Master of the Universe, it is known to you what Bar Yochai said to me."

God said, "Go destroy the world and ignore Bar Yochai."

When he [the angel] returned, Rabbi Shimon saw the angel, and said, "If you do not leave I will decree on you that you will not return to heaven; rather you will be in a place of Aza and Azael [Hell]. Go to God and say to Him: 'If there are not thirty righteous, then twenty should suffice...if not twenty then ten

---

1   Regarding the relative secret stature of Rabbi Shimon, see *Yerushalmi, Sanhedrin* 1:2 (19a): "Rabbi Akiva said [to Rashbi], 'It should suffice if I and your Creator know your power.' "

2   It is likely that the mountain is symbolic of Sinai, which had been forgotten.

should suffice.... If not ten[1] then two should be enough, and there is me and my son...and if two is not good, then one should be enough, and that is me, as it says, "A righteous man is the foundation of the world" (*Mishlei* 10:25).' "

At that moment a voice rang out of heaven and said, "Fortunate is your portion, Rabbi Shimon, for God decrees above, and you rescind below. Certainly about you the verse is written, 'The will of those who fear Him is done' (*Tehillim* 145:19)."

(Zohar, Bereishit, HaShmatot, p. 205)[2]

Rashbi's response seems like the supreme arrogant statement: "I order you — go in front of God and say to Him, 'Bar Yochai is in the world.' " However, when we consider the previous passage in the Talmud, we can understand this statement and begin to penetrate the greatness of Rashbi. When he left the cave the first time, he

---

1 If there are not ten, then it could be argued that this is the result of the massacre of the ten martyrs!

2 This passage is linked thematically with the rainbow by the following passage: *Zohar, Vayikra*, 15a: "What is the meaning of 'This [*zot*] is to Me,' in the verse quoted? Said the Holy One, blessed be He, 'The waters of Noach have caused me to reveal "*zot*" in the world, as it is written, "*Zot* [this] is the sign of My covenant with them.... My bow have I set in the cloud" (*Bereishit* 9:12–13),' as much as to say, there is none who heeds the glory of My Name which is alluded to by the word *zot*. Hence it is one of the signs of a saintly and virtuous man that the rainbow does not appear in his days and the world does not require this sign while he is alive.

"Such a one is he who prays for the world and shields it, like Rabbi Shimon ben Yochai, in whose days the world never required the sign of the rainbow, for he was himself a sign. For if ever punishment was decreed against the world he could annul it. One day he was sitting at the gate of Lod when he lifted up his eyes and saw the light of the sun darkened three times, and black and yellow spots appearing in the sun. He said to his son, Rabbi Eliezer: 'Follow me, my son, and let us see what happens, for it is certain that some punishment is decreed above, and God desires to let me know. For such a decree is kept in suspense thirty days, and God does not carry it out before making it known to the righteous, as it is written, "For the Lord will do nothing but He reveals His secret to His servants, the prophets" (*Amos* 3:7).'

"They came into a vineyard, where they saw a serpent advancing like a coil of fire along the ground. Rabbi Shimon shook his garments and brought his hand down on the head of the serpent, which then came to a halt, though its tongue was still moving. He said to it: 'Serpent, serpent, go and tell that supernal Serpent that Rabbi Shimon is still alive.' It then put its head into a hole in the ground. He said: 'I ordain that just as this serpent has returned to its hole in the ground, so the supernal one shall return to the hollow of the great abyss.'

wanted to destroy all evil. Inconsistency would not be tolerated. After twelve years in a cave, all that he knew was learning, perfection. Anyone not learning should perish. The power of Torah raged within him and poured forth with a vengeance. There was only one problem: God did not concur.

Thereupon a Heavenly Echo came forth and cried out, "Have you emerged to destroy My world? Return to your cave!"

God would not allow the world to be destroyed. "Go back to the cave," God said to him. "Learn one more lesson." When they left the cave the second time, an old man[1] holding myrtle provides the lesson.

Said he to his son, "See how precious are the commandments to Israel."

The world is not black and white; rather it is composed of many hues and shades, like the rainbow. God taught Rashbi this phenomenal lesson: The world is awaiting redemption. Instead of the tzaddik taking a stance of superiority, of judment, he must take responsibility for his generation, and indeed the entire world. When Rashbi confronts the angel of destruction, he tells the angel, "I order you — go in front of God and say to Him, 'Bar Yochai is in the world' " — the same Bar Yochai whom God would not allow to destroy the world, even a small piece of it. Rabbi Shimon now takes responsibility for the world, imperfections and all. Destruction is antithetical to this stance. When the power of his Torah is harnessed, the true tzaddik does not set fires of destruction. Instead, he

"Rabbi Shimon then began to pray. As they were praying they heard a voice say: 'You ministers of evil, return to your place; you band of ruffians, abide not in the world, for Rabbi Shimon ben Yochai annuls your power. Happy are you, Rabbi Shimon, that your Master is solicitous for your honor at all times, above that of all other men.' By this time he saw that the sun was shining again and the blackness had passed. He said: 'Surely the world is safe again.' He then went into his house and expounded the verse: 'For the Lord is righteous, He loves righteousness, the upright shall behold His face' (*Tehillim* 11:8). 'God,' he said, 'loves to do righteous acts when the upright behold His face, that is, pray to Him for their needs.' "

1   Often anonymous old men are Eliyahu in disguise.

achieves a beautiful harmony with all of nature. The world is not evil, merely awaiting elevation.

God has no desire to see the world destroyed. He desires that the righteous take responsibility for their fellow men, providing the leadership and inspiration to help mankind realize its potential. The tzaddik can be that catalyst: Rashbi argues that even one tzaddik can save the world, provided the tzaddik knows how to affect the world without burning it. It is Rashbi's sense of responsibility for his generation, rather than an inflated ego, which prompt the statements recorded by the Talmud and quoted above. Rashbi steps up, accepts the imperfect world around him, and takes responsibility for saving the world. He makes the transition from student to teacher.

Rashbi did not need a rainbow up in the heavens to remind him of God's promise and his own mission; he saw a rainbow[1] down on earth. He saw all the shades of gray and was able to visualize the beautiful rainbow that can be formed from it. Other leaders failed in this same mission: Other generations had no one to speak for them before God, no one to carry the burden as Rashbi did. Noach needed a rainbow[2]; and Rashbi questions other great men as to their ability to step beyond their own lofty intellectual and spiritual plane. Some generations would possess great souls with the power to redeem the world, making the appearance of the rainbow completely unnecessary. On Lag BaOmer, we celebrate the life and teachings of just such a man: Rabbi Shimon bar Yochai.

---

1   The rainbow is the symbol of God's _Shechinah_ (_Bemidbar Rabbah_ 14:3, _Berachot_ 59a, _Chagigah_ 16a). "And the rainbow is therefore called 'covenant' because they embrace one another. Like the firmament it is a supernal resplendent glory, a sight of all sights, resembling the hidden one [the _Shechinah_], containing colors undisclosed and unrevealable. Hence it is not permitted to gaze at the rainbow when it appears in the heavens, as that would be disrespectful to the _Shechinah_, the hues of the rainbow here below being a replica of the vision of the supernal splendor, which is not for man's gaze" (_Zohar, Bereishit_ 71b).

2   See _Explorations_ on _Parashat Noach_, where Noach's failure is discussed in detail.

The Twenty-eighth of Iyar

The Battle for Holiness

In recent years the twenty-eighth day of Iyar is celebrated as Yom Yerushalayim, the day the city of Yerushalayim was re-united. Some Jews respond to this Divine gift publicly, in festive prayer, others more personally,[1] yet almost all agree that the day that the Old City of Yerushalayim became accessible to Jews after thousands of years is a watershed in Jewish history, a day the Creator, in an act of compassion, remembered His children and His city.

In Judaism, days often have a personality of their own, a unique aura. Sad days seem to march ahead inexorably to the beat of the same drum year after year, producing tragic events.[2] Holidays possess an intrinsic holiness, which can be felt and experienced by the spiritually sensitive. These days do not merely commemorate events that took place long ago and far away. It seems that particular events occur on particular days because these days already have a certain color, an appropriate personality.

Does the twenty-eighth of Iyar have its own history, or is it just another day? Throughout history, significant events occurred on this day, giving it a special charisma.

---

1   See *Minchat Yitzchak* 10:10.
2   The Mishnah in the last chapter of *Ta'anit* stresses the repetitive aspect of calamities which befell our people on specific dates.

The *Shulchan Aruch*, section 580, reports that on the twenty-eighth day of the month of Iyar a fast day is observed, marking the anniversary of the death of Shmuel HaNavi.[1] Because this is considered a so-called "minor fast" many Jews are unaware of the significance of this commemoration. However, in antiquity this day was widely celebrated.

In a responsa[2] of the Radbaz, we learn that in the Middle Ages the tomb of Shmuel HaNavi was a site of pilgrimage. People would take their young sons and travel to the burial place of Shmuel to cut the child's hair for the first time. A father who had made a vow to cut his son's hair at the Tomb of Shmuel HaNavi poses a dilemma to the Radbaz: When the time to fulfill the vow arrived the father found that he was unable to ascend to the tomb because the burial place had become off-limits to Jews. The rabbis themselves had forbidden Jews from going there at all; from the context it is unclear if the prohibition was a response to the danger involved, or because the tomb had become a non-Jewish place of worship.

This responsa is particularly interesting in terms of the history of Jewish customs. We learn that in that same period, Jews began to travel to Meron on the eighteenth of Iyar (better known as Lag BaOmer), where they would give their sons their first haircuts. It is possible that this custom, practiced first in the outskirts of Yerushalayim on the twenty-eighth of Iyar, was transported to the outskirts of Tzefat on the eighteenth of Iyar when the tomb of Shmuel became off-limits for Jews.[3] Shmuel was a *nazir*, and as such never cut his hair, which would make his tomb an excellent place for a child to have his hair cut for the first time. Furthermore, the twenty-eighth day of Iyar, which falls after the thirty-third day of the Omer, is a far less problematic date on which to cut hair:

1   See Rav Eliezer Waldenberg for a discussion of the accuracy of this date (*She'eilot U'Teshuvot Tzitz Eliezer* 15:4).
2   *She'eilot U'Teshuvot Ridvaz* 2:608.
3   I believe that I heard this suggestion from Rabbi Professor Daniel Sperber many years ago when I attended a course that he offered in "The History of *Minhagim*." Much of the material we studied was subsequently published in a series of books (by Mosad HaRav Kook), though I did not find this specific suggestion in print.

Sephardi minhag prohibits cutting hair until the thirty-fourth day of the Omer.[1] This, too, seems to support the theory that the custom was transported to the less-desirable, less-logical date of Lag BaOmer when conditions made the original custom untenable.

The history of this *minhag* being as it may, we have a clear testimony that the twenty-eighth day of Iyar was, in antiquity, a day of pilgrimage as well as the yearly remembrance of Shmuel HaNavi. On that day, of all the days in the calendar, Yerushalayim was the destination. We might even venture to say that the power of the prayers uttered all those years ago on this day by the pilgrims at the end of their arduous journey contributed to Yerushalayim's liberation on the very same date, causing it to once again become the day when people venture up to Yerushalayim. Yet there are other, deeper aspects of Shmuel's connection with Yerushalayim that shed light on this special date.

The connection between Shmuel and Yerushalayim is twofold and intertwined. Shmuel was the prophet who anointed David, the founder of Yerushalayim. David and Shmuel together surveyed the region, looking for the proper place to build the Temple.

> What is meant by the verse, "[And he asked and said, 'Where are Shmuel and David?'] And one said, 'Behold, they are at Nayot [name of place; literally it means "beautiful" or "glorious"] in Ramah [name of a place; literally it means "high"]' " (*Shmuel* I, ch. 19)? What connection has Nayot with Ramah? It means, however, that they sat at Ramah and were engaged with the glory [beauty] of the world. Said they, "It is written, 'Then you shall arise and ascend to the place [which God, your Lord, shall choose]' (*Devarim* 17:8). This teaches that the Temple was higher than the whole of Eretz Yisrael, while Eretz Yisrael is higher than all other countries."
>
> They did not know where that place was. Thereupon they brought the Book of *Yehoshua*.[2] In the case of all [tribal

---

1   See *Shulchan Aruch, Orach Chaim* 493:2.
2   See chapters 15–18.

territories] it is written, "And the border went down," "and the border went up," "and the border passed along," whereas in reference to the tribe of Binyamin "and it went up" is written, but not "and it went down." Said they: "This proves that this is its site."

(Zevachim 54b)

Yerushalayim represents both the holiness of the Temple and the seat of the Davidic dynasty; Shmuel was involved in the establishment of both. The date of Shmuel's passing, the twenty-eighth of Iyar, was commemorated each year; how appropriate to honor his memory by bringing one's family, young and old, to this mountaintop overlooking Yerushalayim.

There is, however, an earlier episode in Jewish history which makes an oblique reference to the twenty-eighth of Iyar.

שנאמר ויסעו מאילם ויבאו כל עדת בני ישראל אל מדבר סין (שמות ט"ז א') (והוא אלוש) בחמשה עשר יום לחדש השני לצאתם מארץ מצרים (שם /שמות ט"ז, א'/), ואחד בשבת היה, הא למדנו שראש חדש אייר באחד בשבת היה, ועוד למדנו שהיו ישראל אוכלין מעוגה שהוציאו בידם ממצרים כל שלשים יום, ובו ביום כלתה, ולערב אכלו את השליו ולמשכים לקטו את המן, ובאלוש נתנה להם השבת, ושם עשו שבת ראשונה, שנאמר וישבתו העם ביום השביעי (שם / שמות/ ט"ז/ ל'), באחד בשבת בכ"ג באייר נסעו מאלוש ובאו להם לרפידים, ושם נתנה להם הבאר ונלחמו עם עמלק ושם עשו שבת שניה, נסעו מרפידים ובאו להן למדבר סיני ומצאו עליו ענני כבוד. כל חמשת הימים היה משה עולה לראש ההר ויורד ומגיד לעם את דברי המקום, ומשיב דבריהם לפני המקום, בשלישי בששה לחדש נתנו להם עשרת הדברות, ויום השבת היה.

(סדר עולם רבה [ליינר] פרק ה')

The *Seder Olam* reports biblical chronology, recording the precise dates of ancient events. In detailing the journey immediately following the Exodus, the *Seder Olam* tells us that in the year the Jews left Egypt, Rosh Chodesh Iyar was on a Sunday,[1] and the first Shabbat observed was on the twenty-second of Iyar. The following day the Jews traveled to Refidim, where the battle with Amalek took place and where the second Shabbat was observed.

---

1   *Shabbat 87b.*

Understanding the battle with Amalek reveals a very important relationship with Yerushalayim. In describing the battle the Torah states:

> But Moshe's hands were heavy. And they took a stone and put it under him, and he sat on it. And Aharon and Chur supported his hands, one on one side and the other on the other side; and his hands were steady until the going down of the sun.
>
> *(Shemot 17:12)*

Rashi informs us that in referring to the sun the Torah wishes to communicate that Moshe made the sun stand still.[1] We are perhaps more familiar with another similar occurrence: When the battle of Givon raged, Yehoshua caused the sun to remain in its place. The Sages[2] explain the need for this miracle as follows: The enemies of the Jews, knowing that Shabbat was coming, waited for Shabbat in order to defeat the Israelite army. Therefore, the sun was made to stand still to avoid the onset of Shabbat. Moshe, too, made the sun stand still — for the same reason: Shabbat was coming.[3] This was only the second Shabbat celebrated by the Jews, and Amalek, who despised all that was sacred,[4] was going to use the Shabbat to destroy the Jewish people. But while Yehoshua led the troops below, Moshe stood on a mountain and caused the sun to stand still and "hold off" the onset of Shabbat.[5]

The battle with Amalek, then, indeed took place on *erev Shabbat* and the precise date was the twenty-eighth of Iyar. This association allows us a deeper appreciation of the date and its significance. The battle with Amalek is the archetypical struggle between holiness and depravity. This struggle defines the essence of the twenty-eighth of Iyar. It is its nature, its character, its "personality." The

---

1   *Yalkut Shimoni, Chavakuk* 3:564.
2   *Pirkei D'Rabbi Eliezer* 51, *Yalkut Shimoni, Yehoshua* 10:22.
3   Many things which Yehoshua accomplished are based on miracles which were performed by Moshe. See *Midrash Tanchuma, Parashat Tetzaveh* 9.
4   See *Rashi* on *Devarim* 25:18.
5   See *Sichot* for *Sefer Shemot* based on the talks of Rav Avigdor Nebenzahl, p. 432.

victory of holiness over depravity was achieved when the prayers of Moshe and the nation were answered. When the Beit HaMikdash was eventually constructed on the holy mountain, symbolizing the possibility of human connection with God and holiness, its spiritual foundations are traced back to the prayers Moshe uttered on that hill in the desert.[1]

In the aftermath of that first battle we are told that until Amalek is ultimately and completely defeated, something will remain missing in this world and the celestial spheres:

> And God said to Moshe, "Write this for a memorial in a book, and recite it in the ears of Yehoshua; for I will completely erase the remembrance of Amalek from under heaven." And Moshe built an altar, and called its name Adonai-Nissi, for he said, "Because God has sworn by His throne (*kes*) that God will have war with Amalek from generation to generation."
>
> *(Ibid., 14–16)*

Rashi explains that the word *kes* is used instead of the more common form *kisei*, for as long as Amalek is around, spewing his venom, the throne of God and God's Name are, as it were, incomplete.[2] Evil has a foothold in this world as long as God's holiness is not completely manifest. The symbol of the destruction of evil is the final victory in the epic battle with Amalek. Yerushalayim represents God's throne on Earth; Amalek represents the attack on the throne:

> At that time they shall call Yerushalayim the throne of God; and all the nations shall be gathered to it, to the name of God, to Yerushalayim; and they shall no longer go after the stubbornness of their evil heart.
>
> *(Yirmiyahu 3:17)*

---

1   See previous source. Jerusalem is hinted at in the biblical text: "And Moshe said to Yehoshua, 'Choose for us men and go out, fight against Amalek. Tomorrow I will stand at the top of the hill [*rosh hagivah*] with the staff of the Lord in my hand' " (*Shemot* 17:9). The numerical equivalent of "*rosh hagivah*" is 586, the same as the *gematria* of "Yerushalem" (which is how *Yerushalayim* is spelled in Tanach).

2   God's Name is also incomplete, written "*Yud-hei*" instead of "*Yud-hei-vav-hei.*"

The first king anointed by Shmuel was supposed to defeat Amalek; all subsequent history would have been different had Shaul succeeded, but he failed. Now David would take his place and seek to complete God's throne, in both the physical and spiritual sense. Perhaps now we can better appreciate King David and Shmuel the Prophet looking with prophetic vision for the throne of God. They sought the place that would symbolize the complete destruction of evil. They sought the place for the Temple. They sought Yerushalayim.

Presently the throne of God is incomplete; forces of evil thrive. The struggle for Yerushalayim is not an easy one. It is a battle that began long ago and far away in the desert, waged first by Moshe and Yehoshua, later by Shaul and again by David. If the spiritual foundation of the Temple dates back to the prayers fervently said during the first battle with Amalek, the physical foundation is identified with David and his dynasty.

In the outskirts of Yerushalayim, just beyond the present neighborhood of Ramot, there is a large building that stands majestically on a hill. It is the tomb of Shmuel.[1] Looking north one can see where the sun stood still all those years ago. Today a vibrant neighborhood called Givat Ze'ev stands in the shadows of the biblical Givon. Looking south, the new city of Yerushalayim is spread almost as far as the eye can see.

In ancient and modern days pilgrims make their way to Yerushalayim on the twenty-eighth day of Iyar. In those days they sought holiness, they sought completion; they sought God, just as Shmuel and David did. There were times throughout history when Jews were not permitted to make the journey, to see the holy, aged stones. They mourned for an incomplete Yerushalayim. They mourned for God's throne which was not manifest. For millennia we had to settle for facing Yerushalayim three times a day as we

---

1   Archaeologists are not at all convinced of the veracity of the association of the present Nebi Samuel — Kever Shmuel HaNavi — with the ancient biblical burial plot.

prayed. We remembered her pain even when we celebrated our personal joy.

To this day there are forces seeking to wrest Yerushalayim from our hands, but we will not relinquish control after all these years. We will fight to reveal the true nature of Yerushalayim — the throne of God. We are well aware that the battle is ancient, that it began in the desert many years ago. We see the hand of God in Yerushalayim's liberation on the twenty-eighth day of Iyar. We realize that this is just the beginning. We pray that we may merit the completion of the building of Yerushalayim in our days.

At that time they shall call Yerushalayim the throne of God; and all the nations shall be gathered to it, to the name of God, to Yerushalayim; and they shall no longer go after the stubbornness of their evil heart.

Sivan

Shavuot

The Word of God

A s the Jews awaited the Revelation at Sinai, they gathered at the foot of the mountain, anxiously anticipating the momentous events which would shortly unfold.

In the third month after the people of Israel's departure from the land of Egypt, on this same day they came to the wilderness of Sinai. And they had departed from Refidim, and they came to the desert of Sinai, and they camped in the wilderness; and there Israel camped before the mount.

(Shemot 19:1–2)

Moshe received initial instructions and the people responded enthusiastically:

And Moshe went up to the Lord, and God called to him from the mountain, saying, "Thus shall you say to the House of Yaakov, and tell the people of Israel: 'You have seen what I did to the Egyptians, and how I carried you on eagles' wings and brought you to Me. Now if you will obey My voice indeed and keep My covenant, then you shall be My own treasure among all peoples; for all the earth is Mine. And you shall be to Me a kingdom of priests and a holy nation.' These are the words which you shall speak to the people of Israel."

And Moshe came and called for the elders of the people and

laid before them all these words which God commanded him. And all the people answered together, and said, "All that God has spoken we will do...."

(Ibid., 3–8)

The people agreed to uphold their part of the covenant and heed the word of God. Three days of preparation, both physical and spiritual, passed:

> And it came to pass on the third day in the morning, that there were thunders and lightnings, and a thick cloud upon the mount, and the sound of a shofar exceedingly loud; and all the people who were in the camp trembled. And Moshe brought forth the people out of the camp to meet with God; and they stood at the lower part of the mount.
>
> *(Ibid., 16–17)*

The Rabbinic tradition fills in numerous details of the events: In general, this is considered to be the finest hour of Jewish history, the apex of spiritual experience, which will only be surpassed when all the words of the Torah are fulfilled in the Messianic Age. There are, nonetheless, some expressions which indicate a lowness of spirit and a hesitation in accepting the Divine Word. The Talmud, in *Masechet Shabbat*, describes the scene while focusing on the phrase "stood on the lower part of the mount":

> "And they stood on the lower part of [or, 'under'] the mount": Rabbi Abdimi ben Chama ben Chasa said: "This teaches that the Holy One, blessed be He, overturned the mountain upon them like an [inverted] cask, and said to them, 'If you accept the Torah, it is well; if not, you shall be buried there.' " Rabbi Acha ben Yaakov observed: "This furnishes a strong protest against the Torah." Said Rava, "Yet even so, they reaccepted it in the days of Achashveirosh, for it is written, '[The Jews] confirmed, and accepted upon themselves...' (*Esther* 9:27): [i.e.,] they confirmed what they had accepted long before."
>
> *(Shabbat 88a)*

While the term in question could be rendered either "by the foot of the mountain" or "under the mountain," the exposition seems strange; what made the Rabbis declare that the acceptance of the Torah had not been wholehearted? We have seen that the people expressed complete willingness to adhere to the word of God, when they declared "all that God has spoken we will do."[1] Furthermore, later (in *Parashat Mishpatim*) there are additional expressions of the people's acceptance of Torah. While it should be noted that the exact sequence of events is somewhat challenging, the response of the people recorded is certainly part of the same general discussion — regardless of the specific details:

> And Moshe came and told the people all the words of God and all the judgments; and all the people answered with one voice, and said, "All the words which God has said we will do." And Moshe wrote all the words of God, and he rose up early in the morning and built an altar under the hill and twelve pillars, according to the twelve tribes of Israel. And he sent young men of the people of Israel, who offered burnt offerings and sacrificed peace offerings of oxen to God. And Moshe took half of the blood and put it in basins, and half of the blood he sprinkled on the altar. And he took the Book of the Covenant and read it in the hearing of the people; and they said, "All that God has said we will do and hearken."
>
> *(Shemot 24:3–7)*

The people have responded positively on three occasions. In *Shemot* 19:8, we find: "And all the people answered together, and said, 'All that God has spoken we will do.' " Then again in *Shemot* 24:3, "And all the people answered with one voice, and said, 'All the words which God has said we will do.' " Finally, the most famous response follows in 24:7: "And he took the Book of the Covenant and read it in the hearing of the people; and they said, 'All that God has said we will do and hearken.' "

---

1   See *Tosafot* on *Shabbat* 88a, where this question is posed.

This last response is the impetus for Divine rapture:

> When the Israelites gave precedence to "we will do" over "we will hearken," a Heavenly Voice went forth and exclaimed to them, "Who revealed to My children this secret which is employed by the ministering angels? As it is written, 'Bless God, angels of His, you mighty in strength, that fulfill His word, that hearken to the voice of His word' (*Tehillim* 103:20): first they fulfil and then they hearken."
>
> *(Shabbat 88a)*

On the one hand we notice that the people's acceptance of the Torah was clearly viewed as an act of heroism. On three occasions the people wholeheartedly accept the word of God. The contention that God lifted the mountain and threatened their lives turns the Revelation into the proverbial "offer which they could not refuse." This does not seem consistent with either the Biblical account or the Rabbinic tradition articulated in the other sources.

If we analyze the various responses we will find that the first "we will do" is a response to "all that God has spoken." Here they respond affirmatively to "Now if you will obey My voice indeed and keep My covenant." The Word of God is acceptable to the people.

In the second instance, the positive response is to "And Moshe came and told the people all the words of God and all the judgments." Again, it is the Word of God with which they are in agreement. Apparently, the people are understandably prepared to accept what God says. The awesome word of God is the subject of their acceptance. While this was certainly a lofty response, this is not referred to as "the secret of the angels." Upon reflection one can even ask, what choice did they have? When God speaks — directly to man — does man truly have the ability to reject the Word?

The direct communication at Sinai was most certainly an overwhelming experience. Furthermore, when Moshe descends from Sinai and transmits and explains those words, the people must have perceived the message itself as an extension of the Divine. Perhaps this is what the Rabbis mean when they speak of the mountain being lifted and dangled over them. Standing at Sinai, the people were overwhelmed, awed, unable to escape the immediacy of God's self-revelation.

Significantly, the Talmud relates that the Jewish people accepted the Torah during the era of Achashveirosh, the despotic ruler of the Purim epoch. This period of Jewish history is described as a time of *"hester panim,"* when God's face was hidden. For the first time in Jewish history, the word of God was not heard. The age of prophecy had come to an end. Instead of the Word of God, silence reverberated. It was specifically in this state of spiritual and physical exile that the Jews renewed their collective vows. Now the mountain no longer hung precariously over their heads. Now they were no longer overwhelmed by the word of God. To accept the Torah at this point was totally different than that first time at the foot of the mountain.[1]

Now, despite the silence, the leaders act heroically and choose to anticipate what the Torah would have required of them in such a situation. The relationship with God has shifted somewhat: With the end of the age of prophecy, man must take a proactive role in applying the Divine mandate, values, and mores. This new process of extrapolation, analysis, and application resulted in the institution of the first "Rabbinic" holiday — Purim.[2] The establishment of this holiday indicated man's willingness to become an active partner with God. This was a new type of acceptance of the Torah, a new covenant.[3]

It was, however, the third acceptance of the Torah which elicited the impassioned response from above.

> And he took the Book of the Covenant and read it in the hearing of the people; and they said, "All that God has said we will do and hearken."

---

1   See *Gur Aryeh* on *Shemot* 19:17.
2   See *Or HaChaim* on *Shemot* 19:5.
3   For more on this concept, see Rav Levi Yitzchak of Berdichev in the *Kedushat HaLevi* on Purim.

Upon hearing God's word, the people promise to "do and obey" or, perhaps, to "do and listen." The question that this raises is obvious: clearly, the text seems inverted. "Listen" should logically preceed "do." Man cannot "do" the word of God unless he hears it first. For this reason, translators have such difficulty with the phrase; it seems illogical.[1]

Rabbi Yosef Dov Soloveitchik, in his classic *Beit HaLevi*, explains (based on the *Zohar*) that the "do" implies the performance of the commandments, while the "listen" implies Torah learning or involvement in Torah — attentive listening to the Torah's teachings.

The initial acceptance of the Torah involved the word of God[2]; the Jewish people agreed to listen exclusively to what God had said. This is surely a unique level of adherence, but one which pales in comparison to the level reached subsequently, when they vowed to accept that which emanates from the word of God, even that which will be distilled from the word of God hundreds of years in the future, when the actual word is no longer heard. Perhaps the idea can be explained as follows: The declaration "we will do" implies listening to the word of God, and adhering and acting in accordance with the content of that word. The phrase "we will hearken" implies ongoing listening. Rabbi Yosef Dov Soloveitchik, echoing the words of his great-grandfather and namesake, once explained that the phrase "we will do and we will hearken," "*na'aseh v'nishma*," is in the present tense. We declared at Sinai that we will always listen to God; with great care and attention we will listen to hear what God is telling us in any situation.

This became an issue in the time of Purim, when the people manifested their partnership with God: They listened attentively and added Rabbinic law. Now they were no longer silent partners in their relationship with God. Now they boldly joined God and man-

---

1   See the comments of the Kedushat HaLevi on *Shemot*, where he suggests that the people "heard" without speech. This is often the manner of prophetic and mystic communication and is the meaning of the word *chashmal — chash mal*, spoken silence.

2   See the *Beit HaLevi* on *Shemot* 19:5 and 24:7.

ifested this special relationship. This was the secret which had hitherto been the sole dominion of the angels. Angels are truly partners with God, serving as an extension of the Divine Hand. If man simply obeys and fulfills the word of God, he is not a partner, but an adherent. When man says that he will forever listen to the Divine decree, he states that he will be a partner in the teaching and "production" of Torah. This was the exalted level reached by the Jews at Sinai. They became partners with God. The true fulfillment of this partnership took place in Shushan: With the creation of a Rabbinic law, the leaders of that generation courageously displayed the willingness to manifest a partnership which was formed at the foot of a mountain a thousand years before.

Shavuot

Bikkurim: First Fruits

One of the main mitzvot of Shavuot is to bring the first fruits to a centralized place of worship — later known as the Temple in Yerushalayim.

And it shall be, when you come to the land which God, your Lord, gives you for an inheritance, and possess it, and live in it, that you shall take of the first of all the fruit of the earth, which you shall bring of your land that God, your Lord, gives you, and shall put it in a basket, and shall go to the place which God, your Lord, shall choose to place His Name there.

(Devarim 26:1–2)

We have no trouble understanding the significance of dedicating first fruits to God: The beginning of any venture has uniqueness, a special quality, and the Torah's requirement opens the way for us to use physical bounty as an impetus for religious expression and experience. In expressing our thanks for what we harvest and our hopes for the future, we are given a unique opportunity, a unique vehicle of expression before God. The term used for the first fruits in this passage is *"reishit,"*[1] similar to the word *bereishit,* "in the beginning," the first word in the Torah.

---

1   This term was used in the same context previously in *Shemot* 23:19.

In his comments on the first verse of the Torah, Rashi describes the Torah itself as *"reishit."* Elsewhere, the people of Israel are called *"reishit"* as well.[1] It is not too difficult to distinguish a pattern of uniqueness linking the Torah and the people, yet there is one other thing refered to as *"reishit,"* and this other application is somewhat disturbing.

> And when he looked on Amalek, he took up his discourse and said, "Amalek was the first [*reishit*] of the nations, but his latter end shall be that of everlasting perdition."
>
> *(Bemidbar 24:20)*

How can Amalek, the very antithesis of Torah and Israel, deserve the same appellation? From a purely stylistic viewpoint, the use of the term *"reishit"* for Amalek sheds light on the sequence of teachings, serving as a link between chapters 25 (end of *Ki Teitzei*) and 26 (beginning of *Ki Tavo*) of *Sefer Devarim*, namely *Parashat Zachor* and *bikkurim*. This observation, that Amalek, too, is called *"reishit,"* links two sections of the Torah which seemed thematically independent.

> Remember what Amalek did to you by the way, when you came forth out of Egypt. How he met you by the way, and struck at your rear, all who were feeble behind you, when you were faint and weary; and he did not fear the Lord. Therefore it shall be, when God, your Lord, has given you rest from all your enemies around, in the land which God, your Lord, gives you for an inheritance to possess, that you shall blot out the remembrance of Amalek from under heaven; you shall not forget it.
>
> *(Devarim 25:17–19)*

> And it shall be, when you come to the land which God, your Lord gives you for an inheritance, and possess it, and live in it; that you shall take of the first of all the fruit of the earth, which you shall bring of your land that God, your Lord, gives you and

---

1 See *Bereishit Rabbah* 1:1.

shall put it in a basket, and shall go to the place which God, your Lord, shall choose to place His Name there.

(Ibid. 26:1–2)

The juxtaposition of these teachings leads us to conclude that there must be a deeper relationship between the first fruits and Amalek, the "first nation." Rashi offers three insights on the insidiousness of Amalek. The verse reads *"asher korcha,"* which is usually translated, "how he met you by the way." Rashi explains that the word *korcha* is derived from the word indicating coincidence and thus the phrase *"asher korcha"* should be translated as "who happened upon you." This translation highlights a defining characteristic of Amalek: their worldview is of existence without God. Life and history are a series of coincidences, without a Creator of a master plan.

When the Jews in the desert questioned God's involvement in their lives, thus calling God's existence into question, they mirrored Amalek's worldview and therefore became susceptible to the onslaught by Amalek.

And he called the name of the place Massah and Merivah, because of the strife of the people of Israel and because they tempted God, saying, "Is God among us, or not?" Then Amalek came and fought with Israel in Refidim.

(Shemot 17:7–8)

Rashi's second insight into Amalek's national character revolves around the word *"keri,"* which may also be related to the root *mikreh* ("coincidence" or "happening") but in this usage indicates a nocturnal emission. Amalek pollutes the world as the source of unnatural, illegitimate pleasure.

Rashi's third insight is directly related to the idea of *"reishit"*: After the Exodus, all nations feared Israel. Word of the plagues and the splitting of the sea spread, and the other nations were in awe. Only Amalek was not afraid. The people of Israel were compared to a boiling cauldron, and Amalek jumped in to cool them off. According to this explanation, the word *korcha* comes from the word *kar*, cold. They cooled off the children of Israel by being the first to wage battle against them. In the words of the *Zohar*:

> It is written, "Amalek was the first of the nations, but his latter end shall be that of everlasting perdition." Was, then, Amalek the first of the nations? Were there not many tribes, nations, and peoples in the world before Amalek came? But the meaning is that Amalek was the first nation who was not afraid to proclaim war against Israel, as it says, "and he did not fear the Lord"; while the other nations were filled with fear and trembling before Israel at the time of the Exodus, as it says: "The peoples heard and were afraid; trembling took hold of the inhabitants of Peleshet" (*Shemot* 15:14). In fact, apart from Amalek there was no nation that was not awestruck before the mighty works of the Holy One, blessed be He. Therefore "his latter end shall be everlasting perdition."
>
> *(Zohar, Shemot 65a)*

We know specifically of two non-Jews who heard reports of the Exodus — Yitro and Amalek. Their respective responses stand in stark contrast. Yitro, like Amalek, heard of the amazing happenings in Egypt and on the Red Sea, as well as the terrible punishment decreed for Amalek, and he made his way to the Hebrew encampment. While Amalek desired to squelch any holiness in the world, Yitro wished to join the celebration. The Midrash explains the juxtaposition of the end of *Beshalach* and the beginning of *Yitro*:

> For he said, "Because God has sworn that God will have war with Amalek from generation to generation."
>
> *(Shemot 17:16)*

> Yitro, the priest of Midyan, Moshe's father-in-law, heard of all that the Lord had done for Moshe and for Israel his people, and that God had brought Israel out of Egypt.
>
> *(Shemot 18:1)*

Amalek and Yitro were of the advisers of Pharaoh; but when Yitro beheld that God had wiped out Amalek both from this world and the next, he felt remorse and repented, for first it says, "I will completely erase the remembrance of Amalek from under heaven" (*Shemot* 17:14), and then "Yitro...heard." Said he: "The only thing for me to do is to join the God of Israel."

(Shemot Rabbah 27:6)

Significantly, the portion of *Yitro* contains the Revelation — the giving of the Torah. The first fruits were brought to Yerushalayim on the holiday of Shavuot — the day of the giving of the Torah. While the Torah and Israel represent one type of *reishit*, Amalek represents the antithesis, a completely different type of beginning. The Torah and Israel are a manifestation of God's will, holiness on earth. Amalek represents the opposite, the rejection of God, a worldview of coincidence, a pact with impurity and a desire to attack all that is holy.

Rashi (to *Devarim* 25:18) cites a tradition taught in the *Midrash Tanchuma* that when Amalek enjoyed any military victory they immediately severed the male sexual organs from their victims and threw them heavenward. The very idea of a covenant with God was foreign to them. The idea of holiness and chastity grated on them and caused this atrocious response.

The battle against Amalek is both a physical and a spiritual struggle, and the *bikkurim* offering — the first fruits — represents the defeat of Amalekian philosophy. The individual who appreciates his produce as the work of God and gives thanks for the bountiful harvest rejects the worldview of coincidence.

Immediately following the first fruit declaration, the Torah continues:

This day God, your Lord, has commanded you to do these statutes and judgments; therefore, you shall keep and do them with all your heart and with all your soul.

(Devarim 26:16)

Rashi explains the significance of the term "this day" in this context.

Every day should be new for you, as if on that day you were commanded [given the Torah].

The ability of man to see himself in close proximity to God is the antidote to Amalek. If a person were able to visualize the Revelation taking place each and every day, adherence to the word of God would be infinitely easier.[1]

Amalek, despite a well-earned reputation, was hardly the first instigator against God. That distinction belongs to the original serpent in Eden.[2] The serpent, too, tried to lead man toward belief in an existence without God. The serpent hoped to infect mankind with the ultimate delusion of grandeur: man can be like God, and therefore need not heed the word of God. Rav Nachman of Breslov[3] added that illegitimate pleasure originates with Chavah being convinced that the Tree of Knowledge was desirable. The serpent, who introduced this desire, and Amalek, who fulfilled this same role later in history, are one. Each led a rebellion against God and is responsible for the spread of evil and the rejection of God.

The sin in Eden, after all, consisted of eating the "first fruit." The mitzvah of *bikkurim* may be seen as an antidote for this sin.

In the aftermath of the expulsion from the Garden, man now has to work by the sweat of his brow. With the commandment of *bikkurim*, the serpent's initial victory, and the resultant distance from God, man is called upon to find God through his labor, to return to a higher spiritual plane, and to reestablish intimacy with God through the first fruits.

Later on in history there lived two brothers. One was a man of the field, while the other remained in the tents. The realms seemed separate: the secular and the Divine. Yaakov remained engaged in

---

1   See *Sefat Emet, Ki Tavo* 5639.
2   In *Resisei Lailah*, section 31, Rav Tzadok says that Amalek is the source of all evil manifested in this world.
3   *Likutei Maharan Tanina* 8:1.

spiritual pursuits, while his brother Esav was involved in the mundane. However, in this post-Eden world it was decreed that Yaakov become a man of the field as well. His task was to merge the spiritual and the secular, to take the mundane and elevate it into a spiritual context.

The descendant of Esav, Amalek, continues his war against the spiritual, while the descendant of Yaakov, Israel, attempts to merge the two worlds.

Now we may appreciate the mitzvah of *bikkurim* — the first fruits: Israel enters the Land, so close to fulfilling its destiny. The most crucial of questions emerge: Will the people follow the legacy of the serpent, of Amalek, and see the fruits of their labor independent of God? Or will they bring the fruits to Yerushalayim, part and parcel of their religious experience?

Understanding of this issue will shed light on another issue articulated in the same section in the Torah. Later on we are told of the terrible calamities which will befall the people should they deviate from the word of God. The specific explanation offered by the Torah is:

> Because you did not serve God, your Lord, with joyfulness and with gladness of heart, from the abundance of all things.
>
> *(Devarim 28:47)*

The terms for "abundance" and "all" are *rov* and *kol* respectively. These same terms are found in a fascinating discussion between Yaakov and Esav. After becoming a man of the field, Yaakov returns to Israel. He meets up with his estranged brother. Yaakov offers gifts to Esav, who declines them, saying that he has "*rov*," an abundance. Yaakov, for his part, insists that he has everything, "*kol.*"

> And Esav said, "I have enough, my brother; keep what you have to yourself."
>
> And Yaakov said, "No, I beg you, if now I have found grace in your sight, then receive my present from my hand; for

therefore I have seen your face, as though I had seen the face of God, and you were pleased with me. Take, I beg you, my blessing that is brought to you; because God has dealt graciously with me and because I have everything."

And he urged him, and he took it.

(Bereishit 33:9–11)

Rashi points out the difference in speech: While Yaakov says that he has everything that he can imagine, Esav says merely that he has enough — indicating that he is well aware that there is more and he would like to possess it one day.

The Torah is telling us that when we fail to appreciate the gifts which God gives us, and instead we become fixated on acquiring more and more, we become like Esav. Yaakov focuses on what he has and is satisfied. Esav focuses on what he does not have and is never satisfied. This is how Esav produces Amalek, who represents misanthropy. When Israel becomes like Amalek, then the stay in Israel will come to an end.

Now we understand the significance of being satisfied with the *bikkurim*, the sanctification of the first fruits. Even though this is still the beginning of the season and hopefully more produce will follow, even the first fruits should produce joy in the heart of the Jew, realizing that all the bounty which we have comes from God.

As we saw, this took place on the holiday of Shavuot, the day of the giving of the Torah. For our parts we need to view each day as if the Torah is new, fresh, given that day. This type of consciousness is the opposite of the worldview of the serpent and Amalek.

This was the trait of our forefathers. The Talmud connects the trait of *kol* with the taste of another world:

> There were three to whom the Holy One, blessed be He, gave a foretaste of the future world while they were still in this world, and they are Avraham, Yitzchak, and Yaakov. Avraham [we know] because it is written of him, "[God blessed Avraham] in all" (*Bereishit* 24:1); Yitzchak, because it is written, "[And I ate] of all" (ibid. 27:33): Yaakov, because it is written, "[For I have]

all" (ibid. 33:11). There were three over whom the evil inclination had no dominion, and they were Avraham, Yitzchak, and
Yaakov, [as we know] because it is written in connection with
them, "in all," "of all," "all."

(Bava Batra 17a)

Because Avraham, Yitzchak, and Yaakov saw themselves as privileged, as possessing all good, they had defeated the evil inclination. That wicked serpent had no power over them. They were able
to taste the future world.

As the children of Israel prepare for their entrance to Land of Israel, they are given a strategy which will allow the stay to be enduring and meaningful. God provided the tools needed to create a
society with a God-consciousness, a society which will have tents
of study and fields of labor. But no schism will exist between the
two. God will be found in the fields, marketplaces, and study halls.
Every day revelation would be experienced. Holiness will permeate
the streets and fields. This is what eradication of Amalek is all
about. This is the goal of the mitzvah of the first fruits. This is the
particular holiness of the holiday of Shavuot.

Shavuot

The Holiday of the
Giving of the Torah

havuot is a somewhat elusive holiday. While the Torah
clearly states the historical events commemorated on
Pesach[1] and Sukkot,[2] no such connection is clearly drawn
between Shavuot and any historical event. Rather, the Torah's description of Shavuot is agricultural: The nation is commanded to
bring their first fruits to Jerusalem.

> And the Festival of Harvest, the first fruits of your labors,
> which you have sown in the field; and the Festival of Ingather-
> ing, which is at the end of the year, when you have gathered in
> your labors from the field.
>
> *(Shemot 23:16)*

> And you shall observe the Festival of Weeks, of the first fruits
> of wheat harvest, and the Festival of Ingathering at the year's
> end.
>
> *(Shemot 34:22)*

> To the next day after the seventh Shabbat you shall count fifty
> days; and you shall offer a new meal offering to God....
>
> *(Vayikra 23:16)*

---

1   *Shemot* 12 and numerous other sources.
2   *Vayikra* 23:43.

Also in the day of the First Fruits, when you bring a new meal offering to God, in your Festival of Weeks, you shall have a holy gathering; you shall do no labor.

(Bemidbar 28:26)

Seven weeks you shall count; begin to number the seven weeks from such time as you begin to put the sickle to the grain. And you shall keep the Festival of Weeks to God, your Lord, with a tribute of a freewill offering of your hand, which you shall give as God, your Lord, has blessed you.

(Devarim 16:9–10)

The only description of Shavuot is as the holiday of first fruits; no historical explanation is offered. On the other hand, Pesach and Sukkot, aside from their own agricultural identity, are described in the Torah as the holidays that commemorate the Exodus from Egypt and the sojourn in the desert, respectively. Apparently, the Torah weaves the agricultural date into a historical holiday in order to provide deeper meaning and to heighten the farmers' religious experience: The three yearly pilgrimages were tied into the agricultural cycle, in addition to the historical and theological significance of each holiday, creating a merger of the physical and spiritual realms and heightened historical consciousness.[1]

Of the three major celebrations, only Shavuot is left without a clear historical connection, a fact made all the more striking by the monumental nature of the event which transpired at the same time of year (the beginning of the third month) in the desert that first year after leaving Egypt: the giving of the Torah.

In the third month, when the People of Israel went forth out of the land of Egypt, the same day came they into the wilderness

---

1   See *Pesachim* 68b, where the division of the day in terms of divine service versus personal pleasure is noted. Of specific interest is the declaration that regarding Shavuot it is clear that there is an aspect of human pleasure — a point which is debated regarding the other holidays: "All agree in respect to the Feast of Weeks that we require [it to be] 'for you,' too. What is the reason? It is the day on which the Torah was given."

of Sinai.... And God said to Moshe, "Go to the people, and sanctify them today and tomorrow, and let them wash their clothes. And be ready by the third day, for on the third day God will come down in the sight of all the people upon Mount Sinai."

(Shemot 19:1, 10–11)

Fairly simple mathematics places the giving of the Torah more or less at the same time as the holiday of Shavuot,[1] though arguably not on the exact day:

Our Rabbis taught: On the sixth day of the month [Sivan] were the Ten Commandments given to Israel. Rabbi Yosei maintained: On the seventh thereof.

(Shabbat 86b)

While this may seem strange, we must keep in mind that in the days when the months were consecrated by the courts after witnesses testified that they saw the new moon, it was possible for the holiday of Shavuot to fall on the fifth, sixth, or seventh day of Sivan[2] and still coincide with the giving of the Torah.

Nonetheless, a problem remains: According to the chronology recorded in the Talmud, the Jews left Egypt on a Thursday and the Torah was given on Shabbat, which would be fifty-one days — and not fifty — after Pesach.

The Magen Avraham (*Orach Chaim* 494) insists that the law is actually decided in accordance with the opinion of Rabbi Yosei cited above: the Torah was given on the fifty-first day after Pesach, the seventh day of Sivan. While the Magen Avraham therefore questioned the appropriateness of calling Shavuot "the day the Torah was given," we should note that the liturgy actually calls

---

1 It is worthwhile mentioning that the date in Sivan is not ordained in the Torah as the means of establishing the holiday; rather the holiday is established by counting seven weeks from Pesach. For the Diaspora, if the giving of the Torah was not commemorated by the holiday of Shavuot itself, then it was by the second day observed in the Diaspora. See Joseph Tabori, *Jewish Festivals in the Time of the Mishnah and Talmud* (Jerusalem: Magnes Press, 2000), p. 153.

2 See *Tosefta Arachin* 1:4.

Shavuot "Zeman Matan Torateinu," the time of the giving of the Torah, not necessarily implying the precise day.[1]

Rav Shimshon Rafael Hirsch (commentary to *Vayikra* 23:21) suggested that the essence of Shavuot is not the giving of the Torah but the preparedness of man to accept the Torah. Just as the Jews in the desert prepared themselves to accept the Torah, so must we. This would alleviate the difficulty of assigning the date of the holiday to the sixth day of the month, which is not necessarily the day the Torah was given, but was, in fact, the day the People of Israel prepared themselves to receive it. This understanding is borne out by the choice of Torah reading for Shavuot, chapter 19 of *Shemot*, which begins with the preparations made to receive the Torah.

Rav Kook suggested that we must bear in mind that in the desert God said that the Torah would be given after two days of preparation.[2] Moshe asked the people to prepare for three days.[3] Therefore the Torah was received on the third day, which is indeed the fifty-first day. However, the word of God cannot be changed. Therefore even though the people of Israel were not ready to receive the Torah until the third day, the spiritual aura of the Torah being given appeared on the second day (in a spiritual sense), which is the fiftieth day, as God had declared, and that is the day which is celebrated for posterity.[4]

The Torah itself remains silent regarding the relationship of the giving of the Torah to the bringing of the first fruits. We are not told the date of the holiday — either of Shavuot or the giving of the Torah. Shavuot is fifty days after the Exodus, and the giving of the Torah is in the beginning of the third month. While the connection between Shavuot and the Revelation is obscured in the Torah, the association was maintained by tradition.[5]

---

1   See *Chok Yaakov* (*Orach Chaim* 494); *Chatam Sofer* responsa *Yoreh Dei'ah*, 179; and Rav Kook, *Responsa Daat Kohein, Yoreh Dei'ah*, 80.
2   See *Shemot* 19:10–11.
3   *Shabbat* 87a.
4   See *Responsa Daat Kohein, Yoreh Dei'ah* 80. I have heard this idea also attributed to the Imrei Emet.

One expression of this tradition may be found in the Torah reading, the Sages' means of capturing and transmitting the spirit of the day. This is true for both the primary Torah reading as well as the secondary haftarah reading. Regarding Shavuot, we are told the following:

Mishnah: On Pesach we read from the section of the festivals in *Vayikra*. On Shavuot, "Seven Weeks" (*Devarim* 16:9).

(Megillah 30b)

Gemara: On Shavuot, we read "Seven Weeks," and for haftarah a chapter from *Chavakuk* (ch. 3). According to others, we read "In the Third Month" (*Shemot*, ch.19–20) and for haftarah the account of the Divine Chariot (*Yechezkel*, ch. 1). Nowadays that we keep two days, we follow both courses, but in the reverse order.

(Megillah 31a)

The difference between the two choices of Torah reading is telling: the section in *Devarim* describes the "Festival of Weeks" — Shavuot. This holiday is mentioned in various sections of the Torah. It describes an agricultural holiday, celebrated by bringing the first fruits to Jerusalem. The section in *Shemot* describes the Revelation, which links Shavuot with *matan Torah*. According to the Mishnah and the first opinion expressed in the Talmud, the reading for the first day is about Shavuot — the agricultural holiday — and the second day is about the giving of the Torah. The conclusion of the Gemara is that on the first day of Shavuot we read the nineteenth chapter in *Shemot*, which describes the giving of the Torah, while on the second day (in the Diaspora) we read the description of the holiday of Shavuot in *Devarim* (16:9). The irony is that it

the prayers, which are the formulation of the Men of the Great Assembly. They call Shavuot "Zeman Matan Torateinu," the day of the giving of the Torah. This appellation was used by them in the beginning of the Second Commonwealth. Additionally, the association of the giving of the Torah with Shavuot was retained by the Ethiopians and the Samaritans, both of whom had limited contact with or influence of the Rabbinic authorities. See Tabori, p. 151, note 25.

is possible that the Torah was actually given on what would eventually become the second day of Shavuot — hence the reading on the second day reflected the giving of the Torah, while the first day reflected the holiday of Shavuot.

The haftarah reading for the first day is the description of the Divine Chariot, and for the second day the section of *Chavakuk* which mentions the giving of the Torah[1] (and provides an overview of the years in the desert and the conquest of the Land of Israel). Notably, both choices of the haftarah are related to the giving of the Torah and ignore the agricultural motif. The Rabbis always knew of the relationship between Shavuot and the giving of the Torah; perhaps, taking their cue from the Torah's silence, they too were reticent about openly declaring the relationship.

The final choice for the first day is the Prophecy of Yechezkel known as the Chariot of Yechezkel. This section seems the most appropriate match for the section in *Shemot* that describes the Revelation; by choosing this as the haftarah, the Sages instruct us as to the nature of Shavuot while teaching us an important lesson about the Revelation. There are two distinct aspects of the Revelation to consider: first, the content of the Revelation, and second, the fact that there was a Revelation at all — namely, that the Creator and Sustainer of the universe "descended" upon a mountain and made Himself "known."

Upon reflection, we realize that the fact of Revelation is of primary importance: The content would have no significance had it not been for the fact that God Himself said these things. On the other hand, even had the Revelation been devoid of content, it would still have been of incredible religious significance, in and of itself, as a rendezvous between man and God. It is this theme of revelation per se which is highlighted by the choice of the haftarah of *Yechezkel*.

The *Merkavah* (Chariot) deals with the Revelation witnessed by Yechezkel:

---

1   Compare *Chavakuk* 3:3 with *Devarim* 33:2.

And it came to pass in the thirtieth year, in the fourth month, in the fifth day of the month, as I was among the exiles by the Kevar River, that the heavens were opened, and I saw visions of the Lord.

(Yechezkel 1:1)

The ensuing chapter provides an elaborate description of divinity. The images are stark yet mysterious; the symbols are illusive yet tantalizing. More than any another scriptural prophecy, this section became associated with mystical knowledge and exploration.[1]

There may be another message being communicated by this choice. The Prophecy of the Chariot is actually an unlikely candidate for haftarah reading at any time. The Mishnah teaches that there are those who believe that the Chariot may never be read in public as a haftarah:

The portion of the Chariot is not read as a haftarah, but Rabbi Yehudah permits this.

(Megillah 25a)

Why were the Sages hesitant to publicly read about the Chariot? The Mishnah taught that this section may not be taught in public — not even to a small group of initiates:

The [subject of] forbidden relations may not be expounded in the presence of three, nor the Work of Creation in the presence of two, nor [the Work of] the Chariot in the presence of one, unless he is a sage and understands of his own knowledge.

(Chagigah 11b)

So intense and mystical is the teaching of the Chariot that it was not to be taught or even read publicly. Too much would be revealed.

It is the glory of God to conceal a thing.

(Mishlei 25:2)

The choice of this section for this day speaks volumes: Though

---

1   See *Berachot* 21b, *Shabbat* 80b, *Megillah* 24b, and *Bava Batra* 134a.

on other occasions it would be more prudent to conceal, on this day we may reveal a bit, for on this day Revelation took place. Even post-Revelation man must realize that there is so much about God that we cannot know and indeed will never know. On this day of Revelation, perhaps we should even conceal that something was revealed, yet we boldly read about the Revelation and follow with the description of the Chariot. We know that something — perhaps better concealed — was revealed. By choosing the haftarah of the *Merkavah*, the rabbis were expressing their ambivalence in identifying Revelation as the key aspect of the day and subtly telling us to be careful with our conclusions.

The challenge of Revelation is to avoid hubris; man may become overconfident, deluded into thinking he understands what may actually eluded him. To avoid this pitfall, revelation must be obscured and protected. Ultimately if man wishes to understand God and His ways, the only way to reveal this secret is to learn His Torah and perform His commandments. This is the gift of Revelation with which we are entrusted throughout the year; the content of the Revelation at Sinai is the key to unlocking the secrets of the Revelation itself.

Accessing Revelation is not something that is limited to one day on the calendar; we are enjoined to see every day as if the Torah was given anew on that day.[1] Receiving the Torah is not limited to one day a year.

> "Command you today" (*Devarim* 11:13) — This suggests that they should ever be to you as new commandments, as though you had heard them for the first time on this day.
>
> *(Rashi, Devarim 11:13)*

The Torah writes at the conclusion of the first fruit ceremony:

> This day God, your Lord, has commanded you to do these statutes and judgments; you shall therefore keep and do them

---

1   See *Sichot Maharan*, section 26, where Rav Nachman explains that even forgetting Torah can be positive: when you learn it anew the joy is as if it were the first time.

with all your heart and with all your soul.

(Devarim 26:16)

Rashi's comments are instructive:

"This day God, your Lord, has commanded you" — This suggests that each day they [God's commandments] should be to you as something new [not antiquated and something of which you have become tired], as though you had received the commands that very day for the first time.

(Rashi, Devarim 26:16)

How interesting that specifically on the holiday of Shavuot, at the celebration of the first fruits, we are commanded to think and act as if the Torah was given on that very day! We now know that, in fact, it was.

Our attitude toward Torah should be as if it were given on each and every day. Perhaps this frame of mind takes us back to the first fruits: The man who has worked so hard during the entire year now has the fruits of his labor in his hands. He experiences a sense of renewal and completion. The first fruits were a living example of what man's orientation to Torah should be — a sense of newness and freshness coupled with resolve to continue, a recognition of hard work coupled with an appreciation of its rewards. Remarkably, the ceremony which accompanied the first fruit offering included a revelation — a *bat kol* calling on man to continue onward:

"You shall therefore keep and do them" — A Heavenly Voice ["*bat kol*"] pronounces by these words a blessing upon him [the worshiper] — "You have brought the first fruits today — you will be privileged to do so next year, too!"

(Rashi, Devarim 26:16)

The themes of Revelation and first fruits are inseparably intertwined in the holiday of Shavuot. The window between the revealed and the concealed is opened for us on this singular holiday, and the content and purpose of the Revelation at Sinai, the Torah and its commandments, is wrapped around the more familiar and accessible agricultural aspects of the day. As we offer the first fruits of our physical labor before God, the physical bounty with which we have been blessed serves as a reminder of the personal and national destiny we accepted at Sinai. In the final analysis, the holiday of the First Fruits was about receiving the Torah all along, about the medium and the message of Revelation.

Av

Tishah B'Av

The Three Sins

When the order of Torah readings was established, certain portions were linked to specific events in the Jewish calendar, and the entire cycle of Torah readings was arranged around them. Thus, many portions fall in a more general way at specific times of the year, as a function of their proximity to the parashiyot that are more precisely assigned. *Parashat Devarim* always falls during the Nine Days preceeding Tishah B'Av: Its searing rebuke was deemed appropriate for this time of year, a period of perpetual national disaster. It may therefore seem incidental that *Parashat Va'etchanan* always follows Tishah B'Av, simply because it immediately follows *Parashat Devarim*, yet when we analyze the themes of the parashah we find strong connections to Tishah B'Av, as well as a prescription for avoiding future calamities.

The major message of *Parashat Va'etchanan* is the belief in one God. This idea is conveyed in both a positive and a negative manner. On the one hand the exalted prayer of Shema is found in this parashah. The Shema may be seen as the pinnacle of man's acceptance of one God. The Shema, however, is not an isolated statement. The basic tenet of monotheism is expressed in a number of places in the parashah.

To you it was shown, that you might know that God is the Lord; there is no other beside Him. From heaven He made you hear His voice, that He might instruct you; and upon earth He showed you His great fire; and you heard His words out of the midst of the fire.

(Devarim 4:35–36)

Know therefore this day, and consider it in your heart, that God is the Lord in heaven above, and upon the earth beneath; there is no other.

(Ibid., 39)

Know therefore that God, your Lord, He is the Lord, the faithful Lord, who keeps covenant and mercy with those who love Him and keep His commandments to a thousand generations.

(Ibid. 7:9)

I am God, your Lord, who brought you out of the land of Egypt, from the house of slavery.

(Ibid. 5:6)

The last reference is, of course, from the Ten Commandments, which are repeated in *Va'etchanan*. The entire parashah is a testament to the centrality of the belief in one God. On the other hand, the parashah also stresses the negative aspect of this same faith — the avoidance of idolatry. This, too, is stated clearly in the Ten Commandments, but not exclusively there. The second commandment is not an isolated statement; the polemic against idolatry is reiterated numerous times throughout the parashah. (See 4:15–19, 4:23, 4:25–28, 6:12, and 6:14.)

Parashat Va'etchanan is almost exclusively one of ideas, of basic tenets of faith. The only action mentioned in the parashah, aside from Moshe's act of speech in transmitting the word of God, is the establishment of cities of refuge.

Then Moshe set apart three cities on this side of the Jordan toward the rising suns, that the slayer who killed his neighbor unintentionally and did not hate him in times past might flee there, and that by fleeing to one of these cities he might live: Betzer in the wilderness, in the plain country of the tribe of

Reuven; and Ramot in Gilad, of the tribe of Gad; and Golan in Bashan, of the tribe of Menasheh. And this is the Torah which Moshe set before the people of Israel.

(Ibid. 4:41–44)

There are also a number of references to a particular place where scandalous behavior took place — Pe'or.

So we remained in the valley opposite Beit Pe'or.

(Ibid. 3:29)

Your eyes have seen what God did because of Baal Pe'or, to all the men who followed Baal Pe'or; God, your Lord, has destroyed them from among you.

(Ibid. 4:3)

On this side of the Jordan, in the valley opposite Beit Pe'or....

(Ibid., 46)

While Pe'or was a place where idolatry was practiced, it was also a place where an outrage of a sexual variety was perpetrated. It would therefore be fair to state that the major topic of the parashah is belief in God and avoidance of idolatry, while concern about bloodshed and its effects on society (the inclusion of the issue of the cities of refuge in this parashah) and sexual licentiousness (the references to Pe'or) also make an appearance.

These three could be called the cardinal offences in Judaism, and they are the only principles for which a Jew is required to sacrifice his life.

By a majority vote, it was resolved in the upper chambers of the house of Nitza in Lod that in every [other] law of the Torah, if a man is commanded: "Transgress and you will not suffer death" he may transgress and not suffer death, excepting idolatry, sexual licentiousness, and murder.

(Sanhedrin 74a)

These are the three crimes that caused the destruction of the first Temple:

Why was the first Sanctuary destroyed? Because of three [evil] things which prevailed there: idolatry, sexual immorality, bloodshed.

(Yoma 9b)

Understanding the centrality of these three crimes requires analysis of past failures and their implications for the future. The first sin in the history of the world was that of Adam and Chavah in the Garden of Eden. While technically one could call the sin thievery — they took and ate from something that did not belong to them — the objective of the repast was to become like God. This was the seductive description hissed by the serpent:

For the Lord knows that on the day you eat of it, your eyes shall be opened, and you shall be as gods, knowing good and evil.

(Bereishit 3:5)

The very thought that man could become like God is based on two fallacious assumptions: One, that in order for man to approximate God, he must "emasculate God," cutting God down to human size. On the other hand, the equation of man with God rests upon an incredibly inflated perception of man. Thus, the core of the sin in the Garden was idolatry. This is the Jewish idea of "original sin."

Adam was a heretic, for it is written, "And God, the Lord, called to Adam and said to him, 'Where are you?' " i.e., where has your heart turned? ... He denied God.

(Sanhedrin 38b)

The second sin in *Bereishit* is the fratricide committed by Kayin. It is interesting that these two sins, of Adam and Chavah and of Kayin, both resulted in exile.

The next sin came in the generation of the flood. Here a sexual breakdown is described:

The sons of the powerful people saw the daughters of men that they were pretty; and they took as wives all those whom they chose.... There were Nefilim in the earth in those days; and also after that, when the sons of the powerful people came unto the daughters of men, and they bore children to them, they became mighty men of old, men of renown. And God saw that the wickedness of man was great in the earth, and that every imagination of the thoughts of his heart was only evil continually.

(Bereishit 6:2–5)

The earth also was corrupt before the Lord, and the earth was filled with violence. And the Lord looked upon the earth, and, behold, it was corrupt; for all flesh had corrupted its way upon the earth.

(Ibid., 11–12)

As Ibn Ezra explains these passages, the violence and corruption stemmed from the sexual practices of the powerful men, who took whichever woman they chose.

The three primordial sins are committed in the early chapters of *Bereishit*: idolatry in the Garden of Eden, bloodshed in the next generation, and sexual misbehavior in the generation of the flood. The Torah reports that this same cycle is reinitiated: a tower is built to reach to heaven and wage war on God.

And they said, "Come, let us build us a city and a tower, whose top may reach to heaven; and let us make us a name, lest we be scattered abroad upon the face of the whole earth."

(Ibid. 11:4)

It is at this juncture that Avraham appears and breaks the cycle: He undertakes a war on paganism. A new light shines brightly and new hope for the world is born. Generations later, Avraham's descendants leave Egypt and begin their march toward the destiny that is the product of Avraham's relationship with God. The children of Israel arrive at the foot of Sinai where the Revelation transpires. Moshe then ascends the mountain, where he will remain for forty days and nights. The people wait below, theoretically in great anticipation, awaiting Moshe's descent with the Torah. Instead, they begin to build a calf of gold.

The tragedy is enormous. The tide is turned: The children of Israel abandon the course of monotheism set by Avraham. This historic moment should have been the ultimate expression of monotheism, the unique ability of the children of Avraham to form a covenant with the one God, expunging the stain of the sin in the Garden of Eden and correcting the warped premises of the serpent's worldview. Instead, a new chapter of idolatry is opened, the inexorable cycle of sin is reinitiated. On his way down the mount, Moshe witnesses this great perfidy, and the tablets with the Word of God come falling out of his hands.

The sin of the golden calf was not exclusively one of idolatry. There were other facets to the debacle. When the idea of the calf first arose, the people approached Chur and asked him to oversee the project. Chur refused and was immediately murdered:

> Chur arose and rebuked them: "You brainless fools! Have you forgotten the miracles God performed for you?" Whereupon they rose against him and slew him.
>
> *(Shemot Rabbah 41:7)*

> [Aharon] saw Chur lying slain before him and said [to himself]: "If I do not obey them, they will now do to me as they did to Chur, and so will be fulfilled [the fear of] the prophet, 'Shall the priest and the prophet be slain in the Sanctuary of God?' "[1]
>
> *(Sanhedrin 7a)*

The sin of the golden calf included a third element. The Torah says:

---

1   The Talmud is referring to a verse from *Eichah* (2:20) that describes the destruction of the Temple: "Behold, God, and consider to whom you have done this. Shall the women eat their fruit, their cherished babies? Shall the priest and the prophet be slain in the sanctuary of the Lord?"

And the people sat down to eat and to drink, and rose up to make merry.

(Shemot 32:6)

Rashi (on this verse) cites the *Midrash Tanchuma*, which explains the meaning of "making merry" as an expression of sexual activities.[1]

The sin of the golden calf, then, is actually threefold, containing within it the three cardinal sins of idolatry, murder, and sexual licentiousness.

The Talmud tells us the significance of this tragedy:

Rabbi Eliezer further stated: "What is the purport of the Scriptural text: 'Graven upon the tablets' (*Shemot* 32:16)? If the first tablets had not been broken the Torah would never have been forgotten in Israel." Rabbi Acha ben Yaakov said: "No nation or tongue would have had any power over them; for it says 'graven.' Read not 'graven' [*charut*] but 'freedom' [*cheirut*]."

(Eiruvin 54a)

Now we may begin to understand the severity of this sin. Had the Jews not built a golden calf, the Torah would have been received in a more organic way, "graven" upon the hearts and minds of Israel, and not only on the stone tablets. The Temple, once established in this sort of atmosphere, could never had been destroyed, for the resulting bond between Israel and the one God would have been such that no other philosophy or nationality could have interfered. The three cardinal sins represented by the sin of the golden calf, echoes of the primordial sins of *Bereishit*, are the very same sins that lead to destruction and exile. The Mishnah draws a line between them:

Five misfortunes befell our fathers on the seventeenth of Tammuz.... The Tablets [of the Law] were shattered, the daily offering was discontinued, a breach was made in the city

---

1   The *Midrash Rabbah* (*Shemot* 41:7) discerns only idolatry.

[Yerushalayim], and Apostomos burned the Scroll of the Law
and placed an idol in the Temple.

(Ta'anit 26b)

The seventeenth of Tammuz is the beginning of the three weeks
of mourning for the destroyed Temple. The negative spiritual
power of the day was unleashed when the Jews worshiped the
golden calf. At that moment the *luchot* lost their holiness. The let-
ters fled back to heaven, leaving only stones in Moshe's hands,
rocks devoid of holiness. Now we understand how years later the
walls of the holy city, Yerushalayim, could be breached on the
same day: By their behavior, the people banished the Presence of
God; the *Shechinah* fled. The city had lost its holiness, and the walls
of the city were now just stones, devoid of *Shechinah*, and like the
luchot, they were shattered. The physical reality of the stones was
nothing more than a burden when bereft of *Shechinah*.

Of the three offenses, Judaism sees idolatry as certainly the
worst and most destructive. The individual who has no belief may
subjectively create his own worldview, justifying all his desires and
peccadilloes;[1] the slippery slope to the other cardinal sins is paved
with the idolatrous perspective expressed so succinctly by the serpent in Eden. The axis of Judaism, then, is belief in one God. Therefore Moshe spends the majority of the parashah discussing the
problem of idolatry and the centrality of this belief. If the Jews are
to remain in the land which they are about to enter, they will need
to avoid these three offenses by working on their belief in God,
honing their sensitivity to the oneness of God and their ability to
imitate, not emasculate, Him. Moshe repeats the Ten Commandments, hoping to instill in the people deep, profound faith, awe
and fear of God. For if the people retain God within them, the
Shechinah will never be expelled and exiled.

Today we stand thousands of years later; we have the advantage

---

1   This idea is expressed in a *tosefta* which asks, "Who is the most dangerous man?"
    (Shavuot 3:6). The *Tosefta's* answer is that the atheist, even if he is a moral man, is
    most dangerous because there is no basis for his morality. In the eyes of the *Tosefta*,
    today's moral atheist may be tomorrow's murderer.

of the perspective of history. Today our goal must be to imbue the rocks with their original holiness and to restore our relationship with God, to assure that the *Shechinah* returns to the People and the Land, never to be exiled again.

Tishah B'Av

To Climb the Mountain

O f all the sins which the children of Israel perpetrated in the desert, the one with the most far-reaching consequences was the sin of the spies. While other offenses generated a local, concentrated response, in the case of the spies, though the perpetrators perished, the entire nation suffered for the next forty years by being forced to languish in the desert.[1]

There are a number of basic questions and intrigue which surround the story. The first intrigue is the observation that despite the widespread labeling of the incident as the "sin of the spies"[2] the word *spy* does not appear at any point in *Parashat Shelach*. Rather, the term *tur* is used, which implies touring and not spying. If the sin of the spies did indeed have such dire consequences, then why did God command it, and why did Moshe acquiesce without the slightest discernable hesitation?

> And God spoke to Moshe, saying, "Send men, that they may travel the land of Canaan, which I give to the people of Israel. Of every tribe of their fathers shall you send a man, every one a

---

1   The Rabbinic association of the destruction of the Temples on the same day is a further echo of the same idea. The ninth of Av is recorded as a day of infamy, and through history countless other atrocities, including the Spanish expulsion, took place on that date.
2   For example see *Sanhedrin* 10:3; *Bemidbar Rabbah* 16:2; and *Rashi, Bemidbar* 13:2.

leader among them." And Moshe sent them by the commandment of God from the wilderness of Paran; all those men were
chiefs of the people of Israel.

(Bemidbar 13:1–3)

While most of us are primarily familiar with the episode based
on the description in *Bemidbar,* this may provide a "stilted" reading, and hence our questions. The recounting of the story in the beginning of *Devarim* deals with both of these issues. On the one
hand, the tourists are referred to in retrospect as spies. On the other
hand, far more background is offered to the story.

And I said to you, "You have come to the mountain of the
Amorites, which God, our Lord, gives to us. Behold, God, your
Lord, has set the land before you; go up and possess it, as God,
the Lord of your fathers, has said to you. Do not be afraid or
discouraged." And you came near me, every one of you, and
said, "We will send men before us, and they shall search us out
the land, and bring us word by which way we must go up and
to what cities we shall come." And the saying pleased me well;
and I took twelve men of you, one from each tribe. And they
turned and went up into the mountain, and came to the valley
of Eshkol, and searched [spied] it out.

(Devarim 1:20–24)

The idea of the spies arose from the ranks, and Moshe was en-
thused by the prospect. Now we may understand God's instructions in *Parashat Shelach:* God says, "*Shelach lecha*" — if you really
want to, then go ahead and send them. This is how Rashi explains
the text, even though locally the interpretation may have seemed
somewhat forced and theologically disturbing — why would God
encourage Moshe to send the men to set out on a mission destined
for failure? Rashi explains that God is saying, "If you really would
like to send them, then fine," hence *shelach lecha* — for your edifi-
cation.

While this answers one question, namely God's involvement in the debacle, now Moshe's role becomes more disturbing. By getting God "off the hook" Moshe assumes more responsibility. Indeed, why did Moshe think that this was a wonderful idea? Why did Moshe wish to send spies?

The answer to this question is in the other observation; Moshe never sent spies. Moshe sent men to see the land. The mission was not one of intelligence gathering.

The prototypical spies in the Torah are the accused brothers of Yosef:

> And Yosef remembered the dreams which he dreamed of them, and said to them, "You are spies; to see the nakedness of the land you have come."
>
> And they said to him, "No, my lord, your servants came to buy food. We are all one man's sons; we are honest men, your servants are not spies."
>
> And he said to them, "No, to see the nakedness of the land you have come."
>
> *(Bereishit 42:9–12)*

They were accused of searching the "nakedness of the land," of plotting calculated devious behavior. Moshe did not request that type of mission. Moshe sent the men "*latur et haaretz*," to travel the land. It is true that they were further told to see the land. The question is for what purpose — to produce a conquest feasibility study or to see the land for an alternative reason?

Rabbi Yosef Dov Soloveitchik suggested a completely different purpose of the mission. There is a law taught in the Talmud that it is inappropriate to marry someone unless you met them first. Technically marriage could be executed by sending an agent without a personal meeting. Despite the decidedly unromantic prospect of marriage without any relationship, the "acquisition" would be valid. Marriage, however, should be based on love, and hopefully the love should grow as the years go by.

Rabbi Soloveitchik suggested that the entering of the land by these emissaries, "men of renown," was intended to foster the love between a people and their beloved promised land. The critical approach which they took was therefore completely uncalled for and unexpected. This land was their destiny. For centuries, these people and their ancestors had been pining for the day that they would return home. One can only imagine how tales of this exquisite land, with the beauty of the sea coupled with the majestic mountain ranges, which would once again be home, gave strength to the slave in Egypt exhausted beyond imagination.

Now, as these men return from their mission they articulate the impossible: the land is indeed stunning, but unattainable, and there are plenty of negatives, which apparently got lost in years of idealizing this land in idyllic terms. If we were to return to the metaphor of the young erstwhile lovers, let us imagine that the matchmaker was God, who promises that this is indeed the match of your dreams, the match which was conceived when you were, the proverbial *"bashert."* However, upon meeting, self-doubt overwhelms and anticipation of years of happiness is replaced by the gnawing feeling that this match was not meant to be. When the young people explain their position to friends, they then make disparaging comments about their date, which of course ultimately reflects on the Matchmaker as well.

Now we can understand Moshe's enthusiasm in sending the spies. Moshe saw the meeting in religious, spiritual terms. On the other hand, the spies saw their mission in pragmatic terms. Their mission was cold and calculating; in a word, they thought their mandate was to be "spies." We may discern Moshe's motivation by the instructions that he offers:

> And Moshe sent them to spy out the land of Canaan, and he said to them, "Go up this way southward, and go up into the mountain. And see the land, what it is, and the people who live in it, whether they are strong or weak, few or many. And what the land is that they live in, whether it is good or bad; and what cities they are that they live in, whether in tents or in fortresses. And what the land is, whether it is fat or lean,

whether there are trees in it or not. And you be of good courage, and bring of the fruit of the land." Now the time was the time of the first ripe grapes.

(Bemidar 13:17–20)

Moshe's instructions are interesting. They may be divided into three parts. The first part seems exclusively geographical: "Go up this way southward, and go up into the mountain." The second part seems inquisitive; looking for information: "And see the land, what it is, and the people who live in it, whether they are strong or weak, few or many. And what the land is that they live in, whether it is good or bad; and what cities they are that they live in, whether in tents or in fortresses. And what the land is, whether it is fat or lean, whether there are trees in it or not."

The third part sounds like a request: "and bring of the fruit of the land." However, this statement helps us understand the second part of Moshe's instructions. Rather than asking for fruit in the conditional form, "See what type of land it is — and if you find produce please bring some back," Moshe says definitively: "and bring of the fruit of the land." Thus it is clear that the second part of his instructions was not fact finding; rather, it was rhetorical. When Moshe asks "whether it is good or bad," he knows the right answer, and he assumes these men do as well.

What was the purpose of Moshe's first comments, "Go up this way southward, and go up into the mountain"? From where the Israelites are encamped not that many options are available. Of course they will come from the south, and surely they will soon hit a mountain range. We must listen carefully to Moshe's words, for they are not superfluous or mundane. Moshe's words are intrinsic; they are part of his instructions, and in fact coming first they may be the most important part of the instructions.[1]

---

1   Rabbi Soloveitchik made this point in a lecture delivered June 4, 1975, entitled "*Cheit Miriam U'Meraglim.*"

The term "ascend the mountain" should have an associative meaning, especially when we consider that the duration of the excursion was forty days. Moshe too had gone up a mountain for forty days. Moshe was involved in a profound religious experience; he met God on the mountain. Moshe believes that a similar experience awaits these travelers, as they embark on a mission to the land where God dwells:

> For the land which you enter to possess is not as the land of Egypt from where you came out, where you sowed your seed and watered it with your foot, as a garden of vegetables. But the land which you are going over to possess is a land of hills and valleys that drinks water from the rain of the skies. A land which God, your Lord cares for; the eyes of God, your Lord, are always upon it, from the beginning of the year to the end of the year.
>
> *(Devarim 11:8–12)*

Apparently Moshe does know something about this land, especially its spiritual makeup. He does not need a detailed report. Which specific mountain does Moshe have in mind? Based on an analysis of the Torah, it appears to be Chevron.

> And they ascended by the south, and he came to Chevron.
>
> *(Bemidbar 13:22)*

When they came from the south they arrived at Chevron. This is the mountain range they would have to cross and is clearly what Moshe had in mind. However, readers of the text in Hebrew notice a shift in grammar: "*they* ascended by the south," yet the singular "*he* came" to Chevron.

> "And they ascended by the south and he came to Chevron" — it should have read "and they came"! Raba said: "It teaches that Kaleiv held aloof from the plan of the spies and went and prostrated himself upon the graves of the patriarchs, saying to them, 'My fathers, pray on my behalf that I may be delivered

from the plan of the spies.' "[1]

(Sotah 34b)

Had all these men heeded Moshe's advice they would all have been spared. Had they understood the spiritual nature of their mission they would not have needed to be spared.

There may, however, be a deeper meaning to the significance of Chevron in this context. The exile which they were crawling out of had its origin in Chevron. From Chevron Yaakov sent Yosef to seek his brothers. As we know, he ended up in Egypt.

> And Yisrael said to Yosef, "Are your brothers not feeding the flock in Shechem? Come, and I will send you to them."
>
> And he said to him, "Here I am."
>
> And he said to him, "Go, I beg you, see whether it is well with your brothers and well with the flocks, and bring me word again."
>
> So he sent him out from the valley of Chevron, and he came to Shechem.
>
> *(Bereishit 37:13–14)*

The Midrash poses a question on the topography implicit in the verse:

> "So he sent him out from the valley of Chevron" — But surely Chevron lies on a mountain, yet you say, "out from the valley of Chevron"? Said Rabbi Acha: "He went to bring about the fulfillment of the deep designs which the Holy One, blessed be He, had arranged between Himself and His noble companion who is buried in Chevron [Avraham], which is, 'And they shall serve them, and they shall afflict them' (*Bereishit* 15:13).' "
>
> *(Bereishit Rabbah 84:14)*

The Midrash explains that the term "valley of Chevron" implies something deep in the recesses of Chevron, namely the covenant

---

1   As far as Yehoshua, the Talmud continues: "As for Yehoshua, Moshe had already prayed on his behalf; as it is said: 'And Moshe called Hoshea ben Nun Yehoshua,' [meaning], 'May God save you [*yoshi'acha*] from the plan of the spies.' "

formed between God and Avraham which included a promise of exile. Now it was time to return to Chevron and inform the Patriarchs that the time has arrived for the children to return home. Chevron was the origin of the Jewish ownership of Israel, the plot bought by Avraham for a burial place for his beloved Sarah. Now these great men who were supposed to fall in love with the land of their dreams are told, "return home, ascend the mountain." Yet only one of the men understands his mission. Only Kaleiv comes home to Chevron.

Moshe's itinerary was of the "holy sights." This was to be a religious pilgrimage; therefore of course Chevron must be the first stop, where they are to ascend the mountain.

The spies, however, had a different plan. They thought that they must spy. As we recall, the very idea of entering the land on this mission arose from the people. What were they seeking? The people knew that one day soon the time would arrive for the conquest. Was this conquest meant to be a spiritual experience? Or was this to be a series of epic battles? The people preferred the "normal life" to the pressures of living with God in their midst. They probably therefore envisioned the conquest as a natural process. This would be especially true if they knew that Moshe would not be the leader who takes them into the land.[1]

The Talmud teaches that the prophecy of Eldad and Meidad contained that ominous message:

> They said, "Moshe shall die and Yehoshua shall bring Israel into the land."
>
> *(Sanhedrin 17a, cited in Rashi, Bemidbar 11:28)*

The last time Yehoshua led was the battle against Amalek, when things did not go as well as the people would have wanted:

> Then Amalek came and fought with Israel in Refidim. And Moshe said to Yehoshua, "Choose for us men and go out, fight with Amalek; tomorrow I will stand on the top of the hill with

---

1   See the discussion in *Explorations, Parashat Beha'alotcha.*

the rod of the Lord in my hand."

So Yehoshua did as Moshe had said to him, and fought with Amalek; and Moshe, Aharon, and Chur went up to the top of the hill. And it came to pass, when Moshe held up his hand, that Israel prevailed; and when he let down his hand, Amalek prevailed. But Moshe's hands were heavy; and they took a stone, and put it under him, and he sat on it. And Aharon and Chur supported his hands, one on one side and the other on the other side; and his hands were steady until the going down of the sun.

And Yehoshua discomfited Amalek and his people with the edge of the sword.

(Shemot 17:8–13)

The only power to win was the great Moshe. With only Yehoshua leading the people, the spies felt that they would need greater military prowess. Yet the Talmud stresses that it was not the hands of Moshe which clinched the battle; rather, being with God and focusing on God is what allowed the people to be victorious.

Did the hands of Moshe wage war or crush the enemy? Not so; only the text signifies that so long as Israel turned their thoughts above and subjected their hearts to their Father in Heaven they prevailed, but otherwise they fell.

(Rosh HaShanah 29a)

The spies are unconfident, uncertain what the future holds. Moshe for his part tells them the secret to succeed: if they look to the heavens, if they climb the mountain, they will be victorious. If God is with them, then victory is theirs. The Torah had actually already told the plan for the conquest — immediately prior to Moshe's ascension of the Mountain of Sinai.

Behold, I send an angel before you, to watch you on the way and to bring you into the place which I have prepared. Take heed of him and obey his voice, provoke him not; for he will not pardon your transgressions, for My Name is in him. But if you shall indeed obey his voice and do all that I speak, then I will be an enemy to your enemies and an adversary to your adversaries. For My angel shall go before you, and bring you in to the Amorites, the Hittites, the Perizzites, the Canaanites, the Hivites, and the Jebusites; and I will cut them off....

I will send My fear before you and destroy all the people to whom you shall come, and I will make all your enemies turn their backs to you. And I will send hornets before you, which shall drive out the Hivite, the Canaanite, and the Hittite from before you. I will not drive them out from before you in one year, lest the land become desolate and the beast of the field multiply against you. Little by little I will drive them out from before you, until you are increased and inherit the land.

(Shemot 23:20–23, 27–30)

The passage is complex. On the one hand, God's spirit will be in a force (or person) who leads them, yet the conquest will be gradual. Is this the description of a natural or supernatural conquest? The people evidently felt that they must do the hard work themselves. The Torah, though, was quite clear God will scatter the enemies; He will put fear in their hearts, and they will [slowly] prepare the land for its rightful owners.

The spies did not climb the mountain. They did not join God in a rendezvous as they were to transverse the land as Avraham of old had. Their pragmatism won the day, as their intelligence report concluded that they could not climb the mountain. Of course, had they known the significance of the mountain, they would have realized that indeed they could climb.

The Torah ends the story of the spies by telling us how the spies are sentenced to death, and the rest of the generation would die in the desert. There is then a postscript to the tragedy:

And Moshe told these sayings to all the people of Israel, and the people mourned greatly. And they rose up early in the morning and went up to the top of the mountain, saying, "Behold, we are here and we will go up to the place of which God has spoken; for we have sinned."

And Moshe said, "Why do you now transgress the commandment of God? But it shall not succeed. Do not go up, for God is not among you; so that you should not be struck before your enemies. For the Amalekites and the Canaanites are there before you, and you shall fall by the sword; because you are turned away from God, and therefore God will not be with you."

But they presumed to go up to the hilltop. Nevertheless, the Ark of the covenant of God and Moshe did not depart from the camp. Then the Amalekites and the Canaanites who lived in that hill came down and defeated them, and pursued them, even to Chormah.

(Bemidbar 14:39-45)

These people were known for posterity as the *"ma'apilim,"* a term that implies brazenness or presumptuousness.[1] Now, after the decree has been sealed that they must live and die in the desert, they decide that they wish to go up the mountain, they wish to enter the Land. Moshe tells them that they should not be foolish; they will not succeed. "Do not go up, for God is not among you." The only way to enter the Land is with God — that is what Moshe tried to teach them.

The Midrash, when it explains the logic of the *ma'apilim*, states:

It is written, "You murmured in your tents and said: 'Because God hated us' " (*Devarim* 1:27). The Holy One, blessed be He, said: "I have loved you" (*Malachi* I:2), and they say, "Because God hated us!" They reasoned in this wise: "There is proof positive that He hates us! If a mortal king has two sons and possesses two fields, one dependent on irrigation and the other on rain, will not the king give the irrigated field to the son whom he loves and the one that depends on rain to the son whom he hates? The land of Egypt is dependent on irrigation and we were there. The land of Canaan depends on rain, and He

---

1   The Midrash (*Bemidbar Rabbah* 17:3) also associates the term with darkness.

brought us out of Egypt to give us the land of Canaan!"
(Bemidbar Rabbah 17:3)

The very fact that the land is a place where God may be discerned was what the *ma'apilim* misinterpreted. Of course a people who think that they are hated by God would be disinterested in joining God. When they were sentenced to remain in the desert, the *ma'apilim* refused to take the sentence passively.

They thought the only mistake was their lack of gumption or bravery. They would correct that mistake. What the *ma'apilim* and the spies failed to understand is that the Land of Israel is a land where the presence of God is discernable. It is a land where the *Shechinah* rests. Therefore, the mode of entering the land is to join God, not to fight or force the Divine hand.

The Land indeed is a special land. We should see being in Israel as a love story between a people and their home, a match which has been chosen at the dawn of history. It is a land where the eyes of God are our constant companions: "A land which God, your Lord, cares for; the eyes of God, your Lord, are always upon it, from the beginning of the year to the end of the year." The manner of entering the land is intimately connected with living in the land. As the purpose of living in the land is a rendezvous with the *Shechinah*, the way to enter the land is to ascend the mountain and join God. Neither the spies nor the *ma'apilim* understood that.

Tu B'Av

Dancing in the Streets

The Fifteenth of Av (Tu B'Av) is a holiday of unclear significance. Although certain elements of the celebration of this day have captured the imagination of popular Israeli culture, the day itself remains obscure. While not specifically mentioned in the Torah, it is described by the Mishnah at the end of *Ta'anit* by way of a surprising analogy: This hitherto-unknown day is compared with Yom Kippur, arguably the holiest day of the year.[1]

There never were in Israel greater days of joy than the fifteenth of Av and the Day of Atonement. On these days the daughters of Yerushalayim used to walk out in white garments which they borrowed in order not to put to shame anyone who had none. All these garments required ritual dipping. The daughters of Yerushalayim came out and danced in the vineyards, exclaiming at the same time, "Young man, lift up your eyes and see what you choose for yourself. Do not set your eyes on beauty, but set your eyes on [good] family. 'Grace is deceitful,

---

1   Rav Menachem Azarya Defano and Rav Tzadok HaKohein (*Yisrael Kedoshim* 5) both point at the power of *minhag* — custom — at the core of this day. We know of Torah festivals and Rabbinic festivals; Tu B'Av has its unique charisma as an expression of the power of custom.

and beauty is vain; but a woman who fears God, she shall be praised' (*Mishlei* 31:30). And it further says, 'Give her of the fruit of her hands, and let her works praise her in the gates' (ibid., 31). Likewise it says, 'Go forth, daughters of Zion, and gaze upon King Shlomo, even upon the crown wherewith his mother had crowned him on the day of his wedding and on the day of the gladness of his heart' (*Shir HaShirim* 3:11). 'On the day of his wedding' — this refers to the day of the giving of the Law. 'And on the day of the gladness of his heart' — this refers to the building of the Temple; may it be rebuilt speedily in our days."

(Ta'anit 26b)

This *mishnah* is the concluding *mishnah* of the tractate of *Ta'anit*, which deals with fast days and the laws of fasting. The previous *mishnah* had taught the laws of the Ninth of Av. Now the Mishnah continues to the next day of importance in Av — Tu B'Av. Ostensibly, the intent of the Mishnah is to end on a positive note, especially after all the tragedies enumerated in the previous section. Indeed, the Mishnah concludes with the building of the Temple, clearly a cause for monumental joy.

A scene of dancing and celebration is described, raising two questions: First, the description of Yom Kippur as a day of song and celebration seems dissonant with our understanding of Yom Kippur. And secondly, what is the significance of Tu B'Av, and why did it deserve the same celebration as Yom Kippur?

The Talmud answers the first question while raising the second, explaining the joy of Yom Kippur while pondering Tu B'Av:

I can understand the Day of Atonement, because it is a day of forgiveness and pardon and on it the second Tablets of the Law were given, but what happened on the Fifteenth of Av?

(Ta'anit 30b)

Ecstatic joy, which is absent from our contemporary experience of Yom Kippur, is taken for granted in the Talmud. The experience of Yom Kippur was palpably different in Temple times. We are told that the red string in the Temple turned white, serving as a veritable spiritual barometer of God's forgiveness of man. When the people were shown this tangible sign of forgiveness, celebration erupted.

> But they had another sign, too: A thread of crimson wool was tied to the door of the Temple, and when the goat reached the wilderness the thread turned white, as it is written: "Though your sins be as scarlet, they shall be as white as snow" (*Yeshayah* 1:18).
>
> *(Yoma 68b)*

> They would accompany him [the *kohein gadol*] to his house. He would arrange for a day of festivity for his friends whenever he had come forth from the Sanctuary in peace.
>
> *(Yoma 70b)*

This type of joy was spontaneous, even though it was a yearly occurrence on Yom Kippur. Singing, dancing, and celebration broke out all over. The women of Yerushalayim began dancing in the vineyards. Marriage was on their minds. Perhaps this is the reference at the end of the *mishnah*:

> "On the day of his wedding" — this refers to the day of the giving of the Law.

The Talmud had described Yom Kippur as a day of "forgiveness and pardon and on it the second Tablets of the Law were given." Yom Kippur encapsulates the mutual commitment between the Jewish people and God. It is the day that the Jews finally took their vows and were forgiven for the indiscretion of the golden calf. The seventeenth of Tammuz, the day Moshe first came down with the tablets in hand, should have been the day when the Jews solidified their commitment with God; instead it became a day of infamy. The fate of the entire community was held in abeyance in the following weeks until Moshe was invited once again[1] to ascend the mount on the first day of Elul. Forty days later, on the tenth of Tishrei, the day celebrated henceforth as Yom Kippur, Moshe descended with the second Tablets and with God's message that He had forgiven the Jewish nation. This is what the Mishnah describes as "the day of his wedding."[2]

This idea dovetails with the teaching that one's wedding day is a day of personal forgiveness and has a cathartic, Yom Kippur–like element.[3] For this reason, tradition dictates that bride and groom fast on their wedding day, an additional expression of the atoning powers of the day. This may also explain the choice of Torah reading for Yom Kippur afternoon: The section of the Torah that enumerates forbidden relations. The backdrop of celebration in the streets explains the need, on this day more than others, for a warning against unmitigated, excessive frivolity, and a demarcation of forbidden relations.

While the celebratory aspect of Yom Kippur has been identified, the Fifteenth of Av remains elusive. The Talmud offers numerous explanations for the joy on that day:

Rabbi Yehudah said in the name of Shmuel: "It is the day on which permission was granted to the tribes to intermarry...."

Rabbi Yosef said in the name of Rabbi Nachman: "It is the day on which the tribe of Binyamin was permitted to reenter the congregation [following the episode of the concubine in Givah]...."

Rabbah bar Bar Chanah said in the name of Rabbi Yochanan: "It is the day on which the generation of the wilderness ceased to die out...."

Ulla said: "It is the day on which Hoshea ben Eilah removed the guards which Yeravam ben Nevat had placed on the roads

1. According to tradition, Moshe ascended the mountain three times: the first and last, to receive the tablets, and, in between, to pray for forgiveness for the people. See *Rashi* on *Shemot* 33:11 and *Devarim* 9:18.
1 See Rashi's commentary on *Ta'anit* 26b, s.v. *"Zeh."*
3 This idea may be found in the *Yerushalmi, Bikkurim* 3:3, p. 65c. See *Rashi, Bereishit 36:3; Torah Temimah, Bereishit* 28:9; and *Yechaveh Daat*, vol. 4, section 61.

to prevent Israel from going [up to Yerushalayim] on pilgrimage, and he proclaimed, 'Let them go up to whichever shrine they desire.' "

Rabbi Mattenah said: "It is the day when permission was granted for those killed at Betar to be buried...."

Rabbah and Rabbi Yosef both said: "It is the day on which [every year] they ceased to fell trees for the altar." It has been taught: Rabbi Eliezer the elder says: "From the Fifteenth of Av onwards the strength of the sun grows less and they no longer felled trees for the altar, because they would not dry [sufficiently]." Rabbi Menashya said: "And they called it the 'Day of the Breaking of the Axe.' From this day onwards, he who increases [his knowledge through study] will have his life prolonged, but he who does not increase [his knowledge] will have his life taken away." What is meant by "taken away"? Rabbi Yosef learned: "His mother will bury him."

(Ta'anit 30b–31a)

While the Talmud offers six different causes for celebration on Tu B'Av, many of these reasons seem insufficient to justify the type and intensity of celebration described. At first glance the various explanations seem unrelated, but we may be able to find a common thread running through them by looking back to the first Tu B'Av ever celebrated:

Rabbi Abin and Rabbi Yochanan said: "It was the day when the grave-digging ceased for those who died in the wilderness." Rabbi Levi said: "On every eve of the Ninth of Av Moshe used to send a herald throughout the camp and announce, 'Go out to dig graves' and they used to go out and dig graves in which they slept. On the morrow he sent out a herald to announce, 'Arise and separate the dead from the living.' They would then stand up and find themselves in round figures: 15,000 short of 600,000. In the last of the forty years, they acted similarly and found themselves in undiminished numerical strength. They said, 'It appears that we erred in our calculation'; so they acted

similarly on the nights of the tenth, eleventh, twelfth, thir-
teenth, and fourteenth. When the moon was full they said, 'It
seems that the Holy One, blessed be He, has annulled that decree from us all.' So they proceeded to make [the fifteenth] a
holiday. Their sins caused it [the ninth of Av] to become a day
of mourning in this world, in the twofold destruction of the
Temple. That is what is written, 'Therefore is my harp turned
to mourning, and my pipe into the voice of those that weep'
(*Iyov* 30:31). Hence, 'And the people wept that night'
(*Bemidbar* 14:1)."

(*Eichah Rabbah, Prologue 33*)

   This description is certainly morbid, yet it succeeds in capturing
the pathos of the yearly Tishah B'Av commemoration. The crying
in the desert at the report of the spies created a negative paradigm
for the rejection of the Land of Israel and its holiness, and even
more, the rejection of God. The yearly commemoration of this
breach of faith was systematic, inexorable: The entire generation of
the Jews who had been redeemed from Egypt and crossed the Red
Sea would die out in the desert. They had doubted God's ability to
complete His promise; they had rejected the Promised Land and
their own destiny, and each year on this day of infamy they would
dig their own graves and lie down in them, arising the next morning to take stock of their situation. The character of this day, the
spiritual power of the paradigm unleashed at the sin of the spies,
was revisited on future generations when Jews rejected the sacred.
Tragedy struck over and over on this same date.

   The Fifteenth of Av marked the end of the death sentence for
the sin of the spies. Only on the night of the Fifteenth, by the light
of the full moon, could they be certain that the chapter of the spies
was closed. This alone would be sufficient rationale for the *mishnah* of Ta'anit, regarding Tishah B'Av, to conclude with a teaching
about Tu B'Av: On a conceptual level, the Fifteenth marks the end
of the Ninth of Av.[1] During First Temple times the people certainly

---

1   Whether the Fifteenth of Av marks the end of the sadness of Tishah B'Av is a point

did not fast on Tishah B'Av, but they may have celebrated Tu B'Av. The end of the death sentence is the main cause for celebration offered by the Sages. But what of the other explanations offered by the Talmud? Arguably the strangest of these relates to the pagan king[1] Hoshea ben Eilah. While it may be argued that he displayed remarkably liberal thinking and was not particular whether his constituents served foreign deities wherever they chose or served God in the Beit HaMikdash, he certainly did not lead people toward Yerushalayim, toward the service of God! Why would this be a cause for celebration? Hoshea's decree reversed the nefarious deeds of his predecessor on the throne, Yeravam, yet even this reversal seems insufficient cause for celebration: Hoshea merely removed the guards charged with preventing pilgrimage to Yerushalayim. Furthermore, during Hoshea's reign the ten tribes were carried into captivity. He was not a leader to be remembered in song and celebration.

In order to understand the significance of Hoshea's decree we must first understand the implications of Yeravam's actions. Due to the spiritual failings of Shlomo, God wrested part of the monarchy from the Davidic family.

> And it came to pass at that time when Yeravam went from Yerushalayim that the prophet Achiyah the Shilonite found him in the way. And he had clad himself with a new garment, and the two were alone in the field. And Achiyah caught the new garment that was on him and tore it in twelve pieces, and he said to Yeravam, "Take you ten pieces; for thus said God, the Lord of Israel, 'Behold, I will tear the kingdom from the hand

debated by the halachic authorities. The Mishnah (*Ta'anit* 4:6, 26b) teaches that from the beginning of Av happiness is decreased, and debates whether this sadness continues until Tu B'Av or until the end of the month. See *Shulchan Aruch, Orach Chaim* 551:1; *Mishnah Berurah* 2 opines that the entire month is sad, whereas Chatam Sofer rules that Tu B'Av marks the end of the sadness. See *Piskei Teshuvah* 551:2.

1 For more on this king see *Melachim* II 15:30. "And Hoshea ben Eilah made a conspiracy against Pekach ben Remalyah, and struck him, and killed him, and reigned in his place, in the twentieth year of Yotam ben Uziyah."

of Shlomo, and will give ten tribes to you. But he shall have one tribe for My servant David's sake, and for Yerushalayim's sake, the city which I have chosen from all the tribes of Israel.' "

(Melachim I 11:29–32)

Yeravam ignored God's plan and built an alternative place of worship in an attempt to deter the people from Yerushalayim and, perhaps, allegiance to the Family of David. Motivated by jealousy, totally misdirected and self-centered, Yeravam did the unthinkable: he built places of worship replete with golden calves.

> Then Yeravam built Shechem in Mount Efrayim and lived there; and he went out from there and built Penuel. And Yeravam said in his heart, "Now shall the kingdom return to the House of David. If this people go up to do sacrifice in the House of God at Yerushalayim, then the heart of this people shall turn back to their lord, to Rechavam King of Yehudah, and they shall kill me, and go back to Rechavam King of Yehudah."
>
> And the king took counsel and he made two calves of gold. And he said to them [the people], "It is too much for you to go up to Yerushalayim; behold your gods, O Israel, which brought you out of the land of Egypt." And he set one in Beit El, and the other he placed in Dan.

(Melachim I 12:25–29)

Unlike Yeravam, Hoshea was not afraid or jealous of Yerushalayim or the Davidic dynasty. He may have been an idolater, but he was not filled with spiritually self-destructive hatred. Thus, Hoshea removes the guards stationed by Yeravam, indicating healing from the hatred and jealousy and the possibility of reconciliation.

This observation will help us reveal the message our Sages were trying to convey. The Sages associated the destruction of the Temple with the sin of baseless hatred,[1] which has its roots in the fratri-

---

1   See *Yoma* 9a.

cide perpetrated by Kayin. This strand of baseless hatred is first discerned within the Jewish community in the hatred of the sons of Leah toward the sons of Rachel. Yeravam's scheme should be seen within this context, proving that a son of Rachel could be just as bad, if not worse, than the sons of Leah.

The Temple in Yerushalayim was a manifestation of the unity of Israel, bringing together diverse spiritual attributes within the community of Israel. The primary tribes are Yehudah, descendants of the son of Leah, who would one day be kings, and the tribe of Yosef, descendants of the favorite son, the son of Rachel. It may be argued that had the sons of Yaakov been able to unite, the Temple would have stood in the portion of Yosef (Yosef would have inherited Yerushalayim), and the seat of the monarchy would have been in the realm of Yehudah. With the sons of Rachel and Leah united, this Temple would never have fallen. Unfortunately, the brothers are never able to resolve their differences with Yosef. The son of Rachel who becomes the unifying symbol of the people is Binyamin, and the Temple eventually stands in his portion. This explains the tears of Yosef and Binyamin at the moment when Yosef reveals himself to his brothers:[1]

> And he fell upon his brother Binyamin's neck and wept; and Binyamin wept upon his neck.
>
> *(Bereishit 45:14)*

> He wept for the two Temples destined to be in the territory of Binyamin and to be destroyed. "And Binyamin wept upon his neck" — he wept for the Mishkan of Shiloh which was destined to be in the territory of Yosef and to be destroyed.
>
> *(Megillah 16b; see Rashi, Bereishit 45:14)*

The hatred of the brothers created the spiritual power for the hatred that would one day destroy the Temple. This simmering conflict is what caused the Temple to be built in the portion of Binyamin, and not in the portion of Yosef. This is the same hatred

---

1   See *Explorations, Parashat Vayigash* (p. 104).

that poisoned Yeravam and motivated him to place guards in the path of would-be pilgrims to Yerushalayim. On Tu B'Av, when Hoshea rescinds the evil edict of Yeravam, the division and hatred cease.

On Tishah B'Av the tribes of Yosef and Yehudah were united: When the spies returned, only Yehoshua and Kaleiv, from the tribes of Yosef and Yehudah respectively, remained steadfast in their desire to enter Israel. They serve as the prototypes for the Messiah from Yosef and the Messiah from David (Yehudah), who will usher in the Messianic Era.[1] Tragically, the other tribes did not rally around those two leaders; what should have been the beginning of the great march to Israel became the day the Land of Israel was rejected. What could have been a day of celebration became a day of mourning.

This theme of division and reunion may be the key to some of the other reasons for Tu B'Av festivities offered by the Talmud. Significantly, the prohibition of intertribal marriage began with the daughters of Tzelafchad — from the tribe of Yosef. Surely, this law, which maintained each tribe as insulated and separate, also had a negative impact on interpersonal relationships between Jews. Tu B'Av marked the end of this division. Likewise, the isolation of the tribe of Binyamin: Their role in the episode of the concubine of Givah was certainly an outrage (See *Shoftim*, ch. 19–21). But the isolation of an entire tribe, specifically of the son of Rachel, was even more significant in light of the ongoing division between the sons of Rachel and the sons of Leah. Tu B'Av, in all three of these episodes, marks a reunion of the estranged sons of Rachel with the larger community of Israel.

This, then, is the unifying theme in all the explanations offered by the Talmud for the celebration of Tu B'Av: The battle of Betar was the culmination of the Bar Kochva rebellion, which was doomed to failure because the students of Rabbi Akiva did not treat one another with respect.[2] Without national unity, the Third Tem-

---

1 See *Sukkah* 52a.

ple could not be built: The failure of Bar Kochva's messianic movement was caused by the breakdown of the Jewish community,
represented by Rabbi Akiva's students who could not get along
with one another.

Another of the reasons for Tu B'Av celebrations now seems less
strange: The days begin to get shorter, or in the Talmud's words,
"the sun loses its strength." The Midrash, in recounting the first Tu
B'Av in the desert, noted that on this date the moon is full. The tension between the sun and moon represents the first struggle for
dominance, for leadership. This ancient, primordial struggle between the sun and the moon[1] is the same struggle for dominance as
the struggle between the sons of Yaakov, and between Yeravam and
the Davidic dynasty: two kings cannot share one crown. In fact, the
resolution of this struggle for dominance is one of the harbingers
and prerequisites for the Messianic Age: The Talmud speaks of the
complementary leadership of a Messiah who is the son of David
and a Messiah who is the son of Yosef, which will pave the way to
the Messianic Age.[2]

As we noted above, the first catastrophe of Tishah B'Av was the
failure of the spies and the nation's inability to rally around a
united core of leadership — Kaleiv/Yehudah and Yehoshua/Yosef.
The Land of Israel was forfeited, the Messianic Age passed up, and
the Temple, which cannot tolerate disunity, laid to waste on this
day. The spiritual character of this day is one of discord, internal
struggle. Conversely, Tu B'Av is a day which has the potential to re-
build the community of Israel and, as a result, the Temple. Unity of
the community is a prerequisite for building and preserving the
Temple; this is the message of the last phrase of the *mishnah* with
which we began:

Likewise it says, "Go forth, daughters of Zion, and gaze upon

---

2   See the essay on the Omer, "The Students of Rabbi Akiva."
1   See the essay on Rosh Chodesh.
2   See *Sukkah* 52a. *Rashi* on *Yeshayahu* 11:13 states that the two messiahs will not be
     jealous of one another.

King Shlomo, even upon the crown wherewith his mother had crowned him on the day of his wedding, and on the day of the gladness of his heart." "On the day of his wedding" — this refers to the day of the giving of the law. "And on the day of the gladness of his heart" — this refers to the building of the Temple; may it be rebuilt speedily in our days.

After describing the unique celebration of Yom Kippur and Tu B'Av, the Mishna intertwines the giving of the law and building of the Temple. As we have seen, "the giving of the law" refers to Yom Kippur.[1] Now we understand why the reference to "the building of the Temple" refers to Tu B'Av. On this day the daughters of Yerushalayim would share their clothes and dance merrily in the streets, united. The *Zohar* identifies the type of material the garments are made from:

Scarlet [*tola'at shani*] is connected with the Fifteenth of Av, a day on which the daughters of Israel used to walk forth in silken dresses.

(Zohar, Shemot 135a)

The significance of silk and its connection to the unique spiritual character of Tu B'Av lies in a more mystical message: Silk is not like wool or linen. The Vilna Gaon points out that the prohibition of mixing wool and linen — *shaatnez* — emanates from the hatred between Kayin and Hevel. On these glorious days the daughters of Yerushalayim freely share their clothing, with no hatred or jealousy in their hearts. The distinctions made by the requirements of *shaatnez* are irrelevant on this day. Perhaps this served as a type of healing for the hatred the brothers directed toward Yosef and his coat of many colors. This may also be the significance of the Talmud's description of God's attempt to lure Yeravam back into the fold:

"After this thing Yeravam did not turn from his evil way" (*Melachim* I 13:33) — What is meant by "after this thing"?

---

1 See *Rashi* on *Ta'anit* 26b, s.v. *"Zeh."*

Rabbi Abba said: "After the Holy One, blessed be He, had seized Yeravam by his garment and urged him, 'Repent, and then I, you, and the son of Yishai [i.e., David] will walk in the Garden of Eden.'

" 'And who shall be at the head?' inquired he.

" 'The son of Yishai shall be at the head.'

" 'If so,' [he replied], 'I do not desire [it].' "

(Sanhedrin 102a)

God grabbed Yeravam by his clothing to break his jealousy; alas, Yeravam could only join if he was given center stage and the leading role. Ultimately he was unable to control his self-centeredness. The image of his garment, torn into twelve pieces by the prophet, prevails over the image of God Himself attempting to mend the torn fabric of Jewish community.

This is the secret of Tu B'Av and the reason that marriages abound on this day. Marriage of two individuals, the most basic of all relationships, is only possible if each one controls innate egoism and narcissism. The rebuilding of the Temple is dependent on the community being able to unite in a similar manner. The first step is controlling hatred and jealousy, breaking the boundaries that exist between people. The Talmud therefore associates the mitzvah of bringing joy to the newly married couple with building Yerushalayim:

And if he does gladden him [i.e., the groom], what is his reward?... It is as if he had restored one of the ruins of Yerushalayim.

(Berachot 6b)

Tu B'Av marks, celebrates, even creates this type of healing behavior. Jealousies are broken down, tribal distinctions disappear, new unions are created.

We are taught that in the future the fast days marking the Temple's destruction will be transformed into days of celebration:

Thus says the God of Hosts: "The fast of the fourth month [the seventeenth of Tammuz], the fast of the fifth [the ninth of Av], the fast of the seventh [Yom Kippur], and the fast of the tenth [the tenth of Tevet] shall become times of joy and gladness and cheerful feasts to the house of Yehudah; therefore love truth and peace."

(Zecharyah 8:19)

Rav Tzadok HaKohein from Lublin taught that the ninth of Av will indeed become a holiday — a seven-day holiday similar to Pesach, consisting of festival on the first and last days as well as intermediate days (Chol HaMoed). We may theorize that the first day of the holiday, Tishah B'Av, will commemorate the coming of the Messiah.[1] Then there will be Chol HaMoed, and on the seventh day — Tu B'Av — the Temple will be rebuilt. The day when Jews arose unscathed from their graves in the desert will witness the spiritual rebirth of the entire nation, symbolized by the building of the Temple. This will be followed by the ultimate Resurrection: Once again, the people will climb from their graves, as the world achieves perfection and completion. On that day the joy in the streets will be echoed in the vineyards surrounding Yerushalayim, and it will reverberate throughout the entire world.

---

1   According to Rabbinic tradition, the Messiah is born on Tishah B'Av (*Aggadat Bereishit* 68).

Elul

"Return"

Parashat Nitzavim is always read in close proximity to Rosh HaShanah and the Days of Awe. This would seem to be one of the instances where the choice of reading is not coincidental; rather, the division of the parashiyot is carefully constructed to insure that certain messages are conveyed at specific junctures of the calendar.

During this season *teshuvah* is in the air: personal and collective introspection are the order of the day. In this context, it is evident why this parashah is the chosen message. The idea of *teshuvah* (return), if not the major theme of the parashah, is certainly the parashah's apex.

The term "return" and the root *shav* are utilized in numerous verses:

> And it shall come to pass, when all these things have come upon you, the blessing and the curse, which I have set before you, and you shall *return to your heart* [while in exile] among all the nations, where God, your Lord, has driven you. *And you shall return* to God, your Lord, and shall obey His voice according to all that I command you today, you and your children, with all your heart and with all your soul. Then God, your Lord, will *[re]turn your captivity* and have compassion upon

you, and will *return* and gather you from all the nations, where God, your Lord, has scattered you....

And God, your Lord, will bring you into the land which your fathers possessed, and you shall possess it; and He will do you good and multiply you above your fathers. And God, your Lord, will circumcise your heart and the heart of your seed to love God, your Lord, with all your heart and with all your soul, that you may live....

And you shall *return* and obey the voice of God, and do all His commandments which I command you today. And God, your Lord, will make you abundantly prosperous in every work of your hand, in the fruit of your body, and in the fruit of your cattle, and in the fruit of your land, for good; for God will again rejoice over you for good, as He rejoiced over your fathers. If you shall listen to the voice of God, your Lord, to keep His commandments and His statutes which are written in this book of the Torah, and if you *turn* to God, your Lord, with all your heart, and with all your soul.

(Devarim 30:1–10)

In order to appreciate the number of times the root *shav* is used, the Hebrew text must be consulted. Suffice it to say that the term "return" is repeated time after time in this section. This peculiarity has served as a challenge for the classical commentators, who sought to explain the various "returns," both on the part of man and the part of God. One solution offered is that the text refers to the totality of history; each "return" refers to a different period of exile, from the ten tribes through the eschatological ingathering and the End of Days.

The word *shav* and its more common usage *teshuvah* have often been translated as "repentance," yet the Hebrew word *teshuvah* is both more powerful and more simple. *Repentance* is derived from the word *penance*, which primarily means remorse. The feeling of remorse may be private, personal, even egocentric, describing the feelings of an individual who knows that he has failed himself and perhaps his family or society. When a person feels remorse and utilizes these feelings to spur action, or at least a resolution to redouble his efforts and not return to his erroneous ways, we may also call this process rehabilitation.

The only thing lacking with the process we have described is God. The Jewish concept of return is a return to God. It is a theocentric phenomenon, which serves, in most cases, to heal an egocentric perspective. The defining verse is found in *Parashat Nitzavim* and was cited above: "And you shall return to God, your Lord."

Teshuvah is a gesture that returns man to his pure state — by virtue of connecting man with God. This idea lies behind the Rabbis' insistence that *teshuvah* is metaphysical in a unique sense: *teshuvah* is not part of this world, because it predates Creation.

Six things preceded the creation of the world; some of them were actually created, while the creation of the others was already contemplated.... Rabbi Ahavah ben Rabbi Ze'ira said: "Repentance too, as it is written, 'Before the mountains were brought forth...' (*Tehillim* 90:2), and from that very moment, 'You turn man to contrition, and say: "Repent, you children of man" ' (ibid., 3)."

(Bereishit Rabbah 1:4)[1]

When God was about to create man the Torah remonstrated, saying: "Should man be created and then sin and be brought to trial before You, the work of Your hand will be in vain, for he will not be able to endure Your judgment."

Whereto God replied: "I have already fashioned repentance before creating the world."

(Zohar, Bereishit 134b)[2]

---

1   A similar teaching is found in the *Zohar, Vayikra* 34b.
2   The same idea is taught in *Zohar, Vayikra* 70a:
   "Rabbi Yehudah cited here the verse: 'A song of ascents. Out of the depths have I called You, O Lord' (Tehillim 131). 'We have learned,' he said, 'that when God was about to create man, He consulted the Torah and she warned Him that he would sin before Him and provoke Him. Therefore, before creating the world God created Repentance, saying to her: "I am about to create man, on condition that when they*

Prior to the creation of the world, God created an idea called *teshuvah* — a process that brings man in touch with God, the definitive metaphysical Being. Thus, an idea which eluded many great philosophers becomes clear: Secular philosophy cannot grasp the possibility that remorse can uproot past transgressions.[1] Only if human existence were exclusively physical would the question be appropriate. Judaism, however, insists that there is a metaphysical reality called God, who created and sustains the universe. Additionally, God created a procedure which allows man to relate directly to Him. As God transcends time, so can man's relationship with God transcend time, rendering yesterday's failures a blot in a black hole of time, irrelevant to one's current relationship with God, which is itself transcendent. This is the power of *teshuvah*.

This metaphysical relationship may explain several other teachings in *Parashat Nitzavim* and help explain the dynamics of the future redemption. The parashah begins with a covenant drawn between man and God:

> You stand today, all of you, before God, your Lord; your captains of your tribes, your elders, and your officers, with all the men of Israel.... That you should enter into covenant with the Lord your God, and into His oath, which God, your Lord, makes with you this day. That He may establish you today for a people to Himself, and that He may be to you a God, as He has said to you, and as He has sworn to your fathers, to Avraham, to Yitzchak, and to Yaakov. And not with you alone will I make this covenant and this oath, but with him who stands here with us today before God, your Lord, and also with him who is

return to you from their sins you shall be prepared to forgive their sins and make atonement for them." Hence at all times Repentance is close at hand to men, and when they repent of their sins it returns to God and makes atonement for all, and judgment is suppressed and all is put right. When is a man purified of his sin?' Rabbi Yitzchak said: 'When he returns to the Most High King and prays from the depths of his heart, as it is written, "From the depths I called You.' "

1   Rabbi Yosef D. Soloveitchik, *Halakhic Man* (Philadelphia: JPS, 1983), p. 114f.

not here with us today.

(Devarim 29:9–14)

The idea of a covenant "with those not here" is of particular interest. The various commentators explain that this refers to future generations still unborn. They, too, must live up to their side of the covenant or suffer expulsion. In that event, the Torah speaks of the eventual return of man to God.

And you shall return to God, your Lord, and shall obey His voice according to all that I command you today, you and your children, with all your heart and with all your soul.

The idea of "both you and your children" returning to God seems strange: Either you or a subsequent generation will need to return, but why both? In a terse, enigmatic statement Ramban says that a great mystical secret centers around the teaching that the Messiah cannot come until all the souls are completed. His source is a passage found in numerous places in the Talmud:

The Son of David will not come before all the souls in the body are completed; since it is said, "For the spirit that wraps itself is from Me, and the souls which I have made" (*Yeshayah* 57:16).

(Yevamot 63b)[1]

The ultimate return will take place when all souls reach completion. These souls represent both past and future generations, all of which are part and parcel of the metaphysical nature of the Jews' relationship with God.

Rav Eliyahu Dessler (*Michtav Me'Eliyahu*, vol. 4, p. 120) explained this concept by citing a mystical teaching that in the generations prior to the arrival of the Messiah there are precious few "new" souls, the majority being "used," incomplete souls returned in order to complete their task.

Other twentieth century mystics have attempted to "explain" the Holocaust by stating that prior to redemption all souls need to

---

1   This idea is explored in the *Zohar* as well: see *Bereishit* 28b.

be elevated. The generation of people who died in the desert, despite seeing the work of God with greater clarity than any other generation, failed to sanctify God's name. Therefore they needed to return and die performing a sanctification of God's name. However, it is also taught in *Parashat Nitzavim*:

> The secret things belong to God, our Lord; but those things which are revealed belong to us and to our children forever, that we may do all the words of this Torah.
>
> *(Devarim 29:28)*

Rav Yehonatan Eibeshitz combines these teachings when he explains the significance of the verse, "That God, your Lord, will [re]turn your captivity and have compassion upon you, and will return and gather you from all the nations, where God, your Lord, has scattered you" (ibid. 30:3).

Rav Yehonatan writes:

> This refers to the birthpangs of the Messiah which will be in close proximity to the Redemption, [which are so severe] that many Sages said, "Let him [the Messiah] come, but let me not see him" (*Sanhedrin* 98b). The reason is that the *Shechinah* is with us in exile (*Megillah* 29a), taking care of us like a mother cares for a child. At the time of the Redemption the *Shechinah* will not return together with us at one time; rather, first the *Shechinah* will return to the Land of Israel, and then we shall return. For many things must take place in order for the ingathering of the exiles to take place, and this is impossible without the *Shechinah* in its proper place. Therefore when we remain in exile and God is not in our midst, we will have the most severe horrors, for we will be without a protector. Therefore, the verse teaches that first God will return, and only then will He have compassion "and gather you from all the nations, where God, the Lord, has scattered you."
>
> *(Tiferet Yehonatan, Devarim 30:3)*

This is reminiscent of the idea of the "hiding of God's face," which is also described in *Parashat Nitzavim*.

> Then My anger shall be kindled against them on that day, and I will forsake them, and I will hide My face from them, and they shall be devoured, and many evils and troubles shall befall them; so that they will say on that day, "Have these evils not come upon us because our Lord is not among us?" And I will surely hide My face on that day....
>
> *(Devarim 31:17–18)*

According to Rav Yehonatan, this is part of the process of redemption. Rav Yehonatan then goes on to explain the purpose of the return to the Land of Israel. The verse states:

> And God, your Lord, will bring you into the land your fathers possessed, and you shall possess it; and He will do you good, and multiply you above your fathers.
>
> *(Ibid. 30:5)*

Rav Yehonatan explains that the return to Israel is an opportunity for rectification. The failure of the people took place in the Land of Israel, with the *Shechinah* in their midst. One of the principles of *teshuvah* is obedience in the same situation of previous failure:

> How is one proved a repentant sinner? Rabbi Yehudah said: "If the object which caused his original transgression comes before him on two occasions, and he keeps away from it." Rabbi Yehudah indicated: With the same woman, at the same time, in the same place.
>
> *(Yoma 86b)*

According to this approach, the ingathering of the exiles creates a situation in which the Jews may heal the spiritual damage caused by their ancestors. Significantly, it is in this context that the Ramban mentioned the mystical idea of souls reaching completion. Future generations are bidden to follow the covenant forged with a previous generation and to complete the mission of the previous generation, as they heal the damage which was unleashed by sins committed in antiquity. If the Temple was destroyed due to hatred, the generation brought back to the Land must rise above the petty jealousy and hatred and repair the souls tainted in previous generations.

The Rambam writes (*Hilchot Teshuvah* 7:5) that at the end of days the Jews will do *teshuvah* and return to God. He adds that all the prophets commanded Israel regarding *teshuvah*, and the Torah has already guaranteed that the people will do *teshuvah*. His proof is drawn from the verses we have already examined from *Parashat Nitzavim*. The Rambam also cites these verses when describing the task of the Messiah (see *Hilchot Melachim* 11:1).

According to Rambam, for a Jew not to believe in the collective *teshuvah* of the Jewish people he must reject the promise of the Torah and the belief in the Messiah. Rabbi Soloveitchik added that the naysayer also rejects the Jewish people and has lost belief in them as well.[1]

In our days these teachings are all the more poignant and powerful. This century has seen horrific events, and we pray that those were the worst of the birthpangs which the Sages foresaw and prayed to be spared. We have lived to see an ingathering of the exiles, and we are aware that our communal and personal life in Israel is an incredible opportunity to mend the damage of previous generations. We must never lose faith in the Torah which promised the return, nor faith in the people of Israel who will carry out the complete return to God.

For just as we are imbued with a metaphysical soul which allows us to relate to God as individuals, the collective community, too, has an incredible spiritual capacity which is far more powerful than the sum of all its individual parts. Likewise, just as the individual can perform an act of transcendence by doing *teshuvah*, so can the entire community. *Parashat Nitzavim* contains the promise that

---

1   See *On Repentance*, by Rabbi Yosef Soloveitchik, edited by Pinchas Deli (Jerusalem: Oroth Press, 1980), p. 132ff.

this will happen — it is just a matter of time.

> And you shall return and obey the voice of God, and do all His commandments which I command you today. And God, your Lord, will make you abundantly prosperous in every work of your hand, in the fruit of your body, and in the fruit of your cattle, and in the fruit of your land, for good; for God will again rejoice over you for good, as He rejoiced over your fathers.

It is the promise of *teshuvah* and Redemption that links *Parashat Nitzavim* with this special time of year, providing us with a mission, a method and means of accomplishing that mission, and the promise that we can and will succeed.

Elul

Pursuit of Righteousness

The parashah of *Ha'azinu* stands out from other sections of the Torah due to its form. The parashah is a song, written and spoken by Moshe, and constitutes the penultimate actions taken by Moshe prior to his death. Moshe accepts his lot with dignity, pronouncing a *"tzidduk hadin,"* an acceptance of God's judgment,[1] as other Jews on their deathbeds will pronounce throughout the centuries.[2] We get the sense that the poem is not said in resignation; rather, it is an ecstatic expression of Moshe's sublime spiritual psyche.

Many commentaries have occupied themselves with attempts to decipher the religious message contained in the poem. One fairly recent commentator, who lived in the nineteenth century, Rav Naftali Tzvi Yehudah Berlin, known by his acronym "Netziv," offered a unique approach to this section. The Netziv felt that the section hints at the destruction of the two Temples, the subsequent exile, and the eventual rebuilding. Some of the verses refer to the First Temple period, while others refer to the Second Temple. For

---

1   See *Avodah Zarah* 18a.
2   This aspect of the verse is borne out by the Midrash (*Devarim Rabbah* 11:10): "When Moshe saw that no creature could save him from the path of death, he thereupon exclaimed, 'The Rock, His work is perfect; for all His ways are justice; a God of faithfulness and without iniquity, just and righteous is He' (*Devarim* 32:4)."

example, a verse at the outset declares:

The Rock, His work is perfect; for all His ways are justice; a God of faithfulnes and without iniquity, just and right is He.

(Devarim 32:4)

The verse refers to God, and it seems unexceptional in terms of pointing at future events. However, the next verse contrasts God's attributes with the attributes of a twisted future generation:

Not His [is] the corruption, but His children are blemished; they are a perverse and crooked generation.

(Ibid., 5)

The justice and righteousness of God are directly contrasted with the perversity and crookedness of the people.[1] This, according to the Netziv, describes the generation that caused, and lived through, the destruction of the Second Temple.

These comments are said in passing in the Netziv's local commentary in *Devarim*. However, in his introduction to the book of *Bereishit* the Netziv explains the concept in greater depth: The book of *Bereishit* is also known as the "Book of the Straight" — *Sefer HaYashar*. The term used for God, translated above as "just and right," reads in Hebrew as *tzaddik v'yashar*. The term *tzaddik* is quite common and simple to define — a tzaddik is a righteous person. What is the meaning of "*yashar*"?

While the literal meaning is "straight" or "upright," we remain mystified regarding what is included in this appellation. What does it mean to be "*yashar*"? The Netziv explains that the people who lived during the waning years of the Second Temple were tzaddikim — fastidious in their performance of commandments. Nonetheless, there was something twisted about them. They were not *yashar*.

They were righteous and pious and diligent in Torah — but they were not *yashar* in their dealings in the ways of the world.

---

1   The *Zohar* also contrasts these two verses. See *Zohar, Devarim* 297b.

Because of the hatred in their hearts they suspected anyone who was not identical to themselves in service of God of being a Sadducee or a heretic. This led to the spilling of blood and further division and all calamities in the world, until the Temple was destroyed.... God is *yashar* and does not tolerate such tzaddikim, only those who travel a straight path also in worldly matters, and not in crookedness even if it is for the "sake of heaven," for this [trait] causes destruction....

(Introduction of Netziv to Bereishit)

In this extraordinary analysis, the Netziv forcefully attacks false piety. The ends do not justify the means. Real tzaddikim have a completely different type of relationship with the people around them. The Netziv explains that the most important teaching of the book of *Bereishit* is the upstanding behavior of the forefathers, hence the name "*Sefer HaYashar*." Avraham was spiritually tortured and morally repulsed by the behavior of Sedom and Amorah, yet when God tells him of the impending holocaust, he does not celebrate. He prays that the inhabitants of these cities be spared. The Netziv intimates that other "tzaddikim" would bask in the Divine vengeance, their own ways vindicated, the hated sinners obliterated and punished. Avraham was *yashar*. Arguably, even before Avraham was a tzaddik he was *yashar*.

The Talmud tells the tale of a simple laborer who was similarly "upright":

He who judges his neighbor meritoriously is himself judged favorably. Thus a story is told of a certain man who descended from Upper Galilee and worked for an individual in the South for three years. On the eve of Yom Kippur he requested of him, "Give me my wages that I may go and support my wife and children."

"I have no money," answered he.

"Give me produce," he demanded.

"I have none," he replied.

"Give me land."

"I have none."

"Give me cattle."

"I have none."

"Give me pillows and bedding."

"I have none."

[So] he slung his things behind him and went home with a sorrowful heart. After the festival, his employer took his wages in his hand together with three laden asses, one bearing food, another drink, and the third various sweetmeats, and went to his house. After they had eaten and drunk, he gave him his wages.

Said he to him, "When you asked me, 'Give me my wages,' and I answered you, 'I have no money,' of what did you suspect me?"

"I thought, perhaps you came across cheap merchandise and had purchased it therewith."

"And when you requested me, 'Give me cattle,' and I answered, 'I have no cattle,' of what did you suspect me?"

"I thought, they may be hired to others."

"When you asked me, 'Give me land,' and I told you, 'I have no land,' of what did you suspect me?"

"I thought, perhaps it is leased to others."

"And when I told you, 'I have no produce,' of what did you suspect me?"

"I thought, perhaps they are not tithed."

"And when I told you, 'I have no pillows or bedding,' of what did you suspect me?"

"I thought, perhaps he has sanctified all his property to Heaven."

"By the [Temple] service!" exclaimed he, "it was so." I vowed away all my property because of my son Horkanus, who would not occupy himself with the Torah, but when I went to my companions in the South they absolved me of all my vows. And as for you, just as you judged me favorably, so may the

Omnipresent judge you favorably."

(Shabbat 127b)

A simple worker with a good heart, he left with sadness but without anger. Instead of an altercation or bloodshed, he left for home empty-handed after three hard years of labor and nothing to show for the sweat of his brow. This man displayed incredible greatness of spirit in justifying his employer, and bore no anger in his heart. Despite seeing produce and knowing that there were tracts of land — which he himself had worked for three years — he accepted his employer's answers at face value and returned to his home.

The Talmud does not share with us the identity of this worker or the employer; they remain anonymous characters serving as a vehicle for a powerful message. Yet from the text we may surmise that the Temple still stood at the time of this incident. All that we know is that the employer had a son named Horkanus who did not wish to dedicate himself to Torah.

The story is also recorded in the *Sheiltot of Rav Achai Gaon* (*Parashat Shemot*, 40), one of the most ancient post-Talmudic texts extant. Here, the names of the owner and the worker are revealed. The employer was Rabbi Eliezer ben Horkanus, who named his son after his own father. He is known as "Rebbe Eliezer HaGadol," the great Rebbi Eliezer, and was one of the most important and impressive figures of the Talmudic age.

The worker was one Akiva ben Yosef — the illustrious Rabbi Akiva. The Netziv, who also wrote a commentary on the *Sheiltot*,[1] comments that this story is a rare documentation of the period in Rabbi Akiva's life prior to his metamorphosis to learned sage; he was still an ignorant worker. Yet although he may have been ignorant, he was of superior spirit. He possessed greatness of heart. He was *yashar*. Apparently, the Talmud conceals the identity of the characters to protect the innocent. Yet the fact that Rabbi Akiva

---

1   *Ha'Amek Sh'eilah*, commentary on the *Sheiltot* found in the Mosad HaRav Kook edition.

had superior moral qualities prior to his education is clear from other Talmudic sources:

> Rabbi Akiva was a shepherd of Ben Kalba Savua. The latter's daughter, seeing how modest and noble [the shepherd] was, said to him, "Were I to be betrothed to you would you go away to [study at] an academy?"
> "Yes," he replied.
>
> *(Ketubot 62b)*

Rabbi Akiva was ignorant, yet he was modest and noble. Rabbi Akiva's personal change transpired in the same time frame as the destruction of the Second Temple. As we saw above, the "tzaddikim" of that time were not necessarily on the same moral level as this ignorant shepherd. This observation allows us to understand an incredible statement made by Rabbi Akiva himself about his days as a simple man.

> Rabbi Akiva said: "When I was an *am ha'aretz* [an ignoramous] I said: 'If I had a scholar [before me], I would maul him like a donkey.' "
> Said his disciples to him, "Rabbi, say like a dog!"
> He answered them: "The former bites and breaks the bones, while the latter bites but does not break the bones."
>
> *(Pesachim 49b)*

While we may understand tensions between different socioeconomic classes, hatred seems much more difficult to explain. Why did Rabbi Akiva not tolerate the scholars, the intellectual and religious elite? We must recall that the scholars of that age were the ones described by the Netziv as careful in their relationship with God but twisted in their interpersonal relationships. The ignorant Akiva — the *am ha'aretz* — was of morally superior character. He was *yashar*. He could not tolerate the tzaddik who was not *yashar*.

His wife convinced him that the cause of the hypocrisy he saw around him was not the study of Torah. Knowledge of Torah makes the morally challenged more responsible for their actions and may lead to punishment and destruction. However, when a morally superior person like Akiva learns Torah, he will flourish.[1] Rabbi Akiva eventually becomes both *yashar* and a tzaddik.

Hundreds of years ago, a book on the commandments was written, and it was called *Or Zarua*. The author, who was associated with the school of Tosafists, was named Rav Yitzchak from Vienna. In his introduction he explains why he chose the name *Or Zarua* for his work:

> I called the work as I did due to great love for the verse and that intimated in the verse: "אור זרוע לצדיק ולישרי לב שמחה" — Light is sown for the righteous, and gladness for the upright in heart" (*Tehillim* 97:11). The end of each word spells "R' Akiva" — clearly.[2]

While finding a reference to Rabbi Akiva was surely interesting, what was it that so excited Rav Yitzchak? Surely it was the content of the verse: "Light is sown for the righteous, and gladness for the upright in heart." The verse refers to the tzaddik and the *yashar*; what better description could there be of Rabbi Akiva?

Rabbi Akiva, perhaps more than any other person, represented the eternal optimist. His spirit could not be dampened. He always retained the pure, upright heart — a heart of gold.

> It was taught in the name of Rabbi Akiva: A man should always accustom himself to say, "Whatever the All-Merciful does is for good," [as exemplified in] the following incident. Rabbi Akiva was once going along the road, and he came to a certain town and looked for lodgings but was refused everywhere. He said,

---

1   Rav Mordechai Elon once explained that despite Rabbi Akiva's insistence that "love one's neighbor" is the most important mitzvah in the Torah, his own students died because of their moral failings in this very sphere.

2   In the *Yerushalmi, Akiva* is spelled עקיבה, while the *Bavli* replaces the final *hei* with an *alef*. The question of the Or Zarua was which spelling was the authoritative one. This verse appeared to him in a dream. He was so moved by this divine sign that he named his book *Or Zarua*. For more on revelations in dreams, see *Responsa from Heaven (She'eilot U'Teshuvot Min HaShamayim)*, Margoliot edition, Mosad HaRav Kook, and the introduction by Rav Reuven Margoliot regarding this phenomenon.

"Whatever the All-Merciful does is for good," and he went and spent the night in the open field. He had with him a rooster, a donkey, and a lamp. A gust of wind came and blew out the lamp, a weasel came and ate the rooster, a lion came and ate the donkey. He said: "Whatever the All-Merciful does is for good." The same night some brigands came and carried off the inhabitants of the town. He said to them: "Did I not say to you, 'Whatever the All-Merciful does is all for good?' "

(Berachot 60b)

When others see destruction, Rabbi Akiva sees salvation:

Long ago, as Rabban Gamliel, Rabbi Eliezer ben Azaryah, Rabbi Yehoshua, and Rabbi Akiva were walking on the road, they heard the noise of the crowds at Rome [on traveling] from Puteoli, 120 miles away. They all began to weep, but Rabbi Akiva seemed merry. They said to him, "Why are you merry?"

He said to them, "Why are you weeping?"

They said, "These heathens who bow down to images and burn incense to idols live in safety and ease, whereas our Temple, the 'Footstool' of our God, is burnt down by fire, and should we not weep?"

He replied, "Therefore, am I merry. If they who offend Him fare thus, how much better shall fare they who do obey Him!"

Once again they were coming up to Yerushalayim together, and just as they came to Mount Scopus they saw a fox emerging from the Holy of Holies. They began to weep and Rabbi Akiva seemed merry. "Why," they said to him, "are you merry?"

Said he, "Why are you weeping?"

They said to him, "A place of which it was once said, 'And the common man who draws near shall be put to death' (*Bemidbar* 1:51) is now the haunt of foxes. Should we not weep?"

He said to them, "Therefore am I merry; for it is written, 'And I will take to Me faithful witnesses to record, Uriyah the

Priest and Zecharyah ben Yevarechyah' (*Yeshayah* 8:2). Now what connection has this Uriyah the Priest with Zecharyah? Uriyah lived during the times of the First Temple, while Zecharyah lived [and prophesied] during the Second Temple; but Scripture linked the [later] prophecy of Zecharyah with the [earlier] prophecy of Uriyah. In the [earlier] prophecy [in the days] of Uriyah it is written, 'Therefore shall Zion for your sake be plowed as a field' (*Michah* 3:12). In *Zecharyah* it is written, 'Thus says the God of Hosts, "Old men and old women shall again sit in the broad places of Yerushalayim" ' (*Zecharyah* 8:4). So long as Uriyah's [threatening] prophecy had not had its fulfillment, I had misgivings lest Zecharyah's prophecy might not be fulfilled; now that Uriyah's prophecy has been [literally] fulfilled, it is quite certain that Zecharyah's prophecy also is to find its literal fulfillment."

They said to him, "Akiva, you have comforted us! Akiva, you have comforted us!"

(Makkot 24a–24b)

Even with his life ebbing away Rabbi Akiva retained his dignity and positive attitude:

When Rabbi Akiva was taken out for execution, it was the hour for the recital of the Shema, and while they combed his flesh with iron combs, he was accepting upon himself the Kingship of Heaven. His disciples said to him: "Our teacher, even to this point?"

He said to them: "All my days I have been troubled by this verse, '[You shall love God...] with all your soul' (*Devarim* 6:5), [which I interpret,] 'even if He takes your soul.' I said: When shall I have the opportunity of fulfilling this? Now that I have the opportunity, shall I not fulfill it?" He prolonged the word *echad* until he expired while saying it.

A *bat kol* went forth and proclaimed: "Happy are you, Akiva, that your soul has departed with the word *echad*!"

The ministering angels said before the Holy One, blessed be

He: "Such Torah, and such a reward? [He should have been] from them that die by Your hand, O Lord."
He replied to them: "Their portion is in life."
A *bat kol* went forth and proclaimed, "Happy are you, Rabbi Akiva, that you are destined for the life of the World to Come."

(Berachot 61b)

Now we understand why Rav Yitzchak of Vienna thought that this verse, "Light is sown for the righteous, and gladness for the upright in heart," was so appropriate for Rabbi Akiva. Who more than Rabbi Akiva exemplified *tzidkut* and *yosher* while retaining gladness? The Netziv attacked those who were righteous but lacked uprightness; Akiva, in his early years, was upright but lacked righteousness. It was only when the two traits became combined that the joy with which Rabbi Akiva is so closely identified became manifest. Even when he heroically turned his back on his employer and went home, he did so with a heavy heart: "He slung his things behind him and went home with a sorrowful heart." The Rabbi Akiva with whom we later become acquainted never loses his smile. "Light is sown for the righteous, and gladness for the upright in heart."

On Yom Kippur, the holiest day of the year, we begin the prayers with a statement of incredible hope. Without this hope, prayer would not seem possible: "Light is sown for the righteous, and gladness for the upright in heart." In this statement, we hear the resonance of Moshe's parting words, and attempt to emulate God, who is *tzaddik v'yashar*. We must understand, especially in the month of Elul, that to be a tzaddik, a righteous person, is within our reach. We also must remember that the only way to become a true tzaddik is by having first created the proper moral and spiritual infrastructure. First we must be *yashar*, straight: not conniving, not dishonest, not deceitful, not calculating, not disingenuous. We must be *yashar* like Avraham, Yitzchak, and Yaakov, Sarah, Rivkah, Rachel, and Leah. And even like a simple laborer-shepherd, Akiva.

Light is sown for the righteous, and gladness for the upright in heart.

Tishrei

The Idea of Rosh HaShanah

It is common knowledge that Rosh HaShanah marks the Jewish New Year, but less commonly known that Judaism actually recognizes various different new years. The Mishnah in Tractate *Rosh HaShanah* enumerates the different "New Years," days that mark different types of beginnings in much the same way that secular society marks the first day of school, the first day when the government convenes, the first day of the tax year, and so forth.

> There are four New Years. On the first of Nissan is New Year for kings and for festivals. On the first of Elul is New Year for the tithe of cattle. Rabbi Eliezer and Rabbi Shimon, however, place this on the first of Tishrei. On the first of Tishrei is New Year for years, for *shemittah* and *yovel* years, for plantation, and for [tithe of] vegetables. On the first of Shevat is new year for trees, according to the ruling of Beit Shammai; Beit Hillel, however, place it on the fifteenth of that month.
>
> *(Rosh HaShanah 2a)*

A "New Year's Day" marks a passage of time based on either an objective criteria or a subjective perspective; what, then, does the Jewish New Year, the first of Tishrei, demarcate? The traditional response to this question would be that Rosh HaShanah commemorates the creation of the world. One would therefore assume that

Rosh HaShanah must mark the beginning of time itself.

The Talmud, however, reports the following difference of opinion regarding Creation:

> Rabbi Eliezer says: "In Tishrei the world was created...." Rabbi Yehoshua says: "In Nissan the world was created."
>
> *(Rosh HaShanah 10b–11a)*

The opinion of Rabbi Eliezer is clarified in the Midrash, where it is explained that in fact the world came into existence on the twenty-fifth of Elul.[1] Thus, when Rabbi Eliezer referred to the creation that took place on the first of Tishrei, he was referring to the sixth day and the creation of man — of Adam.

Nonetheless we see that these two great luminaries, Rabbi Eliezer and Rabbi Yehoshua, argue whether Creation took place in the fall or spring. It seems strange that so fundamental an issue as the day of Creation could be subject to debate.[2]

Remarkably, Rabbeinu Tam sees no contradiction between the opinions of Rabbi Eliezer and Rabbi Yehoshua, opining that the two are not mutually exclusive:

> These and these are the words of the living God, and one may say that the thought to create was formed in Tishrei, while the actual Creation did not take place until Nissan.
>
> *(Tosafot, Rosh HaShanah 27a)*

According to Rabbeinu Tam, the two Sages do not disagree. Creation is a process; the question is, do we commemorate the beginning or end of the process? Their argument is only in emphasis: Which aspect of creation is dominant, the thought of Creation or the actual Creation? According to Rabbeinu Tam, Tishrei was the time that God thought of Creation. What is the significance of such thoughts?

This idea of a "thought of Creation" has a parallel teaching

---

1   See the teachings attributed to Rabbi Eliezer found in *Pirkei D'Rabbi Eliezer*, ch. 3–7.
2   In Judaism, Creation — or the "mysteries of Creation" — is a subject that cannot be taught publicly — see *Mishnah Chagigah* 2:1 and the Talmud's comments in *Chagigah* 11b.

which should shed light on this passage. Rashi in his commentary to the very first verse in the Torah notes that the name of God used to describe Creation is *"Elokim,"* which refers to the aspect of God from which justice emanates. Later on in *Bereishit* when the story of Creation is recapitulated, the Torah uses a different terminology to describe God: "God, the Lord," where both the aspects of judgment and mercy are used (*Bereishit* 2:4). The Midrash explains why both terms are used side by side:

> "God, the Lord, [made earth and heaven]" — this may be compared to a king who had some empty glasses. Said the king: "If I pour hot water into them, they will burst; if cold, they will contract [and snap]." What then did the king do? He mixed hot and cold water and poured it into them, and so they remained [unbroken]. Likewise, the Holy One, blessed be He, said, "If I create the world on the basis of mercy alone, its sins will be great; on the basis of judgment alone, the world cannot exist. Hence I will create it on the basis of judgment and of mercy, and may it then stand!" Hence the expression, "God, the Lord."
>
> *(Bereishit Rabbah 12:15)*

The Midrash explains why both terms are used, but it fails to explain why in the first verse in the Torah only the term *"Elokim"* is found, implying that justice alone was used to create the world. Rashi explains that the idea of Creation arose and is represented by *Elokim*, and that idea is based on justice. The actual Creation, though, contains both mercy and justice fused together, as described in the Midrash. Creation requires a Divine recoiling; God needs to make space for man. This process may result in man's perception that God is uninvolved or — God forbid — does not exist. [1]

Rav Gedalyah Shor (*Or Gedalyahu*) suggested that we may draw the following conclusion: The thought of Creation is based on justice, while the actual Creation is based on mercy and judgment.

---

1 Some of these ideas have been explained in *Explorations*, p. 196ff and 442.

The thought of Creation took place in Tishrei, while the actual Creation took place in Nissan. Tishrei is a time of judgment, and Nissan is a time of mercy.

We can take this conclusion one step further: The strict aspect of judgment, based on God's creation via thought, is limited to thought. Hence the strict judgment which man undergoes is for his thoughts. However, when it comes to man's actions, God's judgment is tempered by mercy. This leads to a major conclusion regarding the quality of judgment on Rosh HaShanah and man's obligation before God on this day. If judgment on Rosh HaShanah is related to thought, the major objective of Rosh HaShanah is related to thought: the objective on Rosh HaShanah is to come up with a plan. Just as God designed a plan for Creation, man needs to come up with a plan for his own creation — his life. This plan is judged by God with utmost strictness. Whether man lives up to his plan or not, whether his actions in this world succeed in bringing this plan to fruition, is a matter judged with mercy, for in the world of action God fuses strictness with mercy. God understands human frailty.

Perhaps there is another meaning of the term "Rosh HaShanah" — in its most literal sense, the "head" of the year — the time to think. This is the time of year that each of us has to come up with a plan for living our lives, using our heads, our intellect, the *tzelem Elokim*[1] with which we were created. We are judged strictly for this plan, since it directly reflects the extent to which we recognize and utilize our *tzelem Elokim*. Implementation is another matter. There are times that man fails due to his animal instincts; this is something that God understands. There can be no mistake about it: we are judged for these failings, but the judgment is tempered by mercy.

This concept of a plan seen as an independent entity from the actual reality is reflected in the *akeidah*, where Avraham was called

---

1   See Rambam in *Moreh HaNevuchim* 3:8, where he makes the identification between intellect and *tzelem Elokim*. See *Explorations*, p. 222ff.

upon to sacrifice his son. When Avraham was found willing and set a plan for the deed to be done, it was no longer required of him to follow through with the deed. We are told that God considers the positive thoughts of the righteous as if they were accomplished.[1]

On Rosh HaShanah all mankind stands before God in fear and in dread of the awesome Day of Judgment. May we all have the acumen to formulate the proper plan to lead our lives, may we all be given the strength to implement our plans, and may God judge us with mercy on those occasions when we fail.

May we all be immediately written and sealed in the Book of Life.

---

1   *Kiddushin* 40a.

Rosh HaShanah

The *Akeidah*: Father and Son

O
ne of the most dramatic episodes in the entire Torah, and certainly in the book of *Bereishit*, is the *akeidah* — the binding of Yitzchak. From the moment Avraham receives the directive from God until the angel appears and frees him from his horrific mission, the tension is palpable. The *akeidah* has enchanted and haunted generations of readers, Jewish and non-Jewish[1] alike. While the "story" certainly makes for a good read, we are aware that there are numerous levels on which we can read the text, multiple lessons to be extrapolated.

On a literary level and on a Midrashic level, the story stands by itself; no parallels are needed to explain or embellish the ideas contained within it. There is, however, a textual and Midrashic theme which links the *akeidah* with the Revelation at Sinai, an idea which needs to be understood and explored.

The suggestion of such a relationship with the Revelation should not surprise us, for the *akeidah* was itself a "revelation" of sorts. At Sinai, the people saw the sounds:

And all the people saw the thunder....

(Shemot 20:15)

---

1   Kierkegaard's *The Fear and Trembling* has become a classic in general philosophy, and his term "leap of faith" has entered the lexicon of religious and nonreligious alike. See *Explorations* 32ff.

At the *akeidah* there is also an element of Avraham seeing that which was said:[1]

> And it came to pass after these things, that the Lord tested Avraham, and He said to him, "Avraham."
> And he said, "Here I am."
> And He said, "Take now your son, your only son, whom you love, Yitzchak, and go to the land of Moriah; and offer him there for a burnt offering upon one of the mountains which I will tell you."
>
> *(Bereishit 22:1–2)*

God says that He will tell Avraham the location of the execution; nevertheless, after three days, Avraham and Yitzchak see that which is said:

> "On the third day...and he saw the place afar off" (ibid., 4) — What did he see? He saw a cloud enveloping the mountain, and said: "It appears that that is the place where the Holy One, blessed be He, told me to sacrifice my son." He then said to him [Yitzchak]: "Yitzchak, my son, do you see what I see?"
> "Yes," he replied.
> Said he to his two servants: "Do you see what I see?"
> "No," they answered.
> "Since you do not see it, 'abide here....' (ibid., 5)."
>
> *(Bereishit Rabbah 56:1–2)*

This cloud seen by Avraham and Yitzchak reminds us of the cloud which hovered over the mountain at Sinai:

> And it came to pass on the third day in the morning, that there was thunder and lightning, and a thick cloud upon the mount, and the sound of a shofar exceedingly loud; so that all the people who were in the camp trembled.
>
> *(Shemot 19:16)*

At Sinai, the people see a cloud on the third day, and the Revela-

---

1   The Racanati obliquely makes this reference in his comments on *Yitro*.

tion begins. But the connection is somewhat deeper than merely being revelatory.[1]

The text of the *akeidah* begins with a decree:

> And it came to pass after these things, that the Lord tested Avraham, and He said to him, "Avraham."

Here we are told that God "tested" Avraham; the Hebrew word is *nisah*. This word also appears in the aftermath of the Revelation. The people are afraid of the awesomeness of the experience and recoil:

> And all the people saw the thunder, and the lightning, and the sound of the shofar, and the mountain smoking; and when the people saw it, they were shaken and stood far away. And they said to Moshe, "Speak with us, and we will hear; but let the Lord not speak with us, lest we die."
>
> And Moshe said to the people, "Fear not; for God has come to *test* you, so that His fear may be before your faces, that you do not sin."
>
> *(Shemot 20:15–17)*

In both of these cases the Torah utilizes a word with a double meaning. The word *nisah* can mean both to test and to uplift. God desires to uplift Avraham and the Jewish people respectively by these "tests," each of which are singular experiences in the lives of the forefathers and the nation.

Furthermore, the successful conclusion of the *akeidah* takes place when the angel declares that Avraham's "fear of God" has been established.

> And the angel of God called to him from heaven and said, "Avraham, Avraham."
>
> And he said, "Here I am."
>
> And he said, "Do not lay your hand upon the lad, and do not do anything to him; for now I know that you fear the Lord,

---

1   The "third day" is noted in the Midrash as one of the parallels between the episodes — compare *Bereishit* 22:4 and *Shemot* 19:16 (*Bereishit Rabbah* 56:1).

seeing that you did not withhold your son, your only son, from me."

(Bereishit 22:11–12)

These words are echoed in the text cited above in the aftermath of the Revelation:

...for God has come to test you, so that His *fear* may be before your faces, that you do not sin.

Based on these observations alone one can build the case for some type of relationship between these two sections.

The backdrop of the Revelation was the shofar:

And it came to pass on the third day in the morning, that there was thunder and lightning, and a thick cloud upon the mount, and the sound of a shofar exceedingly loud; so that all the people who were in the camp trembled. And Moshe brought forth the people out of the camp to meet with the Lord, and they stood at the lower part of the mount. And Mount Sinai was altogether in smoke, because God descended upon it in fire; and its smoke ascended as the smoke of a furnace, and the whole mount trembled greatly. And when the voice of the shofar sounded long, and became louder and louder, Moshe spoke, and the Lord answered him by a voice.

(Shemot 19:16–19)

The source of the shofar is, of course, the *akeidah*. The ram which was ensnared in the bushes provided the Jewish people with the shofar:

Rabbi Abbahu said: "Why do we blow on a ram's horn? The Holy One, blessed be He, said: 'Sound before Me a ram's horn so that I may remember on your behalf the binding of Yitzchak ben Avraham, and account it to you as if you had bound yourselves before Me.' "

(Rosh HaShanah 16a)[1]

---

1   See the comments in the Midrash where this idea is both redemptive and

Rashi explains that the sound of the shofar heard at Sinai comes from the shofar of the ram of Yitzchak.[1] The Ramban refers to a mystical secret: The sound which was heard at Sinai was actually the *"pachad Yitzchak"* — the awe of Yitzchak.[2]

If the shofar of Yitzchak, or the awe of Yitzchak, is such an integral part of the Revelation, we understand why the *akeidah* must be seen as some type of precursor to the events at Sinai.[3] In fact, some sources see these events so closely related that they place the *akeidah* at Sinai!

Another exposition of the text, "And God spoke to Moshe in the wilderness of Sinai" (*Bemidbar* 1:1) — This wilderness [Sinai] was called by six names: Mount of God, Mount Bashan,

---

eschatological: " 'And Avraham lifted up his eyes, and looked, and behold behind him [*achar*] a ram' (*Bereishit* 22:13) — What does '*achar*' mean? Said Rabbi Yudan: 'After all that happened, Israel still fall into the clutches of sin and [in consequence] become the victims of persecution; yet they will be ultimately redeemed by the ram's horn, as it says, "And God, the Lord, will blow the horn" (*Zecharyah* 9:14).' Rabbi Yehudah bar Shimon interpreted: 'At the end of [after] all generations Israel will fall into the clutches of sin and be the victims of persecution; yet eventually they will be redeemed by the ram's horn, as it says, "And God, the Lord, will blow the horn." ' Rabbi Chanina ben Yitzchak said: 'Throughout the year Israel are in sin's clutches and led astray by their troubles, but on Rosh HaShanah they take the shofar and blow on it, and eventually they will be redeemed by the ram's horn, as it says, "And God, the Lord, will blow the horn." ' Rabbi Abba bar Rabbi Pappi and Rabbi Yehoshua of Siknin said in Rabbi Levi's name: 'Because the Patriarch Avraham saw the ram extricate himself from one thicket and go and become entangled in another, the Holy One, blessed be He, said to him: "Thus will your children be entangled in countries, changing from Babylon to Media, from Media to Greece, and from Greece to Edom; yet they will eventually be redeemed by the ram's horn, as it is written, "And God, the Lord, will blow the horn...the God of Hosts will defend them" (*Zecharyah* 9:14–15)' " (*Bereishit Rabbah* 56:9).

1   This idea is based on the Midrash in *Pirkei D'Rabbi Eliezer*, ch. 30 or 31 depending on the edition.

2   The term used for revelation is often *"mipi hagevurah."* *Gevurah* is the mystical appellation of Yitzchak. The fear which the people experienced at Sinai is connected to the fear which Yitzchak experienced when he found that he had unknowingly given the blessing to Yaakov. See *Ramban, Shemot* 19:13, and notes by *Chavel*.

3   There are many other connections between Sinai and the *akeidah*. Space does not permit a listing of all of them, but I will mention one more: The servants of Avraham remain at the foot of the mountain, reminiscent of the hierarchy at Sinai.

Mount Gavnunim, Mount Moriah, Mount Chorev, Mount Sinai.

(Bemidbar Rabbah 1:8)[1]

The area which we generally call Sinai is here called Moriah; the place God sent Avraham, which is usually identified with Yerushalayim, is called in the Torah "Moriah."

The Talmud discusses the meaning of the word *Moriah*:

What is [the meaning of] "Mount Moriah"? With regard to this there is a difference of opinion between Rabbi Levi ben Chama and Rabbi Chanina. [One says] because from this mountain instruction went forth to Israel; and the other says because it is the mountain whence fear came upon the heathen.

(Ta'anit 16a)[2]

In the comments of Tosafot,[3] the idea of instruction coming forth presents two possible understandings: First, Yerushalayim, the place from which the law was taught, as the Prophet said, "From Zion Torah shall spring forth" (*Yeshayah* 2:3). The second explanation refers to the original source of instruction: Sinai.[4] There is a *midrash* that makes an even more radical suggestion: Sinai was once part of Moriah (in Yerushalayim):

And where did Sinai come from? Rav Yosei said, "From Mount Moriah it was separated like challah, which was separated from the dough. From the place where Yitzchak our Forefather was bound. God said, 'Since Yitzchak their Forefather was bound there, it is an appropriate place for his chil-

---

1   See also *Otzar Midrashim* by Eisenstein, p. 162.
2   The Midrash (*Bereishit Rabbah* 55:7) echoes this idea.
3   *Tosafot* s.v. "*Har.*"
4   See the explanation of the Chatam Sofer, in *Responsa Chatam Sofer, Yoreh Dei'ah,* section 235. Also see the explanation the Chatam Sofer gives in the name of his revered teacher Rav Natan Adler in section 233, that when Avraham sets out on his journey it says the "land of Moriah," not the "Mount Moriah," because the mountain did not exist yet. Avraham Korman in *Ha'Avot VeHashevatim* develops an entire thesis based on this idea, that volcanic activity formed the mountain during the three days of Avraham's sojourn.

dren to receive the Torah.' "

(Midrash Tehillim 68:9, Buber edition)[1]

Here we see, in the clearest possible terms, the link between the *akeidah* and Revelation. The locale of the two is inexorably linked. The *akeidah* provided the conceptual prototype for the Revelation. Understanding the *akeidah* can shed light on the Revelation and understanding the Revelation can shed light on the *akeidah*.

The Ramchal[2] teaches that the major aspect of the Revelation, receiving the Torah, was the distilling of good from the compound of good and evil which resulted from eating of the Tree of Knowledge of Good and Evil. The fall of man at the very dawn of history was caused by the combination of forces, good and evil. Standing at Sinai, hearing, seeing the word of God, broke that force. The clarity with which they saw the words left them without doubts concerning their collective and individual agenda.

The idea of the *akeidah* is of a person or persons so dedicated to God that personal considerations are not factored into decisions. For that individual, God is not the most important thing in life; God is the only thing in life. God is life. That person is no longer controlled by good and evil; good has been extricated from the insidious mixture.[3]

> And God sat and saw the father binding with all his heart, and the son being bound with all his heart, and the angels were screaming and crying.

> *(Pirkei D'Rabbi Eliezer, ch. 30/31)*

If we extend the idea, we will recall that eating from the Tree of

---

1   The Midrash goes so far as to state that in the future Sinai will return to Moriah in Yerushalayim.

2   See *Maamar HaChochmah*, and see Rabbi Chaim Friedlander, *Siftei Chaim*, vol. 3, p. 57.

3   Avraham achieves this level when he is prepared to sacrifice his beloved son. Yitzchak strives for this level when he asks his father to tie him down, explaining that "the soul is strong but the body is weak." See *Bereishit Rabbah* (56:8): "When Avraham wished to sacrifice his son Yitzchak, he said to him: 'Father, I am a young man and am afraid that my body may tremble through fear of the knife and I will grieve you. The slaughter may be rendered unfit and this will not count as a real sacrifice. Therefore, bind me very firmly.' Forthwith, 'He bound Yitzchak' (*Bereishit* 22:9): can one bind a[n unwilling] thirty-seven-year-old man?"

Knowledge of Good and Evil brought death into the world. The Gemara teaches that when the Jews stood at Mount Sinai they were "cured" of the metaphysical venom with which the serpent of old had infected them.[1]

Our Sages teach us that at Sinai the entire nation perished. The awe was apparently too great and the people could not sustain such a level of spirituality. Afterward God sprinkled dew upon them and the entire nation was resurrected.

> At every word which went forth from the mouth of the Holy One, blessed be He, the souls of Israel departed, for it is said, "My soul went forth when He spoke" (*Shir HaShirim* 5:6). But since their souls departed at the first word, how could they receive the second word? He brought down the dew with which He will resurrect the dead and revived them.
>
> *(Shabbat 88b)*

This return to life is a symbol of a spiritual rebirth: The purity lost in Eden is regained. The nation is now cleansed from all evil, radiant and virginal.

The theme of resurrection is also present at the *akeidah*, in a general sense. Yitzchak, bound to the altar, with the blade quickly making its way to his jugular, is saved from the brink of death at the last second. Yitzchak has "one foot in the grave," a knife at his throat. He is all but dead when the epiphany brings the message that Yitzchak may live.

The Midrash goes even further, opining that Yitzchak did, in fact, die on the altar![2]

> When the sword got to his neck Yitzchak's soul departed. When he heard the sound from between the cherubs, saying, "Do not lift your hand...," his soul returned. He stood on his feet and...said, "Blessed are You, God, who revives the dead."
>
> *(Pirkei D'Rabbi Eliezer, ch. 30/31)*

---

1   *Shabbat* 146a.
2   This idea is also discussed in the essay on Chol HaMoed Pesach, "These Bones Will Live!"

Just as the nation perished at Sinai and is brought back to life, so does Yitzchak die and return to life. This theme of resurrection is also the major theme of the haftarah:

> And when Elisha came into the house, behold, the child was dead, lying upon his bed. He went in and closed the door upon the two of them, and prayed to God. And he went up, and lay upon the child, and put his mouth upon his mouth and his eyes upon his eyes and his hands upon his hands; and he stretched himself upon the child; and the flesh of the child became warm. Then he returned and walked in the house to and fro; and went up, and stretched himself upon him; and the child sneezed seven times, and the child opened his eyes.
>
> *(Melachim 4:32–35)*

The opportunity lost at the dawn of history is "fixed" at the Revelation. The *akeidah* serves as the conduit of this divine benevolence, introducing the human ability to change one's fate, to worship God completely and wholeheartedly.

Why is the *akeidah* such a watershed? Why does this event stand out from all the deeds of the *avot*? The Torah has no trace of communication between Adam and his descendants. Whatever he saw or experienced in that celestial garden remains a mystery. Neither does Noach engage in dialogue with his children. The only time we see him speaking to them is when he curses his son. In contradistinction, Avraham takes Yitzchak into his world. The Torah stresses that the two "walk together."

> And Avraham took the wood of the burnt offering and laid it upon Yitzchak, his son, and he took the fire in his hand and a knife, *and both of them walked together.*
>
> Yitzchak spoke to Avraham his father, and said, "My father."
>
> And he said, "Here I am, my son."
>
> And he said, "Behold the fire and the wood; but where is the lamb for a burnt offering?"

And Avraham said, "The Lord will provide Himself a lamb for a burnt offering, my son." *And both of them walked together.*

(Bereishit 22:6–8)

They were on the same path, the same "wavelength," possessing a common destiny.

Perhaps this is the lesson of the *akeidah*: There was no generation gap between the two. They shared a common goal and path. In the words of the Midrash:

"And both of them walked together" — one to bind and the other to be bound, one to slaughter and the other to be slaughtered.

(Bereishit Rabbah 56:3)

At all events, " 'The Lord will provide Himself a lamb — and if not, you are for a burnt offering, my son.' "And both of them walked together": one to slaughter and the other to be slaughtered.

(Ibid., 4)

Avraham and Yitzchak formed the first intergenerational bond, a living lesson in continuity. Sinai, too, is a place that binds all generations of the Jewish people together. All souls stood at Sinai and took part in the theophany. The root of the Sinai experience was at the *akeidah*, where the first two generations of our people, Avraham and Yitzchak, become bound together in their love of God.

The Arizal teaches (*Sefer HaLikuttim*, p. 63) that the response to Yitzchak's query regarding the object which would be slaughtered is instructive: "God will provide himself *a lamb for a burnt offering, my son.*" In Hebrew, the words are השה לעולה בני. The first letter of each word spells "Hevel," drawing a clear line between Adam's failure to engage the next generation in dialogue and Avraham's succeess. This sets the stage for Sinai, where all Jewish people are linked for eternity by a common mission, a common destiny.

And both of them walked together.

The Ten Days of Repentance

The Three Books

The days between Rosh HaShanah and Yom Kippur are known as the Ten Days of Repentance. These are days of introspection and hopefully growth and change.

Three books are opened [in heaven] on Rosh HaShanah: one for the thoroughly wicked, one for the thoroughly righteous, and one for the intermediate. The thoroughly righteous are forthwith inscribed definitively in the Book of Life. The thoroughly wicked are forthwith inscribed definitively in the Book of Death. The doom of the intermediate is suspended from Rosh HaShanah until the Yom Kippur. If they are found deserving, they are inscribed in the Book of Life; if they do not deserve well, they are inscribed in the Book of Death.

(Rosh HaShanah 16b)[1]

While the entire community faces these days of awe with trepidation and angst, this passage indicates that these ten days are provided specifically, if not exclusively, for the mediocre, during which time they must justify their existence. The sentences of the clearly righteous and completely wicked are already signed and sealed. Only those individuals who completed the year as neither

---

1   There is another passage, on page 32b in *Rosh HaShanah,* which speaks of two books being opened on Rosh HaShanah and Yom Kippur.

righteous nor wicked are given an extension of ten days to break the "tie" and clearly determine their righteousness.

Logically, a positive outcome could result either by adding mitzvot or subtracting sins. Nonetheless, when the Rambam codifies this law he states unequivocally that the only path toward inscription in the book of life is *teshuvah*. Numerous Rabbinic commentaries have noted this decision of the Rambam, and various suggestions have been put forth to explain why the Rambam deviated[1] from the simple understanding of the Talmudic passage, which implies that even one more mitzvah should be sufficient to tip the scales.[2]

This question was made famous by Rav Yitzchak Blazer, the eminent student of the founder of the Mussar Movement, Rav Yisrael Salanter.[3] Rav Blazer explains that the commandment to repent is the major obligation during that time of year: God is close and accessible. Forgiveness is there for the asking.[4] Consequently, when a person chooses not to take advantage of this opportunity, one more transgression is added to his list and as a result his fate is sealed.

While this may explain why a particular sinner who does not repent is inscribed in the Book of Death, is this true in every instance? For a marginal individual whose year ended in a tie between his good and bad deeds, will his failure to do *teshuvah* outweigh any conceivable good that he may do in those ten days? If he involved himself in learning, prayer, charity, redeeming captives, and general *chesed*, while avoiding temptation and sin, will his lack of actual *teshuvah* per se[5] condemn him? Such a conclusion seems difficult.

1   The Rambam also changed the phrase "completely righteous" of the Talmud to simply "righteous." This may be due to his understanding that righteousness indicates even a slight advantage compared to the wicked.
2   Various commentators, including Rav Yitzchak Blazer (*Kochvei Or*, 5), Rav Yitzchak Hutner (*Pachad Yitzchak, Rosh HaShanah, ma'amar* 18), Rav Chaim Shmuelevitz (*Sichot Mussar* 5732), Rav Yitzchak Mirsky (*Hegyonei Halachah* p. 170), have all offered fascinating insights to explain this passage of Rambam.
3   It should be noted that early authorities offer explanations for this ruling, including the *Lechem Mishneh*, whose commentary may be found in most standard editions of *Mishneh Torah*.
4   *Devarim Rabbah* (Lieberman edition), *Parashat Ha'azinu*.

Rav Chaim Shmuelevitz suggests that the *beinoni*, the intermediate person, was already found guilty and is given ten days to seek
a stay of his execution. He notes the term used in the Talmud,
teluyim v'omdim, which literally means "hanging yet standing"[1]:
The *beinoni*, the individual who has not been able to justify his existence, has not fulfilled the minimal requirement of performing
more good deeds than evil; he is sentenced to death on Rosh
HaShanah for the crime of not making this world a better place.[2]
This obligation was the basic mandate of Adam and every human
being who has subsequently graced this planet. Failure means
death. In the case of a stalemate, God gives the *beinoni* ten days to
show why the noose should be removed from his neck and he
should be allowed to descend from the gallows.

If this analysis is correct, the requirement of *teshuvah* is understood: the stay of execution requires remorse for mistakes of the
past, while a lack of remorse allows the execution to proceed as
scheduled. However, our question remains: Why is the stalemate
not broken by good deeds? Why does a "stay of execution"[3] order
ignore such deeds as would tip the balance in the condemned
man's favor, requiring *teshuvah* specifically?

The *Emek Berachah* suggests a very simple yet elegant solution to
the question: The year begins on Rosh HaShanah and ends on the
last day of Elul. If a person is "intermediate" at the conclusion of
the year, then another mitzvah will not change the balance sheet
for last year's tally. The new mitzvah will be counted on the new
year's ledger.[4] The only thing that can change last year's tally is

5   Assuming that the core of *teshuvah* is regret of past misdeeds and dedication toward
    not sinning in the future; see Rambam, *Hilchot Teshuvah* 2:2.
1   This may also explain why a tie is not automatically decided in a person's favor —
    which is an assumption some earlier authorities assume is a rule of the spiritual
    universe. See *Rosh HaShanah* 17a and *Tosafot, Kiddushin* 39b.
2   Let us note that according to a Rabbinic tradition recorded in the *Pesikta Rabbati* (*Ish
    Shalom* 40), Adam sinned on the first Rosh HaShanah — and forgiveness was
    afforded on Yom Kippur. This would imply a universal understanding of this time
    period and not a parochial Jewish one.
3   Unless this is a question of Divine etiquette which dictates that a stay of execution
    requires a formal request on the part of the petitioner.

teshuvah, which wipes prior sins off the slate altogether. With this in mind, we see quite clearly why the Rambam would understand the Talmudic passage as referring exclusively to *teshuvah*: A new mitzvah is certainly a good thing to do, but it will be irrelevant to last year's tally.

There is another simple solution to our problem, albeit one which may lack the elegance of some of the other explanations. In the parallel passage in the Talmud *Yerushalmi*,[1] the requirement to do *teshuvah* in these ten days is very specific. Apparently the Rambam learned the *Bavli* in light of the unequivocal language of the *Yerushalmi*.[2] Yet this "solution" merely pushes our question up one level; rather than asking why the Rambam acknowledged *teshuvah* alone as the remedy for the *beinoni*, we can now pose the question regarding the theology of *teshuvah* as taught in the Rambam based on the *Yerushalmi*. Why does the fate of the mediocre person rest on *teshuvah* and not on the performance of additional good deeds?[3]

Rav Yitzchak Hutner grapples with this problem and offers a unique solution. According to the Rambam, a righteous person is not one with more good than bad deeds; rather it is someone whose good outweighs his bad. And the wicked person is not someone with more bad than good; rather, his bad outweighs his good. The Rambam explains that the evaluation is based upon qualitative standards and not technical addition. One good deed may outweigh many negative actions, while one negative action has the ability to eclipse many good deeds (*Hilchot Teshuvah* 3:2).

Thus, being righteous or wicked are qualitative, not quantitative, categories. A righteous person may be defined as someone who is fundamentally an *"eved Hashem,"* someone who is commit-

---

4   *Emek Berachah*, cited in *Hegyonei Halachah.*
1   *Yerushalmi, Rosh HaShanah* 1:3, p. 57, col. 1. Also see *Pesikta Rabbati (Ish Shalom)* 40.
2   This opinion may also be found in the Commentary of Rabbenu Chananel on the aforementioned passage in *Rosh HaShanah.*
3   By virtue of calling the days the "Ten Days of Repentance," we can surmise that the major theme is *teshuvah.*

ted to the word of God. It is true that in the realm of reality, circumstances or weakness may cause this committed individual to fail even more often than he succeeds; nonetheless, his self-definition, his orientation and outlook are those of a servant of God. This is not a delusion; at his core, this is who he is! While in absolute terms he may have committed more transgressions, his good nonetheless outweighs his bad. On the other hand, there may be someone who does more good than bad — but again he is a victim of his own (positive!) circumstances, unable to do what he really wishes. His success is illusory; he himself values his transgressions more than his mitzvot.[1]

Rav Hutner insists that we define the *beinoni* in the same fashion—not as a quantitative state, a mathematically exact sum of minutiae. After all, how many people will finish the year with an equal number of accomplishments and failures? Just as tzaddik and *rasha* are qualitative categories, so is *beinoni* describing individuals whose goodness and badness do not outweigh one another. Such an individual does not know if he wants to be an *eved Hashem* or to rebel against the Divine Word; he sits on the fence. Even if he performs more mitzvot, such an individual remains mediocre.

Although many such people become swept up in the spirit of this time of year, perhaps taking a more active role in Jewish life or even performing acts of charity or other mitzvot traditionally associated with these days in the Jewish life cycle, their lack of consistency, their "unholistic" approach to God, indicates dysfunction. The Days of Awe may inspire sporadic gestures, but by winter the tune of *Kol Nidrei* becomes a distant memory, eclipsed by the beat of a more seductive drum.

In order to break his mediocrity, the *beinoni* must do *teshuvah* — from his mediocrity. He must decide that he wishes to get off the

---

1   In a separate discussion, Rav Hutner explained a teaching of Rabbeinu Yonah as follows: A person can be defined based on what truly energizes him. In his example, a businessman who is excited to meet with a sage is on a higher level than a sage who gets energized by meeting a business tycoon. What a person values is part of the definition of who a person is (*Pachad Yitzchak, Purim, ma'amar* 1).

fence and become an *eved Hashem*. Such a decision requires contemplation, introspection and strength — in a word, *teshuvah*. Only ceasing to be mediocre, not adding more mitzvot, can change his situation, changing the outcome by changing the outlook. A person is thus required to inspect and analyze his entire orientation and outlook, his goals, his essence rather than his actions. Individual, isolated deeds, be they mitzvot or *aveirot*, are not the main point. The *beinoni* must take stock and take an active decision not to be mediocre. This is *teshuvah*, and only such a decision has the power to add significance to his actions.

We may conclude that according to the Rambam, *teshuvah* is superior to all other actions during these ten days. Nonetheless, the Rambam in the very next law states that other deeds aside from *teshuvah* are customary:

> Because of this matter, it is the custom of the entire Jewish community to give greater amounts of *tzedakah*, and [do more] good deeds, and to be involved in mitzvot from Rosh HaShanah through Yom Kippur, more so than the rest of the year. It is the custom to arise in the night during these ten days to pray...until the day dawns.
>
> *(Hilchot Teshuvah 3:4)*[1]

If in the Rambam's opinion *teshuvah* is the only act that can tip the scales, what purpose is there for the other activities he describes? Why would the Rambam speak of giving *tzedakah* during these ten days in the very next law?

A parallel question may be posed based on a different section in the Rambam's *Hilchot Teshuvah*.

> All the prophets command *teshuvah*, and Israel will only be redeemed via *teshuvah*....
>
> *(Hilchot Teshuvah 7:5)*

On the other hand, the Rambam writes elsewhere:

---

1   The idea the Rambam expresses can be found in *Pesikta D'Rav Kahana* (Mandelbaum edition), ch. 26.

We must be more careful in regards to *tzedakah*, more than all other positive commandments. For *tzedakah* is [the] sign of righteous progeny of Avraham our Forefather.... And the throne of Israel is established and the true belief is based only on *tzedakah*. And Israel will be only be redeemed via *tzedakah*.

(Matanot L'Aniyim 10:1)

What, then, will bring about redemption, *teshuvah* or *tzedakah*? This may be the same question with which we have already grappled regarding the Ten Days of Repentance. Obviously, in the Rambam's thinking, there is some type of relationship between *teshuvah* and *tzedakah*, which we may describe as follows: *teshuvah* causes sin to be wiped away, but once the sin has been eradicated, where does the penitent stand? When the bad deeds have been expunged from the record, the person remains an empty vessel. This is not the type of *teshuvah* that can bring redemption to the world.

David HaMelech expresses this basic tenet of Judaism as "Depart from evil, and do good" (*Tehillim* 34:15). "Depart from evil" is *teshuvah*, but to this David adds "and do good." After *teshuvah*, man must redouble his efforts to mend and perfect the world. Only a perfected world can be redeemed, and this perfection will take place via *tzedakah*. We can therefore conclude that *teshuvah* itself is not sufficient to bring about redemption, though it is certainly an essential component: Without *teshuvah*, the *tzedakah* would not be enough, and conversely, without *tzedakah*, *teshuvah* would be insufficient.

Perhaps the same may be said regarding the ten days between Rosh HaShanah and Yom Kippur. We must separate ourselves from evil, but doing good is also necessary; not because it tips the scales in our favor (only *teshuvah* can do that), but because *tzedakah* is connected with the new, redeemed personality. The penitent has left his evil actions behind, and the void in his personality is now filled with good deeds.[1]

---

1   See *Yechezkel* 33:19, *Yoma* 86b, and the next essay.

In the classic work on *teshuvah* penned by Rabbeinu Yonah we find the following comments, which shed light on our discussion:

The seventeenth principle is to pursue acts of kindness, as it says, "By loving kindness and truth iniquity is purged; and by the fear of the Lord men depart from evil" (*Mishlei* 16:6). Now let us meditate on the secret of this verse. If the sinner does not return to God [via *teshuvah*] the kindness which he performs will not purge his iniquity.... "[For God, your Lord, is God of gods and Lord of lords, a great God, mighty and awesome] Who favors no person, nor takes bribes" (*Devarim* 10:17), and as our Sages have explained this verse, " 'Nor takes bribes' — even a mitzvah will not help to disregard sin" (*Yalkut Mishlei* 11:947). Therefore the verse which said, "By loving kindness and truth iniquity is purged" refers to a penitent, for there are sins which are not completely purged by *teshuvah* and Yom Kippur, but suffering completes the purging....

(Shaarei Teshuvah 1:47)

Rabbeinu Yonah describes a fascinating dynamic in the relationship between *teshuvah* and *chesed*. Here, *chesed* is seen as the completion of *teshuvah*, in the sense that the *chesed* counteracts some of the ramifications of sin. *Teshuvah* has the ability to rekindle one's relationship with God, but *chesed* can completely mend the rift caused by sin. This idea of suffering as a component of the *teshuvah* process is mentioned in other sources as well, notably the Rambam himself, who writes:

[A person] will not have complete forgiveness until suffering comes upon him, as it is written, "Then I will punish their transgression with the rod, and their iniquity with strokes" (*Tehillim* 89:33).

(Hilchot Teshuvah 1:4)

There is some discussion among the commentaries whether these words in the Rambam apply to all sins or only some types; in either case, the idea that suffering is a necessity in the rehabilitation process is represented in the thought of the Rambam.

The Mabit (Rav Moshe ben Yosef MiTrani) explains how the suffering works:

> The idea behind suffering bringing about [spiritual] cleansing — this serves to counteract the pleasure that the person had during the sin. The pain will serve to weaken the physical desires, in order to assure that the person will not sin again.
>
> *(Beit Elokim, Gate of Teshuvah, ch. 8)*

Judaism does not see the physical as inherently evil. Quite the opposite is the case: the physical was created by God in order for man to accomplish his mission on this earth. The basic gesture in Judaism is to elevate the mundane. Man has the ability to take the physical and transform it into something spiritual. When man sins, the delicate balance between spiritual and physical is disturbed. As part of the process of rectification, equilibrium must be reestablished. This is accomplished by suffering. When man sees that the physical is not what he thought it was at the time of sin, he is healed.

In *teshuvah* we ask forgiveness for our rebellion against God and resolve not to return to the sin. Suffering purges sin from the soul that has become tainted by its rebellion.

This idea will give us insight into the spiritual dynamic of Yom Kippur, when the Torah speaks of afflicting our souls. The person who erred throughout the year asks of God forgiveness on this holy day, and the fasting and other afflictions help to purge our souls from the insidious effects of sin.

Rabbeinu Yonah's insight may now be understood: Just as affliction may purge our souls, so may acts of kindness, for sin often contains an aspect of self-centeredness. The sinner puts himself and his own desires over everything else. The act of giving to others indicates that this person is no longer controlled by destructive self-centeredness. While this is not a replacement for *teshuvah*, it can replace the need for suffering. Either suffering or giving to others achieves the spiritual equilibrium described earlier, returning the soul — via different avenues — to a state of purity.

It is now clear why the Rambam stressed that these ten days are meant for *teshuvah*, but in conjunction with other deeds: These deeds complete the *teshuvah* and alleviate the need for suffering. The Rambam, however, did not speak of redemption being the result of acts of kindness in general; *tzedakah* was singled out. Why was *tzedakah* given special status compared to all other acts of kindness?

In his *Moreh HaNevuchim*, Rambam discusses the difference between *tzedakah* and *chesed*. *Chesed* are acts of kindness of which the recipient is not really worthy. On the other hand, *tzedakah* is based on *tzedek* — justice; *tzedakah* implies that the recipient deserves the gift.[1]

When a Jew gives *tzedakah* he is in a sense confirming a partnership with God to care for others. This is an obligation; it is not *chesed*. This idea is spelled out in the *Zohar*:

> Hence he that gives charity [*tzedakah*] to the poor makes the Holy Name complete as it should be above, since *tzedakah* is the tree of life, and when it gives to *tzedek* the Holy Name becomes complete. Hence he who sets this activity in motion from below, as it were, completes the Holy Name. It has been stated elsewhere that this is the place of the poor man. Why is it so? Because the poor man has nothing of his own, save what is given him, and the moon has no light save what is given her by the sun.
>
> Why is a poor man counted as dead? Because he is found in the place of death. Therefore, if one has pity on him and gives him charity, the tree of life rests upon him, as it says, "*Tzedakah* [charity] saves from death" (*Mishlei* 10:2). This applies only to charity done for its own sake, for then the doer links together *tzedakah* with *tzedek* so that the whole forms the

---

1   Rabbi Soloveitchik has pointed out that the English translation "charity" is inappropriate, as the word *charity* is based on the Latin *charitus*, which implies the performance of an act of kindness to which the recipient is unentitled. See *Y'mei Zikaron*, p. 43–44.

Holy Name, since *tzedek* is not established without *tzedakah.*

(*Zohar, Vayikra 113b*)

The *Zohar* assumes, as did the Rambam, that the root of the word *tzedakah* is indeed *tzedek.* The only difference between the two concepts is the letter *"hei,"* which the *Zohar* states is derived from the Divine Name. The person who gives *tzedakah* thus enters a partnership with God; his actions are permeated with divinity here on earth, while he completes the Divine Name above.

Furthermore, the *Zohar* states that when man becomes a partner with God, the manner in which Divine Judgment is adjudicated shifts:

> Observe how merciful the Holy One, blessed be He, shows Himself towards all beings, and especially toward those who walk in His paths. For when He is about to execute judgment on the world, before doing so He puts in the way of His beloved the occasion of performing a good act. We have thus been taught that when the Holy One loves a man, He sends him a present in the shape of a poor man, so that he should perform some good deed to him, through the merit of which he shall draw to himself a cord of grace from the right side which shall wind round his head and imprint a mark on him. Thus, when punishment falls on the world, the destroyer, raising his eyes and noticing the mark, will be careful to avoid him and leave him alone.

(*Zohar, Bereishit 104a*)

This idea of a reciprocal relationship between man and God may be illustrated by the following passage:

> [Rabbi Eliezer] once descended before the Ark and recited the twenty-four benedictions [for fast days] and his prayer was not answered. Rabbi Akiva descended after him and exclaimed: "Our Father, our King, we have no King but You; our Father, our King, for Your sake have mercy upon us;" and rain fell. The Rabbis present suspected [Rabbi Eliezer], whereupon a Heav-

enly Voice was heard proclaiming, "[The prayer of] this man [Rabbi Akiva] was answered not because he is greater than the other man, but because he is a forgiving person, and the other is not."

(Ta'anit 25b)

The kindness with which Rabbi Akiva treated others dictated the way God would respond to his plea.

When man sins, not only has he rebelled against God, but he has also failed to accomplish his mission on this earth. God created a wonderful world, full of both physical pleasures and spiritual opportunities. Man, by virtue of his sins, creates a world that is dark and full of pain. Sinning, choosing the physical over the spiritual, causes a warped world to emerge. When man follows that path, he fails to accomplish his mandate here on earth.

The Jewish people as a whole also have a mission: to recreate that exquisite garden which God created at the dawn of history — to mend the world. The sinner who truly repents is surely forgiven. But the ugly stains of sin are often more difficult to cleanse than the sin itself. Collectively, when the Jewish people sin, stains are left — often deep, communal stains. The best way to cleanse those stains is via *tzedakah*. Every sinner separates himself from the community to some extent; *tzedakah* helps bind the individual to the community anew. As the Rambam wrote:

> And the throne of Israel is established and the true belief is based only on *tzedakah*. And Israel will be only be redeemed via *tzedakah*.

By giving *tzedakah* man takes a proactive stance in his partnership with God, which can only occur after a spiritual renaissance, an awakening and return to God. Only this active stance can usher in the Messianic Era.

> Zion shall be redeemed with judgment, and those who return to her with *tzedakah*.

(Yeshayah 1:27)

May we all purge our sins on this Yom Kippur with our fasting. May we all take responsibility in our "partnership" with God, thereby guaranteeing personal redemption. May we all be sealed in the Book of Life, and merit greeting the Messiah — soon and in our days!

The Ten Days of Repentance

Teshuvah from Love and Fear

One of the most exalted teachings of Judaism is the concept of *teshuvah*. The belief that one's present or future need not be devastated by past mistakes is one of the most important and uplifting ideas in Jewish thought. While it is certainly true that there are actions whose ramifications are unchangeable,[1] *teshuvah* does provide a cathartic cleansing of the soul which uplifts the penitent and transforms the sinner into beloved friend of God. The Rambam's poetic description of the impact of *teshuvah* is spiritually breathtaking:

> Yesterday he was hated, distant, despised by God, abhorred and loathed and cast far away; and today he is loved and desired and close at hand; a friend.[2]
>
> *(Hilchot Teshuvah 7:6)*

A theological/philosophical question emerges: What is the precise effect of *teshuvah*? Does the negative action vanish as if it never happened, or is the negative behavior somehow retained and transformed?

---

1   The Sages described this concept with the verse from *Kohelet* (1:15): "That which is crooked cannot be made straight; and that which is wanting cannot be numbered." See *Mishnah Sukkah* 2:6, *Chagigah* 1:6, 9b, and *Yevamot* 22b.
2   See Maharal, *Netivot Olam, Netiv HaTeshuvah*, ch. 2.

The Talmud discusses this question:

Reish Lakish said: "Great is repentance, for because of it pre-meditated sins are accounted as errors, as it is said: 'Return, O Israel, to God, your Lord, for you have stumbled in your iniquity' (*Hoshea* 14:2). 'Iniquity' is premeditated, and yet he calls it 'stumbling.' " But that is not so! For Reish Lakish said that repentance is so great that premeditated sins are accounted as though they were merits, as it is said: "And when the wicked turns from his wickedness, and does that which is lawful and right, he shall live thereby!" (*Yechezkel* 33:11). That is no contradiction: One refers to a case [of repentance] derived from love, the other to one due to fear.

(Yoma 86b[1])

Here both sides of the "argument" are opinions of Rav Shimon ben Lakish, better known as Reish Lakish. We are told that there is more than one type of *teshuvah*: one type is motivated by love, and the other by fear. One type of *teshuvah* transforms the sin into an accident, while the other type transforms the sin into merit. Interestingly, in neither case does the sinful action simply dissipate or disappear with the advent or completion of repentance.

A careful reading of the text does not reveal which is which (the text read: "There is no contradiction: One refers to a case [of repentance] derived from love, the other to one due to fear"). However, logic would dictate that love is associated with merit, while fear is associated with accident. This logic is "associative": love is greater than fear[2] and meritorious behavior is surely greater than any accidental action; ergo, *teshuvah* motivated by love must render the act

---

1   See *Bemidbar Rabbah* 10:1.
2   See Rambam, *Hilchot Teshuvah*, ch. 10. Rabbi Soloveitchik notes that the Rambam does not mention the teaching of Reish Lakish regarding the two types of *teshuvah*, although he does speak of relating to God via love as the culmination of the ten-chapter discussion of *teshuvah*. Rabbi Soloveitchik therefore posited that the Rambam's entire book of *teshuvah* should be studied along these lines — the earlier chapters as a discussion of *teshuvah* by fear and the later ones of *teshuvah* by love. See Michel Shurkin, *Harerei Kedem*, section 37, pp. 78–80.

in question a merit, while *teshuvah* motivated by fear causes sin to be redefined as accident.

This logic is clear in hindsight, but what brought Reish Lakish to this understanding initially? More importantly, what is the intrinsic relationship between love and merit, and fear and accident? What is the meaning of this relationship for us, as potential penitents? What is the spiritual dynamic which retrospectively turns a rebellion against God into a meritorious deed? Furthermore, why would a rebellion against God consequently be considered an accident simply because the sinner becomes consumed with fear of God? How does this process work?

Of the two, the process of turning a sin into a merit seems more daring and therefore more difficult to explain. One would be tempted to say that the merit in question is the merit of *teshuvah*,[1] but this suggestion is untenable: *Teshuvah* motivated by fear is also *teshuvah*, albeit of a somewhat less impressive variety, and should therefore yield the same rewards. The merit of *teshuvah* motivated by love must therefore be independent of the act of *teshuvah* per se, and must lie in a different realm.

Rabbi Soloveitchik posited that the different types of *teshuvah* depend upon the attitude of the individual — whether he sees his past misdeeds as a source of inspiration for the future or as a mistake best forgotten. While this distinction seems accurate, it does not necessarily correlate with fear and love.[2]

There is a teaching cited by Rav Elchanan Wasserman in the name of the Chafetz Chaim which may provide a more direct correlation. In *Mesillat Yesharim*, Ramchal points out that without God's incredible capacity for forgiveness, mere "regret" would have no effect whatsoever. Logically, remorse should, at most, impact future behavior, but is powerless to "undo" prior deeds. In the Ramchal's

---

1 This would assume that *teshuvah* is a mitzvah, which is a thesis not universally accepted. See Rambam's *Hilchot Teshuvah* 1:1, and commentaries, notably the *Avodat Hamelech* by Rabbi Menachem Krakowsky and the *Minchat Chinuch*, mitzvah 364.

2 See *On Repentance*, p. 273.

view, this is where the Divine aspect of forgiveness comes into play. However, the Talmud also teaches that a person may forfeit the merit of mitzvot he performed by later regretting and rejecting these positive deeds:

> Rabbi Shimon bar Yochai said: "Even if he is perfectly righteous all his life but rebels at the end, he destroys his former [good deeds], for it is said: 'The righteousness of the righteous shall not deliver him in the day of his transgression' (*Yechezkel* 33:12)." ...Said Reish Lakish: "It means that he regretted his former deeds."
>
> *(Kiddushin 40b)*

This teaching, codified in *Hilchot Teshuvah* 3:3, is what troubled Rav Elchanan Wasserman: If regret can nullify good deeds, why can't regret simply expunge the bad as well? If regret is a spiritual dynamic which erases the past, why is it selective? Rav Elchanan Wasserman posed this question to his teacher, the Chafetz Chaim: Why does *teshuvah* necessitate the intervention of Divine compassion, rather than acting as an automatic mechanism for deleting the past?

The Chafetz Chaim explained that when a person repents, what he actually fears is punishment. In fact, had he received "inside information" from above that he will not be punished for this offense, the person would have felt no need to repent. People reject punishment, not sinful actions; the ramifications of sin are frightening, not sin itself. The penitent (due to fear of punishment) never really rejected the action — only the punishment.

This is the reason that all *teshuvah* requires some degree of Divine compassion: Not only does God rescind the sentence and repeal the punishment, but He also forgives the sinner for the action for which he should have been punished. This also explains the mechanics of repentance, providing the link between *teshuvah* motivated by fear and accidental transgression: As a result of God's compassion, a misdeed goes unpunished; this is also the case in unintentional sins.

Rav Elchanan did not accept this answer of his mentor, for it assumes that all *teshuvah* is motivated by fear.[1] Rav Elchanan himself suggested that we consider various facets of sin and adherence, taking into account both the action and the impact such action has on the relationship between man and God. When, for example, a person eats nonkosher food, he has ignored the word of God and ingested spiritual poison.[2] *Teshuvah* — expressing regret and accepting upon oneself not to repeat the action itself — repairs the relationship but does not remove the spiritual toxins. Here is where God's compassion steps in: God eradicates the poison of the sin once the relationship has been healed.

On the other hand, fulfilling a positive commandment means fostering a relationship with God as well as doing a good deed. When a person rejects his good deeds he destroys the relationship. To give a harsh example: if a husband presents his wife with flowers and declares that he does not love her, nor has he ever loved her, it is unlikely that those flowers will end up in a vase. Similarly, Rav Elchanan concludes that a good deed is of no value in the absence of a relationship.[3]

This helps us understand the first half of Reish Lakish's dictum: *teshuvah* motivated by fear turns the sin into an accident. *Teshuvah* is the effort to mend the relationship, and God's compassion tends to the residual effects of the action itself. However, the second part of the dictum remains obscure. Why would *teshuvah* motivated by love transform a rebellion into a meritorious deed?

Another source may offer some insight. Reish Lakish's attitude

---

1   See *Kovetz Maamarim*, p. 23ff. See also the comments of Rav Hutner in *Pachad Yitzchak, Rosh HaShanah*.

2   According to tradition, eating nonkosher food causes *timtum halev*, spiritual confusion. See Rabbeinu Bechayei on *Shemot* 23:19.

3   See *Ha'amek Davar, Bemidbar* 15:39, and *Pachad Yitzchak, Pesach* 7:3 and 53:5. Presumably the nonbeliever who performs a good deed is rewarded — not for doing a mitzvah but for doing a good deed. The difference may be whether the reward is received in this world or the next. Mitzvot are generally rewarded in the World to Come (see *Kiddushin* 39b), while good deeds may be rewarded in this world. See *Berachot* 7a and *Seforno* on *Devarim* 7:9.

toward *teshuvah* should be considered in light of the fact that he himself may have been the most important *ba'al teshuvah* in the annals of the Talmud and perhaps in all of Jewish history.[1] There is, to be sure, a certain danger in interpreting an individual's teachings and opinions in light of the life and times the subject lived. We assume that our spiritual heroes had the ability to transcend their subjective experience, and that their opinions are not merely based on limited scope and experiences but rather contain existential truths that make them timeless. Nonetheless, Resh Lakish, being a *ba'al teshuvah*, may have had a more profound understanding of the process of *teshuvah* than did other Sages. We would be well-advised to be especially attentive to his expressions regarding *teshuvah* and to carefully study his personal metamorphosis.[2]

In order to appreciate the enormity of his return, we need to understand who Reish Lakish was. According to the composite that emerges from various primary and secondary sources, Reish Lakish's early education was befitting a young Jewish man.[3] Later he left his study and spent time as a circus performer and a gladiator, and eventually became a thief and murderer[4] and apparently

---

1　Generally everyone's first choice for most celebrated *ba'al teshuvah* is Rabbi Akiva, although according to Rabbeinu Tam technically the term *ba'al teshuvah* would be inappropriate for Rabbi Akiva who, though ignorant, was always a practicing Jew. See *Tosafot* on *Ketubot* 62b ("*D'hava*"). For more on Rabbi Akiva, see my comments above in "Pursuit of Righteousness."

2　In a lecture given on *Parashat Bo,* January 10, 1976, Rabbi Soloveitchik made a similar point, as recorded in notes of that lecture: "We find one important thing lacking with Rabbi Yochanan. He never had the experience of sin and *teshuvah*. He had always lived a saintly life. Rabbi Shimon ben Lakish, on the other hand, originally was a sinner, rather an underworld personality, who fortunately came under the influence of Rabbi Yochanan and rose to great heights. Rabbi Yochanan could not understand Reish Lakish's position, much as we may not be able to understand why a person turns to drugs or to alcohol."

3　This is Rabbeinu Tam's understanding. See *Tosafot* on *Bava Metzia* 84a. Rabbeinu Tam writes that Reish Lakish had studied and then rejected Judaism, becoming a robber, before beginning his studies with Rabbi Yochanan. His early education would account for the occasions when Reish Lakish has different traditions from his mentor Rabbi Yochanan. See *Tosafot* on *Yevamot* 57a and on *Eruvin* 65b.

4　*Gittin* 47a: "Reish Lakish once sold himself to the Lydians. He took with him a bag

leader of his "gang."[1]

Perhaps the most amazing tale is told in *Pirkei D'Rabbi Eliezer*:

Ben Azzai[2] said: In order to understand the power of *teshuvah*, come and see from Rabbi Shimon Lakish. He and his two companions [lived] in the hills and robbed and abused anyone who passed their way. What did Rabbi Shimon do? He left his companions to rob [by themselves] and returned to the God of his fathers with a full heart, with fasting and prayer. He would arrive early every morning and evening, spending his time in the house of prayer in front of the Holy One, blessed be He, and he spent all his days involved in learning Torah and gave gifts to the poor. And he never returned to his previous nefarious ways, and his *teshuvah* was accepted.

The day he died his two former companions, the robbers from the hills, died as well. Rav Shimon was placed in the treasure of life [Heaven], while the two companions were placed in the lower recesses of Hell. The two companions said to God, "Master of all worlds, you play favorites! He who robbed with us was placed in Heaven while we were sentenced to the lower recesses of Hell!"

He responded, "He did *teshuvah* while alive and you did not."

---

with a stone in it because he said, 'It is a known fact that on the last day they grant any request [of the man they are about to kill] in order that he may forgive them his murder.' On the last day they said to him, 'What would you like?' He replied: 'I want you to let me tie your arms and seat you in a row and give each one of you a blow and a half with my bag.' He bound them and seated them, and gave each of them a blow with his bag which stunned them. [One of them] ground his teeth at him. 'Are you laughing at me?' he [Reish Lakish] said. 'I have still half a bag left for you.' So he killed them all and made off."

1   *Rashi, Bava Metzia* 84a.

2   This tradition, reported in the name of Ben Azzai, creates an historical problem: According to our understanding, Ben Azzai died long before Reish Lakish was born. One of the two figures in question is mistakenly placed in this story. Being that we know from other sources that Reish Lakish was a criminal, we may safely assume that that part of the tradition is accurate, and it must have been reported in the name of Ben Azzai erroneously. See comments of Rav David Luria to *Pirkei D'Rabbi Eliezer*.

[They said,] "Allow us and we will do incredible *teshuvah*."
He said, "*Teshuvah* is only possible until the day of death."

(Pirkei D'Rabbi Eliezer, ch. 42)

The extent of Rabbi Shimon's metamorphosis from gang member to righteous scholar is striking. The Talmud describes the transitional moment:

One day Rabbi Yochanan was bathing in the Jordan, when Reish Lakish saw him and leaped into the Jordan after him. Said he [Rabbi Yochanan] to him, "Your strength should be for the Torah."

"Your beauty," he replied, "should be for women."

"If you will repent," said he, "I will give you my sister [in marriage], who is more beautiful than I."

He undertook [to repent]; then he wished to return and collect his utensils[1] but could not. Subsequently, [Rabbi Yochanan] taught him Bible and Mishnah and made him into a great man.

(Bava Metzia 84a)

This description, which almost sounds like a comedy of errors, describes the moment that Rabbi Shimon returned to the Jewish community. From a distance he saw a figure bathing in the Jordan River; mistakenly he thought he had spied on an attractive woman. Accordingly he performed an impressive leap and landed in the river right near his prey. Much to his shock, he had actually seen a good-looking rabbi from afar, not an attractive woman.[2]

The exchange between them seems obscure: Rabbi Yochanan says, "Your strength[3] should be better employed for learning To-

---

1   The Aramaic word is *manei*, literally meaning utensils, but the contextual meaning is most likely "clothing," which is the translation found in the ArtScroll Shottenstein edition. Steinzaltz also renders it "clothing"; indeed, this word is used later on in the same passage where is says that Rabbi Yochanan tore his *manei* – there in context it certainly means clothing. The Soncino translation renders it "weapons."

2   The attractiveness of Rabbi Yochanan was legendary. The Talmud a few lines before this story tells us that he did not have a beard — yet he would stand in front of the *mikveh* and bless the women that their children should be as attractive as him.

rah," indicating that he recognizes this wayward member of the community. Reish Lakish's retort sounds as if his only regret is that he would have preferred finding a beautiful woman rather than a sharp-tongued rabbi. Yet this simple exchange was the beginning of a great relationship and paved the way for the emergence of an exemplary scholar, Rabbi Shimon ben Lakish.

Something seems missing, though; where is the spiritual upheaval? Where is the soul searching, introspection, self-analysis? Where is the internal change? Reish Lakish's reason for this decision does not seem terribly lofty. After all, his motivation was an attractive woman, Rabbi Yochanan's available sister. The entire description seems disappointing: A major life change to "get the girl" doesn't seem to be the type of *teshuvah* that has the capacity to reach the very throne of God.

But if we pay careful attention to the words of Rabbi Yochanan, perhaps we can learn something profound about *teshuvah*. He says (initially) two words: *"cheilach l'oraita"* — use your strength for Torah. With great simplicity Rav Yochanan reveals the highest level of *teshuvah* — the use of all of one's capabilities in the service of God. He doesn't say "reject who you were" — rather, "transform who you were."

In the aftermath of this meeting we are told that Reish Lakish attempted to return to the other side of the river, but he could not, as if he no longer had the strength and dexterity to perform the sort of feat which he performed moments before. Perhaps *teshuvah* motivated by ulterior motives creates an individual who sees *teshuvah* as a total rejection of who he once was. Rashi explains that merely accepting upon himself Torah rendered him unable to make impressive leaps anymore. At this point, he is not yet described as a learned or great man. He has only gone so far as to merely accept upon himself a plan of action.

We may conclude that this is a description of an inferior type of *teshuvah* — motivated by mundane desires, coupled with a rejec-

---

3   See *Chullin* 125a.

tion of personality. Yet Rabbi Yochanan gave him the key to elevated *teshuvah*: "Use your strength for Torah."

The continuation of the Talmud's narrative is tragic; it illustrates the power of words and the capacity we have to hurt one another:

> Now, one day there was a dispute in the house of study [with respect to] a sword, knife, dagger, spear, hand-saw, and a scythe — at what stage [of their manufacture] can they become impure? When their manufacture is finished. And when is their manufacture finished? Rabbi Yochanan ruled: When they are tempered in a furnace. Reish Lakish maintained: When they have been furbished in water.
>
> Said he to him: "A robber knows his trade."
>
> Said he to him, "And wherewith have you benefited me? There [as a robber] I was called 'master,' and here I am called 'master.' "
>
> "By bringing you under the wings of the *Shechinah*," he retorted.
>
> Rabbi Yochanan became depressed, and Reish Lakish became physically ill. His sister [i.e., Rabbi Yochanan's, the wife of Reish Lakish] came and wept before him: "Forgive him for the sake of my son," she pleaded.
>
> He replied, " 'Leave your fatherless children. I will preserve them alive' (*Yirmiyahu* 49:11)."
>
> "For the sake of my widowhood then!"
>
> "And let your widows trust in Me' (ibid.)," he assured her.
>
> Reish Lakish died, and Rabbi Yochanan was plunged into deep grief.[1] Said the Rabbis, "Who shall go to ease his mind? Let Rabbi Elazar ben Pedat go, whose disquisitions are very subtle."
>
> So he went and sat before him; and on every dictum uttered by Rabbi Yochanan he observed: "There is a *beraita* which supports you."

---

1 Subsequently Rabbi Yochanan apparently entertained the idea of learning with the son of Reish Lakaish but was rebuffed by his sister (*Ta'anit* 9a).

"Are you as the son of Lakisha?" he complained. "When I stated a law, the son of Lakisha used to raise twenty-four objections,[1] to which I gave twenty-four answers, which consequently led to a fuller comprehension of the law; while you say, 'A *beraita* has been taught which supports you.' Do I not know myself that my dicta are right?"

Thus he went on rending his garments and weeping, "Where are you, O son of Lakisha? Where are you, O son of Lakisha?" And he cried thus until he lost his sanity. Thereupon the Rabbis prayed for him, and he died.[2]

(Bava Metzia 84a)

It is overwhelming how three words (in Aramaic, five in English) could destroy two lives and leave many more victims. Rabbi Yochanan surely did not intend to insult or harm his friend and colleague — indeed as soon as he understood that Reish Lakish was hurt by his words, Rabbi Yochanan became depressed and ill.[3] Despite all these years as a committed Jew and scholar, the pain of Rabbi Yochanan dredging up his sordid past was overwhelming for Reish Lakish. Rabbi Yochanan most likely wanted to impress on the other students that when it comes to the area of weapons, Reish Lakish was the expert.[4] However, his choice of words,[5] which may have been said in a humorous or ironic manner, were devastating.[6]

1 See *Menachot* 93b.
2 The Rabbis prayed for mercy, which God in His infinite wisdom interpreted as death. Regarding the permissibility of prayer for someone's death, see *Ketubot* 104a, *Nedarim* 40a, and the comments of the Ran. The *Aruch HaShulchan* rules like the Ran, while Rav Moshe Feinstein limits the scope of the Ran's ruling. See *Iggrot Moshe, Choshen Mishpat,* vol. 2, section 74.
3 The Talmud reports that on another occasion Rav Yochanan caused the demise of a scholar due to his perceived slight — see *Bava Kama* 117a. In that instance, Rabbi Yochanan did pray and Rabbi Kahana returned to the living.
4 Rabbi Yochanan may have been a smith; he is called on occasion "bar Napcha," which means "son of a smith." Alternatively, his father was a smith or the term is a euphemism for his beauty. See *Rashi, Sanhedrin* 96a.
5 One is not permitted to remind a *baal teshuvah* of his previous nefarious deeds; see *Bava Metzia* 58b. Perhaps Rabbi Yochanan was focusing on the positive aspects of the former thief utilizing his knowledge to teach Torah.
6 We do find the emphasis Rabbi Yochanan put on the crime of robbery in his lessons

However, a passing comment which a depressed Rabbi Yochanan makes may clarify for us the power of *teshuvah*. When the other scholars see the condition that Rabbi Yochanan is in, they correctly observe that they need to replace Reish Lakish.[1] They bring an able scholar who is ridiculed by Rabbi Yochanan for being a sycophant. When the competent Rabbi Elazer ben Pedat supported the teachings of Rabbi Yochanan, he was dismissed as being unnecessary. But more than unnecessary, he was told that he could not compare to Reish Lakish,[2] for Reish Lakish attacked every idea that Rabbi Yochanan put forward. This is why he was loved. Rabbi Yochanan did not need students who agreed with everything he said — rather the student who could generate an attack was cherished. For when thesis and antithesis collide, an enriched synthesis is the result.

An incredible observation emerges. The reason Rabbi Yochanan loved Reish Lakish was for his attacking, aggressive style. It was the ruffian in Reish Lakish that he loved, the ruffian with one caveat, that he channel his attacking style for the use of Torah, not for the sake of money, intimidation, or fear. "Use your strength for Torah — *cheilach l'oraita*." Moreover, the word *cheilach* doesn't merely mean strength — the connotation is from the realm of soldiering. "Use your attacking skills in a *beit midrash* and not on a dark, abandoned road." Rabbi Yochanan encourages the wayward Shimon ben Lakish not to abandon who he is — rather to channel his gifts in the service of Torah, to become a soldier in the army of God.[3]

We noted initially that before Reish Lakish had learned and become "a great man" he rejected who he was. Perhaps embarrassed by his previous exploits, he rejects that part of his personality. He can no longer leap to the "other side" — he has lost the agility and strength to leap and the other side is a place rejected, a place which represents the person he no longer wishes to be. However, we now

---

with Reish Lakish. See *Kohelet Rabbah* 3:12.

1   Rabbi Yochanan described Reish Lakish as being his equal; see *Ketubot* 84b.

2   See *Yevamot* 72b.

3   See *Makkot* 10b, where Reish Lakish teaches that Divine retribution awaits sinners.

know that over the years Rabbi Yochanan brought out and nurtured the perceived darker side of Reish Lakish's character and taught him to use them in the service of God. This is what *teshuvah* motivated by love of God is about — not a rejection of the past, but rather an elevation of the past motivated and punctuated by deep love of God.

There is an obscure passage in the *Talmud Yerushalmi* which bears out this idea in remarkable fashion.

> Rabbi Isi[1] was caught through an act of treachery. Rabbi Yonatan[2] said, "Let the dead be wrapped in his shrouds" [i.e., there is no hope for him].
>
> Rabbi Shimon ben Lakish said, "I will kill or be killed[3] [for his release], I will go and return him by force." He went and appeased them [i.e., the captors].
>
> *(Yerushalmi, Terumot 8:4, 46b)*

In this remarkable passage we witness the fusion of the former highwayman and present sage: Rather than rejecting his past, he uses it — not to take life but to preserve life. This heroic action is undertaken by Rabbi Shimon ben Lakish the rabbi — who held human life with great esteem; Shimon the Robber never would have been interested in a mission with no payoff. But Shimon the Rabbi never would have succeeded at this mission had his youthful years not been spent honing his skills of sword and mayhem.[4]

This life-saving act transpired because the robber became a rabbi. Such is *teshuvah* motivated by love of God: It allows the sinner to transform himself, the sinful behavior of the past becoming something positive when seen through the prism of new context

---

1   Some texts read "Imi."
2   Some have suggested that the text should read "Yochanan." See Z. Frankel, *Mevo HaYerushalmi*, p. 130, and Rabbi Y. Lau, *Responsa Yachel Yisrael*, section 73.
3   Skoloff, in *A Dictionary of Jewish Palestinian Aramaic* (Bar Ilan University Press, 1990, p. 487), translates this phrase "before I kill and am killed." A modern English colloquial usage would be "over my dead body." See page 386. My thanks to Dr. Leib Moscovitz, who aided me with the translation of this passage.
4   In the same section a second tale relates how Reish Lakish once interceded and liberated some money which had been stolen from Rabbi Yochanan.

and purpose. When Rabbi Shimon underwent a metamorphosis and began serving God exclusively through love, his former transactions became transposed well into meritorious action.[1] Had Rabbi Shimon never learned to use a sword, had he not known how robbers think and act, Rabbi Isi never would have been liberated. Rabbi Isi was saved due to Rabbi Shimon's misspent youth, which in retrospect became the foundation for future meritorious action.

Whether or not his own experiences changed or enhanced Reish Lakish's perspective on the laws of *teshuvah* is a question we cannot answer.[2] But his personal experience certainly serves as a model of the possibilities of *teshuvah*, one where mistakes of the past become reinterpreted as a foundation for mitzvot in the future.

We can certainly imagine Reish Lakish sitting alone in the *beit midrash* the night after Rabbi Isi was liberated. The celebration of the improbable rescue had ended, and now Reish Lakish is alone with his thoughts. The greatest rabbi of the age had given up the prisoner for dead, because the greatest rabbi did not himself know how to handle a weapon. On the other hand, the former bandit/circus performer/gladiator did know how to use a weapon and how to speak with some degree of intimidation in negotiations for the release of his colleague. Such is *teshuvah* motivated by love; the use of all of one's skills and experience in the single-minded attempt to serve God. Such *teshuvah* turns sins into merits.[3]

---

1   The Talmud in *Bava Metzia* 85b reports that Reish Lakish made marks by the cemetery of graves of the righteous in order to insure that *kohanim* not become defiled. One wonders if this was some sort of rectification for previous behavior.

2   In *Sanhedrin* 58b Reish Lakish teaches that even to lift one's hand to strike a neighbor is criminal. Is this pronouncement somehow motivated by his past?

3   See Rabbi Yosef Soloveitchik in *Halakhic Man* (Philadelphia: JPS, 1983), p. 116f.

Yom Kippur

The Inner Sanctum

T he *avodah* — the special once-a-year service performed on Yom Kippur, which helps bring forgiveness for the entire community of Israel — is described in the Torah in the book of *Vayikra*:

> God spoke to Moshe after the death of Aharon's two sons, when they approached before God and they died: And God said to Moshe, "Speak to Aharon, your brother — he shall not come at all times into the Sanctuary, within the curtain, in front of the cover that is upon the Ark, so that he should not die; for in a cloud I will appear upon the Ark-cover."
>
> *(Vayikra 16:1–2)*

After the death of the two sons of Aharon, who perished when they approached God in an inappropriate fashion, the Torah provides instructions for the proper entrance to the holy area "within the curtain." This is a place where God is manifest; the symbol of the epiphany is a cloud. The inner sanctum, the place of extreme holiness, can only be approached when performing the proper rites; the consequence of inappropriate entrance is death.[1] Toward the end of the narrative we are told that this service may only be

---

1   Rashi writes, "For if he comes into the Holy of Holies at any time other than Yom Kippur he will die" (*Rashi, Vayikra* 16:2).

performed on one day a year, a day that has become known as Yom Kippur:

> This shall remain for you an eternal decree — in the seventh month, on the tenth of the month, you shall afflict yourselves and you shall not do any work, neither the native nor the proselyte who dwells among you, for on this day He shall provide atonement for you to cleanse you from all your sins; before God shall you be cleansed. It is a sabbath of complete rest for you, and you shall afflict yourselves; an eternal decree.
>
> *(Ibid., 29–31)*

The Torah enumerates many rites that must be performed on that day, but the inner sanctum, the cloud, and the death sentence for violating it are mentioned only in the context of one action — the entry into the area behind the curtain, which is therefore considered the apex of the ritual.

> He shall take a shovelful of fiery coals from atop the Altar that is before God and his cupped handsful of finely ground incense-spices and bring it within the curtain. He shall place the incense upon the fire before God — so that the cloud of the incense shall blanket the Ark-cover that is atop the [Tablets of the] Testimony — so that he shall not die.
>
> *(Ibid., 12–13)*

The cloud that envelops the area is a result of the *ketoret* — the incense that is brought inside. Regarding this central service we find a difference of opinion between mainstream Rabbinic authorities and the Sadducees. Two groups, called by historians Pharisees and Sadducees, vied for control of the Temple and religious leadership during Second Temple times.[1] Each claimed to know the

---

1 The Rambam (commentary to *Pirkei Avot* 1:3) understood that the Sadducee leadership was for the most part the former Hellenized Jews who preferred new Greek ideas to "old" Jewish ones. When the Greeks were expelled, these Jews — who in reality had rejected the oral and the written Torah — felt unable to publicly reject the written Torah, so they rejected what they could, namely the oral tradition. Whether this analysis would stand up to critical scholarship, especially in light of

proper way to perform the Yom Kippur service; each claimed to be the bearer of the true tradition.

The mainstream approach to the argument has been that the Pharisees followed the Torah as explained by the rabbis through the generations, while the Sadducees felt themselves unconstrained by Rabbinic exegesis.[1] The Rabbis taught that the *kohein gadol* should enter the inner sanctum and then perform the service, namely the incense should be offered only in the Kodesh HaKedashim, while the Sadducees taught the incense was prepared outside and carried in already lit. This "minor" distinction sufficed to pit the two groups against one another.

As far as we can ascertain, the Pharisaic approach was almost always the one performed, even though the high priesthood became a position that could be bought for money[2] during the Second Commonwealth, and many a corrupt or unlearned priest[3] craved the opportunity to be bedecked in finery and be the star of the production. Yearly, the leaders would instruct the *kohein gadol* in the laws which he needed to know to represent the people. At the end of the instructions they would make the *kohein* vow that he would perform the procedure according to tradition and not in the manner of the Sadducees:

The elders of the court handed him over to the elders of the priest-

the scrolls unearthed in the Judean Desert, is questionable, unless the Rambam is only describing the beliefs of the originators of the sects, but not the actual sect.

1   The Sadducees should not be confused with the Kararites, both for historical reasons and for ideological reasons. These heretical groups were separated by hundreds of years. The Kararites rejected the existence of oral Torah, while the Sadducees rejected the Rabbinic tradition of the oral Torah; Sadducees did follow an oral "tradition," though it was not the same as the Rabbinic tradition.

2   The Talmud (*Yoma* 18a) tells of one transaction: "A tarkabful of denars did Martha the daughter of Boethus give to King Yannai to nominate Yehoshua ben Gamla as one of the high priests."

3   The ignorance of some of these priests is illustrated by the fact that at times they didn't even know how to read: "If he [the high priest] were a sage he would expound, and if not, the disciples of the sages would expound before him. If he was familiar with reading [the Scriptures] he would read. If not, they would read before him. From what would they read before him? From *Iyov*, *Ezra*, and *Divrei HaYamim*" (*Yoma* 18b).

hood and they took him up to the upper chamber to the house of Avtinas. They adjured him and took their leave, as they said to him: "Sir High Priest, we are messengers of the court and you are our messenger and the messenger of the court. We adjure you by Him who made His Name dwell in this house that you do not change anything of what we said to you." He turned aside and wept and they turned aside and wept.

(Yoma 18b)

Why this became the center of the controversy is unclear; perhaps the Sadducees felt the need to express their beliefs and dictate and control the service on this holiest of days more than any other. However, other episodes reported in the Talmud indicate that the difference went beyond the technical, beyond any struggle for control. In one of the most tragic episodes of the Second Temple period, the longstanding incumbent *kohein gadol* abandoned Rabbinic tradition, which he had himself had practiced for many years:

Have we not learned: Do not believe in yourself until the day of your death? For lo, Yochanan Kohein Gadol officiated as high priest for eighty years and in the end he became a heretic.[1]

(Berachot 29a)[2]

What was it that pulled this religious leader to abandon his own long-held traditions and practices? Perhaps it is significant that the method of the service according to the Sadducee rite was technically simpler: Performing the service as mandated by the halachah required far greater dexterity. Could ease alone have provided the motivation? Such a position may be supported by evidence of the arguments raised by a different,[3]

---

1   The generic term for heretic, min, is used here in some published texts, implying Sadducee. In his commentary to *Kiddushin* 66a, the Ritva quotes this passage, actually using the term "Sadducee," a reading found in various published editions.

2   See *Yoma* 9a and *Sotah* 33a, 47a–b.

3   One must use caution in any discussion of either the Sadducees or Pharisees, for positions associated with one in any particular source are associated with the other in other sources. For a more comprehensive discussion of this subject, a presentation of the primary materials, and analysis of the secondary sources, see Joseph Tabori, *Jewish Festivals in the Time of the Mishna and Talmud*, pp. 259–274.

contemporaneous sect regarding a different issue:

> For the Boethusians held that Shavuot must always be on the day after Shabbat. But Rabbi Yochanan ben Zakkai entered into discussion with them, saying, "Fools that you are! From where do you derive it?"
> Not one of them was able to answer him, save one old man who commenced to babble and said, "Moshe our teacher was a great lover of Israel, and knowing full well that Shavuot lasted only one day, he therefore fixed it on the day after Shabbat so that Israel might enjoy themselves for two successive days."
>
> *(Menachot 65a)*

While the convenience of long weekends is no trifle, it is hard to believe that such an argument would tempt a long-standing *kohein gadol* to adopt Sadducean practice. Moreover, the Talmud records a case of a Sadducee who finally had the chance to perform the rite according to his beliefs, with devastating results:

> There was a Sadducee who had arranged the incense without, and then brought it inside. As he left he was exceedingly glad. On his coming out his father met him and said to him: "My son, although we are Sadducees, we are afraid of the Pharisees."[1]
> He replied: "All my life was I aggrieved because of this scriptural verse: 'For in a cloud I will appear upon the Ark-cover.' I would say: When shall the opportunity come to my hand so that I might fulfill it? Now that such opportunity has come to my hand, should I not have fulfilled it?"
> It is reported that it took only a few days until he died and was thrown on the dungheap and worms came forth from his nose. Some say: He was smitten as he came out [of the Holy of Holies]. For Rabbi Chiya taught: "Some sort of a noise was

---

1   In the *Tosefta Yoma* 1:8, the same story is told of "a certain Beitusi" whose father explained that their position is theoretical and not practical: "Even though we expound [thus], we do not [so] practice; we heed the words of the Sages. I wonder if you will live long...."

heard in the Temple Court, for an angel had come and struck him down on his face [to the ground], and his brethren the priests came in and they found a trace like that of a calf's foot on his shoulder, as it is written: 'And their feet were straight feet, and the sole of their feet was like the sole of a calf's foot' (_Yechezkel_ 1:7).

(Yoma 19b)

It is hard to believe that small pleasures or convenience would be worth forfeiting one's life for, as did this renegade _kohein gadol_. Can it be possible that any _kohein_, or any Jew, did not know the consequences of improper service in the Holy of Holies on Yom Kippur?[1] Surely, this _kohein gadol_ must have believed that his method of performing the Yom Kippur ritual was the correct one; indeed, this _gemara_ reflects the well-known tradition that the death sentence for inappropriate service in the Holy of Holies is both absolute and, according to some, immediate.

The two versions of the demise of the _kohein_ recorded in this _gemara_ may be associated with two different aspects of the sin. The first, "worms came forth from his nose," relates directly to the _ketoret_ and its pleasant scent: this person who performed the rite in an inappropriate manner had worms come from his nose. The sense of smell was the only one of the senses not corrupted in the sin of eating from the Tree of Knowledge of Good and Evil.[2] This last, pure sense may be the vehicle through which mankind regains purity Yom Kippur. The Sadducee _kohein gadol_, then, sullies the _ketoret_, transgressing with the sense of smell, and is therefore punished in kind.

The second approach spoke of an imprint of a calf's foot on his shoulder. The calf relates to the sin of the golden calf (which was confused with the calf's foot from the vision of Yechezkel). The

---

1 Following the Rambam's identification of the Sadducees with Hellenized Jews, we might see hints of hedonism in this position. Nonetheless, such a position is incongruous with the life-ending gesture taken by this _kohein_, unless he never believed that he would perish. See Rambam's commenary to _Avot_ 1:3.

2 _Bnei Yissachar_, Purim.

golden calf is the prototype of inappropriate worship; therefore it is the calf from the vision of Yechezkel that comes down to stomp on this "golden calf" worshiper. We must recall that Yom Kippur was the day that the Jews were finally forgiven for the sin of the golden calf.[1]

The Sadducee *kohein gadol* in this episode sounds incredibly sincere: He attests to having waited his entire life for this moment, to fulfill this verse. Mere pragmatism, even fear of retribution by the Pharisees, could not sway him. He insisted on fulfilling the Torah as he understood it. This should be our strongest indication that the difference between the two methods of Yom Kippur service are more than cosmetic, more than technical. The divergence between Rabbinic practice and Saducean practice was based upon something much deeper, much stronger.

Amazingly, the speech given by this *kohein gadol* is echoed by none other that the great Rabbi Akiva when he chooses death over submission to the Roman decree to cease Torah study:

> When Rabbi Akiva was taken out for execution, it was the hour for the recital of the Shema, and while they combed his flesh with iron combs, he was accepting upon himself the Kingship of Heaven. His disciples said to him: "Our teacher, even to this point?"
>
> He said to them: "All my days I have been troubled by this verse, 'with all your soul' (*Devarim* 6:5), [which I interpret,] 'even if He takes your soul.' I said: When shall I have the opportunity of fulfilling this? Now that I have the opportunity, shall I not fulfill it?" He prolonged the word *echad* until he expired while saying it.
>
> *(Berachot 61b)*

Both speakers express a lifelong ambition to fulfill a verse, and now with the opportunity presented it would not be lost. How

---

1   The clothes worn by the *kohein gadol* on Yom Kippur in the inner sanctum were not to be made of gold so as not to serve as a reminder of the sin of the golden calf. See *Rashi, Vayikra* 16:4, based on *Rosh HaShanah* 26a.

ironic that the great gesture of martyrdom of Akiva is thus linked to this wrongheaded rebellious priest. The literary allusion was most likely not lost on Akiva's audience: Their master was subtly telling them what is worth dying for, and what is a sad waste of life. People are willing to sacrifice their lives for all types of causes; who is the true martyr and who the fool?

What, then, is at the heart of the argument between the Sadducees and tradition? The Rabbis claimed that the *ketoret* was burned inside, while the Sadducees argued that it was to be lit outside and then carried in. Apparently, the Sadducees felt that only when covered by a cloud of smoke can man enter that awesome place; it is inappropriate for man to stand before God in the Holy of Holies while uncovered. Perhaps the deaths of Aharon's sons served as a warning to stay away from brazenly approaching holiness.

Rabbinic tradition stands in contrast to this viewpoint: When man follows the Word of God, he is sufficiently equipped to enter the Holy of Holies and then to create the cloud within it.[1] We recall that in Eden, only after partaking of the forbidden fruit did man feel the need to hide from God.

> And they heard the voice of God, the Lord, walking in the garden in the cool of the day; and Adam and his wife hid themselves from the presence of God, the Lord, among the trees of the Garden.
>
> *(Bereishit 3:8)*

The cloud of *ketoret* alludes to Torah as the link between man and God: This image of entering the cloud reminds us of the Revelation, when Moshe entered the cloud to receive the Torah. Rashi explains the relationship:

> "For in a cloud I will appear" means for I constantly show Myself there with My pillar of cloud, and because the revelation of My *Shechinah* takes place there he should take care not to make

---

1 Rabbeinu Bechaya (commentary to *Vayikra* 16:2) says that once inside the cloud is needed so that one not look brazenly at the holiness.

it his habit to come there. This is the literal meaning of the verse. The halachic explanation is: He shall not come into the Holy of Holies except with a cloud of incense on the Day of Atonement.

(Rashi, Vayikra 16:2)

Rashi draws a line between this cloud of incense and the cloud that hovered above Sinai, the "pillar of cloud." The Ramban goes even further, explaining that the entire idea of a Temple was for the cloud from Sinai to have a permanent resting place: This singular Sinaitic experience was meant to have a yearly repetition. The date of Yom Kippur also points in this direction, for on the tenth of Tishrei the people of Israel were forgiven for the sin at Sinai, the golden calf. It is the day that the Torah was finally accepted on earth, when Moshe descended with the new tablets.[1]

The Sadducee *kohein gadol* felt the need to cover himself, to enter the Holy of Holies hidden in the cloud of *ketoret*. In this view, God's greatness makes Him unapproachable; even on that one day a year when man does come close he must cover up. Perhaps this argument represented the entire Sadducee approach: Man must be distant from God because of His greatness. Man therefore cannot be a part of the halachic process, creating new interpretations and applications of the Word of God. In the philosophy of the Sadducees, man is incapable of ongoing dialogue with God.

While the Sadducees saw God as overly distant and ultimately nonapproachable, the Rabbis taught that man could enter, as Moshe did, and form a partnership with God, and even have a say in the understanding of Torah. Through the study of Torah we can approach God. All of this is encapsulated within the ritual of the *ketoret* on Yom Kippur and is expressed by the order in which the various steps are carried out: Does the *kohein gadol* enter "as is" or covered by the cloud of *ketoret*?[2]

---

1   See *Ta'anit* 26a and *Rashi* s.v. *"Zeh Matan Torah."*
2   This suggestion was arrived at while discussing this topic with my brother, Rav Yair Kahn.

It is no coincidence that the story of Rabbi Akiva's martyrdom for the sake of Torah study is read each year as part of the *mussaf* prayer on Yom Kippur, immediately following the description of the rites of the day performed by the *kohein gadol*. The verse of Shema which perturbed Rabbi Akiva, declaring God's oneness and unity, also commands us to be one with God, and is the most universal and enduring refutation of the philosophy of the Sadducees.

As the Yom Kippur service comes to an end, there is a moment of special closeness with God. The Ark is open and the entire congregation stands, looking at the Torah within. We conclude our prayer with the Shema, then calling out in unison "Blessed be the glorious Name of the King forever and ever." With perfect faith we declare, "God is the Lord"; the shofar is sounded,[1] harkening us back to the moment when the Torah was given at Sinai, and we conclude: "Next year in Yerushalayim!" The entire community returns to their homes purged of sin, cleansed. They feel one with God. This time, the hour of *ne'ilah*, is our own version of the inner sanctum, the closest we can get to God on this special day of approaching Him. The vehicle of the *ketoret* is no longer available to us, but God maintains His ties to us, and we may draw near to Him through Torah. Rabbi Akiva must surely be quite proud.

> For on this day He shall provide atonement for you to cleanse you from all your sins; before God shall you be cleansed.
>
> *(Vayikra 16:30)*

The key to the cleansing process on Yom Kippur is the belief that despite God's greatness and man's inadequacy, we can stand in front of God and be thus cleansed. When man sinned the very first time he hid from God;[2] now to heal that sin man needs to feel the ability that indeed he can stand in front of God and be cleansed.

---

1   The Torah was given with a shofar blast; see "The *Akeidah*: Father and Son."

2   *Bereishit* 3:8: "Adam and his wife hid themselves from the presence of the Lord God among the trees of the garden."

Sukkot

A Universal Holiday?

T he Talmud relates that in the future, when the nations of the world will complain about the apparent discrimination against non-Jews as compared to the treatment enjoyed by the Jews, they will be told that the difference stems from the Jews' adherence to the Torah.

> The nations will then plead, "Offer us the Torah anew and we will follow it."
>
> "You foolish people," God will answer, "he who prepares on the eve of Shabbat can eat on Shabbat, but he who made no preparations, what can he eat? Nevertheless, I have an easy commandment called sukkah, go and fulfill it...."
>
> Why is it called an easy commandment? Because it has no expense. Immediately each one will build a sukkah on his roof, but God will cause the sun to blaze as if it were the summer solstice. Each one will then kick his sukkah, and leave....
>
> Thereupon God will laugh, as it is said, "He that sits in heaven and laughs" (*Tehillim* 2:4).
>
> *(Avodah Zarah 3a–b)*

Although this passage is a difficult one, I would like to focus on one of its main themes: that non-Jews will not be able to keep the commandment of sukkah. The reason that this is so strange is that of all the holidays, Sukkot has been perceived as the most universal. The Talmud teaches:

> Why are seventy offerings brought on Sukkot? For the [merit of the] seventy nations of the world.[1]
>
> *(Sukkah 55b)*

Rashi explains:

> To bring forgiveness for them [the seventy nations], so that rain shall fall all over the world.

The Sages stressed that Sukkot has a universal element which is clearly absent in the other festivals: Pesach represents the Exodus from Egypt and the emergence of a Jewish nation, while Shavuot celebrates the giving of the Torah. It seems paradoxical to find this expression of the inability of the nations of the world to relate to God specifically in the context of Sukkot. We may theorize that specifically on Sukkot, when the Jews concerned themselves with the welfare of non-Jews, the non-Jews were expected to respond and to relate to God directly. There is, however, another passage which makes this approach untenable.

> And it shall come to pass, that everyone who is left of all the nations who came up against Yerushalayim, shall go up from year to year to worship the King, the God of Hosts, and to keep the holiday of Sukkot. And whoever does not come...to Yerushalayim...upon them there will be no rain.
>
> *(Zecharyah 14:16–17)*

This passage from the prophecy of Zecharyah describes the aftermath of apocalyptic battles, when the vanquished nations will celebrate Sukkot. How, then, can the Talmud suggest that the nations will be given the commandment of sukkot and fail, when the biblical passage describes their successful adherence to this precept

---

1   The concept that there are seventy nations is a popular one in Rabbinic thought. See *Bereishit Rabbah* 66:4. The seventy nations are associated with the seventy names mentioned in the eleventh chapter of *Bereishit*.

in the future? While the Talmud contains many explanations of biblical teachings, the Talmud does not have the mandate to argue with the prophets.[1] Our question, then, is quite simple: How can the Talmud relate that in the future the nations of the world will be unable to keep Sukkot when the prophet tells us that they will keep Sukkot in the future?

I believe that in the resolution of this apparent contradiction lies the essence of Sukkot.

There are two distinct aspects to the holiday of Sukkot, represented by two commandments in the Torah:

> On the fifteenth of the seventh month, when you have gathered in the fruit of the land, you shall keep a festival for God seven days.... And you shall take for yourselves on the first day the fruit of a hadar [etrog], branches of palm trees [lulav], the boughs of thick-leaved trees [aravot], and willows of the brook [haddasim], and you shall rejoice before your God seven days. And you shall keep it as a holiday seven days a year; it shall be a statute forever to celebrate. You shall sit in booths [sukkot] seven days, every citizen of Israel shall sit in the sukkot, in order to inform all generations that in sukkot the Jews dwelled when I liberated them from Egypt.
>
> (Vayikra 23:39–43)

The Torah speaks on the one hand of "gathering fruit" and, as a response, "taking" produce, while on the other hand it speaks of sitting in the sukkah, as the people who left Egypt had done. We see two commandments: 1) taking the four species, and 2) living in booths or "sukkot." One commandment has an agricultural impetus, the other a historical one. The agricultural aspect of the holiday is clearly universal, while the historical aspect is particular to the Jews.

The relationship between the gathering of the fruit and the four species seems clear: After gathering the new fruits, to express our

---

1   See the comments of Rashi in Zecharyah, where he attempts to reconcile the sources.

gratitude to God, we collect these four species. The species which we gather are a tool used for prayer, in order to thank God for the produce we have just harvested and implore that a generous amount be allocated for the coming year. Our Rabbis teach that the allocation of water for the year takes place on Sukkot:

> On Chag [Sukkot] we are judged regarding water.
>
> *(Rosh HaShanah 16a)*

In fact, much of the celebration which took place in Yerushalayim on Sukkot was connected to water, including the Simchat Beit HaSho'eivah ceremony. This, too, was a ritual connected to water, of which the Mishnah says:

> Whoever did not see the Simchat Beit HaSho'eivah never saw real joy in his life.
>
> *(Mishnah Sukkah 5:1)*

The verse spoke of "rejoicing before your God," referring to the Temple in Yerushalayim. Sukkot was uniquely celebrated in Yerushalayim: Armed with the four species, the Jews would come to the Temple and pray for more rain and bounty.[1]

What, however, is the meaning of the other aspect of Sukkot? We are commanded to dwell in booths, because God delivered us in booths. What is the symbolism of these booths? The Talmud records two opinions. Rabbi Eliezer likened God's protection of the Jews, described by the biblical term "sukkah," to a cloud of glory. Rabbi Akiva taught that the Jews were liberated from Egypt they lived in actual booths which protected them from the elements. Both opinions agree that the sukkot signify the special relationship which the Jews have enjoyed with God. The difference lies in respect to the historical reality. Were we protected metaphysically, by a cloud, or were we protected via a physical entity — a sukkah?

Either way, the Jews ventured into the desert, vulnerable to the

---

1   The four species were used in the Temple for all seven days of the Festival. In the rest of the Land of Israel they were used only on the first day. The Rabbis legislated the use of the four species for the duration of Sukkot even outside of the Temple.

elements, putting their faith in God. This is what we commemorate today.[1] This faith in God is the key to Sukkot. For the Jew to leave the comforts of his home and live in a booth, a temporary abode, is the essence of the sukkah experience. We are commanded to make these temporary abodes into our homes for the duration of the seven days of Sukkot. This serves as a reminder of the temporary nature of our existence, helping us focus on the proper relationship between the physical and the spiritual. But most importantly, the sukkah is an expression of trust, the trust that we had in the desert and the trust which we hopefully have today.

Now perhaps we can resolve the inconsistencies. There are two sides to Sukkot: the need for the physical, on the one hand, and the rejection of the physical, in favor of trust in God, on the other. The need for physicality is real, and nothing is as representative of our physical needs as rain. The Hebrew word for rain is *geshem*, which means physical. Yet the source of rain is the clouds referred to by Rabbi Eliezer, clouds of glory, symbolizing the spiritual, the metaphysical.

Clouds are ethereal,[2] beyond our grasp, beyond our understanding. Specifically on Sukkot, we pray for rain. In the wake of Rosh HaShanah and Yom Kippur, when we prayed for our very existence, on Sukkot we are concerned with "quality of life." We pray for the physical; we pray for rain. With dialectical elegance a synthesis is created: We are commanded to leave our homes, the physical anchor in our lives, and enter a home under the clouds, protected by our trust in God.

Our physical existence is brought into sharp contrast with our spiritual life, and the two aspects of Sukkot coexist.[3]

---

1   According to many authorities, remembering the reason for sitting in the sukkah is an integral part of the commandment. Therefore, on Sukkot, aside from sitting in the sukkah, one should mention both opinions regarding the meaning of Sukkot: 1) Sukkot as an extension of the Exodus story, and 2) As a testament to the mighty clouds with which God protected us. See *Mishnah Berurah* 625:1.
2   Revelation often takes place via a cloud. See *Shemot* 13:21, 24:15–16, and 40:38; *Vayikra* 16:13, *Bemidbar* 9:15–23, 12:5, and 14:14; *Devarim* 31:15; *Yeshayah* 4:5; *Yechezkel* 1:4 and 30:3; and *Tehillim* 97:2.

Now we return to our original question: Will the nations of the world be able to observe the holiday of Sukkot? Surely, the answer must consider each aspect of the holiday separately. The passage in *Zecharyah* that spoke of observance by non-Jews of Sukkot stressed that it was in Yerushalayim — "before God." This aspect of Sukkot finds unique expression in Yerushalayim; this is the aspect of thanks and prayer for rain. In fact, the verse continued:

> And whoever does not come...to Yerushalayim...upon them there will be no rain.

The reason for coming to Yerushalayim was to receive the blessing for rain. This aspect of Sukkot surely can be fulfilled by non-Jews. It is, in essence, a recognition of cause and effect; it is pragmatic. The nations of the world can perform this type of service.[1]

However, the other aspect of Sukkot, the building of the sukkah, what the Talmud called a "simple mitzvah," is what the non-Jewish religions, and certainly the pagan religious experience, found so foreign. Here there was no pragmatism, merely trust — trust and love.

> Go and cry out in the ears of Yerushalayim, saying, "Thus says God, 'I remember in your favor the devotion of your youth, your love as a bride, when you followed Me into the wilderness, into land that was not sown.' "
>
> *(Yirmiyah 2:2)*

The sukkah is testimony to that love. Simply being "with God," away from the physical, perhaps only minimizing our physical side, is foreign to the pagan mindset. They were accustomed to difficult commandments which involved giving, sacrificing something dear, in order to find favor with the gods. Conversely, the Talmud asks why it is called an "easy mitzvah."

3 The two elements of sukkah operate in independent spheres with almost no overlap. A notable exception is discerned in the custom of the Arizal to bless the four species specifically in the sukkah.

1 See *Zecharyah* 14:18–19, where it is recounted that not all the peoples of the world will be willing to keep Sukkot in Yerushalayim.

Why is it called an easy commandment? Because it has no expense.

This the pagans found bizarre: What is a God who asks for nothing?

The Talmud further relates:

But does not Rabba say whoever is vexed [by the sukkah] is freed of the obligation of sukkah?

(Avodah Zarah 3b)

A law of sukkah is that someone extremely bothered by the sukkah is exempt; therefore, the non-Jews who found themselves in a hot sukkah were technically exempt. This is even more alien to pagan ideas; if a god asks for something difficult, are you exempt? The response of the non-Jews was to kick down the sukkah, as if to say, "Enough is enough. How can man be expected to relate to such a deity?"

This aspect of sukkah is a uniquely Jewish experience: living with God, remembering the days of our youth when we followed God like a lovesick bride, not questioning, accepting, trusting. This aspect of Sukkot cannot be enjoyed by the non-Jews who will, in Messianic times, seek equal treatment. To our great joy and pleasure, we may enjoy this unique and exclusive relationship with God each year on the occasion of Sukkot.

Simchat Torah

"Chazak"

With the parashah of *V'Zot HaBerachah*, the Torah reaches its conclusion. While the vast majority of the parashah contains the blessing pronounced by Moshe prior to his death, the parashah also records the death of Moshe. Surely the death of such an unparalleled leader created a vacuum that is hard for us to imagine. Moshe wore many hats; he was teacher, warrior, and perhaps king.[1] Moshe was a spiritual and religious leader par excellence. He was also the visionary who helped facilitate the transfer of an enormous population from servitude in Egypt to within a hairsbreadth of the Promised Land.

Of all the facets of Moshe's multifaceted personality, the one which is recorded for posterity as his appellation is "Moshe Rabbeinu" — the teacher, the rebbe. He is the man who ascended Sinai and brought down the Torah. Any person who would take his place would do so with the knowledge that in any comparison he would fall short. Others could learn Torah — but who else could wrest it from the hands of angels and bring a piece of divinity to earth?[2]

---

1   The verse "And he was king in Yeshurun, when the heads of the people and the tribes of Israel were gathered together" (*Devarim* 33:5) may apply to Moshe. See Ibn Ezra on the verse. Rashi opines that the verse refers to the King of Kings. However, see *Rashi* on *Sanhedrin* 36a s.v. *"Bemakom echad."*

The task of following Moshe fell upon Yehoshua bin Nun. The leaders of that generation indeed lamented their plight:

"And You shall put of Your honor upon him" (*Bemidbar* 27:20) — but not all Your honor. The elders of that generation said: "The countenance of Moshe was like that of the sun; the countenance of Yehoshua was like that of the moon. Alas, for such shame! Alas for such reproach!"

(Bava Batra 75a)

Yehoshua glowed — but his glow was dim in comparison to Moshe. When Moshe died, the people stopped learning.

When a *chacham* dies, his house of study is idle; when the *av beit din* dies all the study houses in his city are idle and [the people of the synagogue] enter the synagogue[s] and change their [usual] places: those who [usually] sit in the north sit in the south and those who [usually] sit in the south sit in the north. When a *nasi* dies, all the study houses are idle and the people of the synagogue enter the synagogue.

(Moed Katan 22b)

How much more so when Moshe died. *Tosafot* (*Menachot* 30a) report that the custom to say *tziduk hadin* on Shabbat at *minchah* emanates from the death of Moshe. There is still a custom not to be involved in the study of Torah after *minchah* time on Shabbat to commemorate the death of Moshe.[1]

The Rabbis articulate the loss of Moshe also in quantitative terms. With Moshe's death, learning and knowledge were severely affected.

---

2   See *Shabbat* 88b: "When Moshe ascended on high, the ministering angels said before the Holy One, blessed be He, 'Sovereign of the Universe! What business has one born of woman amongst us?' 'He has come to receive the Torah,' answered He to them. Said they to Him, 'That secret treasure, which has been hidden by You for 974 generations before the world was created, You desire to give to flesh and blood? What is man, that You are mindful of him, and the son of man, that You visit him? O God, our Lord, how excellent is Your name in all the earth! Who has set Your glory [the Torah] upon the Heavens!' "

1   See *Orach Chaim* 292:2 and *Mishnah Berurah* 6–8.

A thousand and seven hundred *kal vachomers* and *gezeirah shavahs* and specifications of the Scribes were forgotten during the period of mourning for Moshe. Said Rabbi Abuha: "Nevertheless, Otniel ben Kenaz restored [these forgotten teachings] as a result of his dialectics, as it says: 'And Otniel ben Kenaz, the brother of Kaleiv, took it...' (*Yehoshua* 15:17)."

(Temurah 16a)

With the demise of Moshe Torah was forgotten. It is interesting that it was not Yehoshua who restored the learning, but Otniel. Perhaps Yehoshua took the death of Moshe in a harder manner than others did.[1] Nonetheless, the people lamented Moshe's demise and therefore Yehoshua's ascension.

What was it about Yehoshua that merited his filling Moshe's enormous shoes? When it comes to scholarship arguably Otniel was superior.

Rashi in his commentary to *Avot*[2] implies that in scholarship Pinchas was the superior to Yehoshua. He cites a verse in *Malachi* and applies it to Pinchas:

The Torah of truth was in his mouth, and iniquity was not found in his lips; he walked with Me in peace and uprightness, and he turned many away from iniquity. For the priest's lips should guard knowledge, and they should seek the Torah from his mouth; for he is a messenger [or angel] of the Lord of Hosts.

(Malachi 2:6–7)

The priest in question who had the true Torah in his mouth was

---

1   From *Sanhedrin* 68a, we see that Rabbi Akiva took the death of his teacher Rabbi Eliezer in a harder manner than his colleagues: "On the conclusion of the Sabbath Rabbi Akiva met his bier being carried from Keisaria to Lod. [In his grief] he beat his flesh until the blood flowed down upon the earth. Then Rabbi Akiva commenced his funeral address, the mourners being lined up about the coffin, and said: 'My father, my father, the chariot of Israel and the horsemen thereof; I have many coins, but no money changer to accept them [I have many questions on Torah, but no one to answer them].'"

2   This commentary has been attributed to Rashi, an attribution which has been debated.

Pinchas. The verse is associated in the following passage, where an additional aspect of his nature is revealed.

No other people sent to perform a religious duty and risking their lives in order to succeed in their mission can compare with the two men whom Yehoshua bin Nun sent; as it says, 'And Yehoshua bin Nun sent out of Shittim two spies to spy secretly' (*Yehoshua* 2:1). Who were they? Our Rabbis taught: They were Pinchas and Kaleiv....

When they [the people of the city] came to seek them, what did Rachav do? She took them away to hide them. Pinchas said to her: "I am a priest and priests are compared to angels, as it says, 'For the priest's lips should guard knowledge, and they should seek the Torah from his mouth; for he is an angel of the Lord of Hosts,' and an angel, if he wishes, can be visible, and if he wishes he can be invisible."

How can we infer that prophets are compared to angels? From the fact that it says in reference to Moshe, "And He sent an angel, and brought us forth out of Egypt" (*Bemidbar* 20:16). Was it not Moshe who brought them out? Certainly; but you can infer from this that prophets are compared to angels. Similarly it says, "And the angel of God came up from Gilgal to Bochim. And he said:... 'I made you go up out Egypt' " (*Shoftim* 2:1). But was it not Pinchas who said this? Yes, but you can infer from it that the prophets are called angels.

Pinchas, then, said to Rachav: "I am a priest and do not need to be hidden. Hide Kaleiv, my companion. I will stand before them and they will not see me."

(Bemidbar Rabbah 16:1)

Not only does Pinchas speak true Torah, but he is also compared to an angel of God. Moshe, too, was angelic in his subsisting without food or drink, when he behaved as the angels during the duration of his stay on Sinai.

The proverb runs, "When you enter a town, follow its customs." Above [in the celestial sphere] there is no eating and drinking; hence when Moshe ascended on high he appeared like them [the angels], as it says, "Then I lived on the mountain forty days and forty nights; I did not eat bread nor drink water" (Devarim 9:9).

(Bereishit Rabbah 48:14)

Yet Rashi stresses that Moshe passed the Torah to Yehoshua. Specifically, exclusively Yehoshua. Other studied and perhaps excelled, but the mesorah was passed on to Yehoshua.

Moshe received the Torah at Sinai and transmitted it to Yehoshua, Yehoshua to the elders, and the elders to the prophets, and the prophets to the men of the great assembly.

(Avot 1:1)

Surely there were others who learned at the feet of Moshe. Why is Yehoshua singled out — especially if others may have been superior? The Talmud describes the scene of the Torah being taught in the beit midrash of Moshe:

What was the procedure of the instruction in the oral law? Moshe learned from the mouth of the Omnipotent. Then Aharon entered and Moshe taught him his lesson. Aharon then moved aside and sat down on Moshe's left. Thereupon Aharon's sons entered and Moshe taught them their lesson. His sons then moved aside, Elazar taking his seat on Moshe's right and Itamar on Aharon's left....

Thereupon the elders entered and Moshe taught them their lesson, and when the elders moved aside all the people entered and Moshe taught them their lesson. It thus followed that Aharon heard the lesson four times, his sons heard it three times, the elders twice, and all the people once. At this stage Moshe departed and Aharon taught them his lesson. Then Aharon departed and his sons taught them their lesson. His sons then departed and the elders taught them their lesson. It thus followed that everybody heard the lesson four times.

From here Rabbi Eliezer inferred: "It is a man's duty to teach his pupil [his lesson] four times. For this is arrived at a minori ad majus: Aharon, who learned from Moshe, who had it from the Omnipotent, had to learn his lesson four times, how much more so an ordinary pupil who learns from an ordinary teacher."

(Eruvin 54b)

Where, was Yehoshua during this process? He seems nowhere to be found. When the Rambam describes the process of the Torah being taught, he states:

Elazar, Pinchas, and Yehoshua all three received from Moshe. To Yehoshua, who was Moshe Rabbeinu's student, he [i.e., Moshe] transmitted the oral Torah, and commanded him regarding it.

(Rambam, Introduction to Mishneh Torah)

We see from the Rambam's formulation that while Moshe taught many people, only Yehoshua was his student. And only Yehoshua was entrusted with the *mesorah*, the oral tradition. Evidently, this is the Rambam's understanding of the *mishnah* in *Avot* — "Moshe received the Torah at Sinai and transmitted it to Yehoshua." In a subsequent paragraph the Rambam writes that Pinchas received the tradition from Yehoshua, which is remarkable considering that Pinchas, too, had studied directly from Moshe. As we saw above, Moshe Rabbeinu had one primary student, Yehoshua.

This formulation remains difficult in terms of the Talmudic statement which left out Yehoshua from the entire process. Where was Yehoshua when the Torah was being taught?

When the daughters of Tzelafchad inherited from their father, Moshe argued: "The time is opportune for me to demand my own needs. If daughters inherit, it is surely right that my sons should inherit my glory."

The Holy One, blessed be He, said to him: " 'Whoever keeps

the fig tree shall eat its fruit, and he who waits on his master shall be honored' (*Mishlei* 27:18). Your sons sat idly by and did not study the Torah. Yehoshua served you much and he showed you great honor. It was he who rose early in the morning and remained late at night at your house of assembly; he used to arrange the benches, and he used to spread the mats. Seeing that he has served you with all his might, he is worthy to serve Israel, for he shall not lose his reward. 'Take for yourself Yehoshua bin Nun' (*Bemidbar* 27:18)." This serves to confirm the text, "Whoever keeps the fig tree shall eat its fruit."

(Bemidbar Rabbah 21:14)

The Midrash tells us that Yehoshua never left Moshe's presence. This is based on the passage found in the book of *Shemot*:

And it was when Moshe entered into the Tent, the pillar of cloud descended and stood at the door of the Tent, and the [God] talked with Moshe. And all the people saw the pillar of cloud stand at the entrance to the Tent; and all the people rose up and worshiped, every man in the entrance to his tent. And God spoke to Moshe face to face, as a man speaks to his friend. And he returned to the camp. And his servant Yehoshua bin Nun, a young man, did not depart from the Tent.

(Shemot 33:9–11)[1]

Yehoshua never left his teacher's side. Therefore, even though arguably Moshe may have had more talented followers, the task of replacing Moshe was the lot of Yehoshua.[2] Yehoshua was the one who set out the benches and tables in Moshe's *beit midrash*. Before the other students arrived and after the other students left, Yehoshua was still there at Moshe's side.[3] This type of dedication is

---

1 See *Bemidbar* 11:28, where the term is also used.
2 Many of the issues discussed in this *shiur* were taught by Rabbi Soloveitchik in a class given March 5, 1957. The Rav cited a Rabbinic source which eludes me that Yehoshua himself insisted that he was inferior to the other students and did not deserve the mantle of leadership.
3 Rashi in *Avot* goes on to explain that Yehoshua displayed more dedication than the others.

institutionalized in the Talmud:

Our Rabbis taught: Who is an *am ha'aretz* (ignoramus)? Anyone who does not recite the Shema evening and morning. This is the view of Rabbi Eliezer. Rabbi Yehoshua says: "Anyone who does not put on tefillin." Ben Azzai says: "Anyone who does not have a fringe on his garment." Rabbi Natan says: "Anyone who does not have a mezuzah on his door." Rabbi Natan ben Yosef says: "Anyone who has sons and does not bring them up to the study of the Torah." Others say: "Even if one has learned Scripture and Mishnah, if he has not ministered to a *talmid chacham*, he is an *am ha'aretz*." Rabbi Huna said: "The halachah is as laid down by 'others.' "

(Berachot 47b)

To be scholarly "book smart" in the absence of serving a sage is insufficient at least, dangerous at worst. Knowledge is not simply a process of assimilating information; it requires far more subtle skills which can only be acquired by sitting at the feet of a sage. There was never a greater sage than Moshe, nor a greater, more dedicated student than Yehoshua. Therefore, when the time came to replace Moshe, God chose Yehoshua.

And Moshe spoke to God, saying, "Let God, the Lord of the spirits of all flesh, set a man over the congregation, who will go out before them and who will go in before them, and who will lead them out, and who will bring them in; so that the congregation of God will not be as sheep which have no shepherd."

And God said to Moshe, "Take Yehoshua bin Nun, a man in whom is spirit, and lay your hand upon him."

(Bemidbar 27:15–18)

Yehoshua received the ultimate *semichah* (ordination) at the commandment of God by the hand of Moshe (*al pi Hashem b'yad Moshe*), just like the Torah itself.[1] The task of Yehoshua would not

---

1 When the Torah is lifted in shul, two verses are recited in combination: "And this is the Torah which Moshe set before the people of Israel" (*Devarim* 4:44) and "at the

be easy. The comparison with Moshe, as we saw, made for a difficult situation. And the fall off in Torah study with the demise of Moshe compounded the problem.

The way of dealing with the problem was by biding Yehoshua to be strong:

> And Moshe called to Yehoshua, and said to him in the sight of all Israel, "Be strong and courageous; for you will go with this people to the land which God has sworn to their fathers to give them; and you shall cause them to inherit it."
>
> *(Devarim 31:7)*

> Moshe therefore wrote this poem the same day, and he taught it to the people of Israel. And he gave Yehoshua bin Nun a charge and said, "Be strong and courageous; for you shall bring the people of Israel into the land which I swore to them; and I will be with you."
>
> *(Devarim 31:22–23)*

Not only did Moshe instruct Yehoshua to be strong, but so did God:

> And it was after the death of Moshe, the servant of God, that God spoke to Yehoshua bin Nun, Moshe's minister, saying, "Moshe My servant is dead; now therefore arise, cross over the Jordan, you and all this people, to the land which I give to them, to the people of Israel....
>
> "Be strong and courageous; for you shall cause this people to inherit the land, which I swore to their fathers to give them. Only be strong and very courageous, that you may observe to do according to all the Torah, which Moshe My servant commanded you; do not turn from it to the right hand or to the left, that you may prosper wherever you go.
>
> "This Book of the Torah shall not depart from your mouth; you shall meditate on it day and night, that you may observe to do according to all that is written on it; for then you shall

commandment of God by the hand of Moshe" *(Bemidbar 9:23).*

make your way prosperous, and then you shall have good success. Have I not commanded you? Be strong and courageous; do not be afraid nor dismayed, for God, Your Lord; is with you wherever you go."

(Yehoshua 1:1–9)

We are told that Yehoshua never left Moshe's tent, and now, with the very same language, Yehoshua is told that the Torah will never leave him. The same word, *yamush*, is used both to describe Yehoshua's never leaving Moshe and the Torah not departing from his mouth.

Completing any endeavor can induce mixed feelings — joy from accomplishment, yet fear of the future. As we complete the yearly Torah cycle, we must pay attention to God's call for strength, and forge ahead and meet new challenges with joy and awe, not self-satisfaction and complacency. We will start the Torah anew, dedicated to delving into our tradition to find more meaning, and take full advantage of the unparalleled opportunity to peek into God's mind.

Four things require strength, namely, [study of] the Torah, good deeds, praying, and one's worldly occupation. Whence do we know this of Torah and good deeds? Because it says, "Only be strong and very courageous, that you may observe to do according to all the Torah": be strong in Torah.

(Berachot 32b)

Kislev

Chanukah

"Bringing Down the Shechinah"[1]

The holiday of Chanukah is of Rabbinic origin: When the Second Temple was violated by the Greeks, Jews, mainly of the priestly family, liberated the Beit HaMikdash and a holiday was established.

The Torah itself mandates consecration of a completed Temple or Mishkan and describes just such events in earlier periods of Jewish history. These earlier accounts should be examined and compared to the case of Chanukah.

The first "Chanukah" — or consecration of a Temple — is described at the end of the book of *Shemot* with the establishment of the Mishkan. In a sense, the consecration of the Mishkan, and especially the resting of the *Shechinah* within its walls, is a sign of healing in the aftermath of the golden calf tragedy. The personal revelation to Moshe at the burning bush thus was transformed into a national revelation for the entire people. The Revelation at Sinai, which was a singular event, becomes institutionalized and ongoing in the building of the Mishkan. The Ramban writes that the sublime secret of the Mishkan is that the presence of God that hovered

---

1   I originally heard many of the ideas in this essay from my brother, Rav Yair Kahn.

about Mount Sinai now will be placed on "permanent display" in the Mishkan.

With the building completed, the book, too, can come to an end. The Torah describes the completion with the following words:

> And he [Moshe] erected the court around the Tabernacle and the altar, and set up the screen of the court gate. So Moshe finished the work. Then a cloud covered the Tent of Meeting, and the glory of God filled the Tabernacle. And Moshe was not able to enter into the Tent of Meeting because the cloud abode on it, and the glory of God filled the Tabernacle. And when the cloud was taken up from over the Tabernacle, the children of Israel went onward in all their journeys. But if the cloud was not taken up, then they did not journey until the day that it was taken up. For the cloud of God was upon the Tabernacle by day, and fire was on it by night, in the sight of all the House of Israel, throughout all their journeys.
>
> *(Shemot 40:33–38)*

The glory of God had entered the building. This was surely seen by the people as a sign of Divine benevolence. God was with the people, His presence palpable.

A similar description is given of the completion of the permanent address, the Temple in Yerushalayim:

> Now when Shlomo finished praying, fire came down from heaven and consumed the burnt offering and the sacrifices; and the glory of God filled the house. And the priests could not enter the house of God because the glory of God had filled God's house. And when all the people of Israel saw how the fire came down and the glory of God [was] upon the house, they bowed with their faces to the ground upon the pavement, and worshiped, and praised God, saying, "For He is good; for His loving kindness endures forever."
>
> *(Divrei HaYamim II 7:1–3)*

There was nothing in the Ark save the two tablets of stone,

which Moshe put there at Chorev, when God made a covenant with the people of Israel, when they came out of the land of Egypt. And it came to pass, when the priests came out of the holy place, that the cloud filled the house of God. And the priests could not stand to minister because of the cloud; for the glory of God had filled God's house. Then said Shlomo, "God said that He would dwell in the thick darkness. I have surely built You a house to dwell in, a settled place for You to abide in forever."

(Melachim I 8:9–13)

We see the same essential response: Man reaches out to God from below and follows the word of God by building the Temple. The Divine response is to fill the earthly structure with a bit of heaven. The same Divine cloud that hovered on the mountain during Revelation was now in Yerushalayim.

Both sources speak of man's inability to enter into the newly completed structure. The Talmud questions this by introducing a "contradictory" passage:

One passage reads: "And Moshe was not able to enter into the Tent of Meeting because the cloud abode on it" (*Shemot* 40:35), whereas another verse says: "And Moshe entered into the midst of the cloud" (ibid. 24:18). It teaches us that the Holy One, blessed be He, took hold of Moshe and brought him into the cloud.

(Yoma 4b)

The holiness of the situation was so profound that man was unable to enter; God Himself had to lead man in. The *Zohar* describes the essence of the cloud as a remnant of the primordial light:

On the day when the Tabernacle was set up on earth, what do we read concerning it? "And Moshe was not able to enter into the Tent of Meeting because the cloud abode thereon." What was that cloud? It was a thread from the side of the primordial light, which, issuing forth joyously, entered the *Shechinah* and descended into the Tabernacle below. After the first day of Creation it was never again made fully manifest, but it performs a function, renewing daily the work of Creation.

(Zohar, Shemot 149a)

This description strengthens the understanding that the book of *Shemot* is a new beginning, a new creation. The book of *Bereishit* begins with a resounding "Let there be light," but the light is quickly dimmed by the failures of man. Now, at the conclusion of the book of *Shemot*, God's final act is in a sense the very same action which began the first book all those years before. The Mishkan creates a new/old reality: God's presence becomes visible, accessible, as it was in the Garden of Eden before the sin. A new beginning is set in motion, and God Himself ushers man into this new era, this new relationship.

There is a third instance when man built a structure for the purpose of housing or hosting the Divine Essence, yet that description seems somewhat different from the first two. The setting is the end of the first exile, in the period between the First and Second Temples. Led by Ezra and Zerubavel, the people build the Temple anew:

And this house was finished on the third day of the month of Adar, which was in the sixth year of the reign of Daryavesh the King. And the people of Israel — the priests, the Levites, and the rest of the returned exiles — celebrated the dedication of this house of the Lord with joy. And they offered at the dedication of this house of the Lord one hundred bulls, two hundred rams, four hundred lambs; and for a sin offering for all Israel, twelve male goats, according to the number of the tribes of Israel. And they set the priests in their divisions, and the Levites in their courses, for the service of God, at Yerushalayim, as it is written in the Book of Moshe.

And the returned exiles kept Pesach on the fourteenth day of the first month. For the priests and the Levites had purified themselves, all of them were pure; and they slaughtered the Paschal lamb for all the returned exiles and for their brothers the priests and for themselves. And the people of Israel, who had returned from exile, and all those who had kept themselves apart from the impurity of the nations of the land to seek God, the Lord of Israel, ate, and they celebrated the Festival of Matzot seven days with joy; for God had made them joyful and turned the heart of the king of Assyria to them, to strengthen their hands in the work of the house of the Lord, the Lord of Israel.

(Ezra 6:15–22)

Read on its own, the description seems glorious: The Temple is rebuilt! The hopes, aspirations, and dreams that had kept the people throughout the exile had come to wonderful fruition. Nonetheless, we have an uneasy feeling about the description. Something is missing. Where is the Divine response? Where is the cloud, the heavenly expression that God had allowed His presence to return and fill the structure? Regarding God's response the verses offer only deafening silence.

There was a problem with this new Temple. Most of the exiles chose not to return and be a part of this historic project; they remained in the Diaspora. The Talmudic sage Reish Lakish (*Yoma* 9b) opines that the reason the Divine Presence did not dwell on the Second Temple was that the majority of Jews did not care enough to return and take part in the building of the Temple and, by the same token, of the entire land. There was something amiss with the foundation of this Temple. This deficiency was sensed as the foundation was built:

And when the builders laid the foundation of the Temple of God, the priests in their vestments came forward with trumpets, and the Levites, the sons of Asaf, with cymbals, to praise God, according to the directions of David, King of Israel. And they sang responsively in praising and giving thanks to God: "For He is good, for His grace endures forever towards Israel." And all the people shouted with a great shout when they praised God because the foundation of the House of God was laid.

But many of the priests and Levites and chiefs of the fathers' houses, old men who had seen the first Temple, wept with a loud voice when the foundation of this temple was laid before their eyes, though many shouted aloud for joy. And the people could not distinguish the sound of joyful shouting from the sound of people weeping because the people shouted loudly, and the sound was heard from far away.

(Ezra 3:10–13)

The masses cheered in ecstasy. The foundation was set. However, the elders sensed something amiss. Where was the cloud? Where was the Divine Glory? Where was the *Shechinah?* It seems that the Second Temple never did reach the spiritual stature of the First Temple or of the Mishkan.

The Second Temple did not have a wonderful track record: Soon after being built, during the Greek period, the Temple became defiled to the extent that no holiness could be found, save one flask of oil. The story is well known.

What is [the reason for] Chanukah? For our Rabbis taught: On the twenty-fifth of Kislev [commence] the days of Chanukah, which are eight, on which lamentation for the dead and fasting are forbidden. For when the Greeks entered the Temple, they defiled all the oils therein, and when the Hasmonean dynasty prevailed against and defeated them, they searched and found only one cruse of oil which lay with the seal of the high priest, but which contained sufficient oil for one day's lighting only. Yet a miracle was wrought therein and they lit [the lamp] with it for eight days. In another year these [days] were appointed a festival with [the recital of] Hallel and thanksgiving.

(Shabbat 21b)

Rabbi Soloveitchik noted an interesting turn of phrase at the conclusion of this passage — "in another year" (*"leshanah acheret"*)[1]: At the time, the people did not realize the significance of

---

1   Although the Rambam writes "the sages of that generation" (*Hilchot Chanukah* 3:3), the same generation could still be understood as a subsequent year.

the events they had witnessed. It is often the case that we have difficulty understanding historic events that unfold before our eyes. At times we need distance in order to gain historical perspective. In just this manner, the Rabbis eventually came to realize that the events of Chanukah should be celebrated.

But what was to be the focus of the celebration? The military battle? Surely not, for this battle contained a nasty secret: it began as fratricide — a veritable civil war. A civil war can be won, but not celebrated. The miracle of the lights was different. It generated within the people a different response: Perhaps a bit of that Divine Light which had been absent for the first few hundred years of the Second Temple's existence had finally come down.

Now we can also appreciate the name *Chanukah*, which means "consecration." *This* was the consecration of the Second Temple, not the great ceremony recorded in the book of *Ezra*. Only now had that primordial light, which had dissipated on the very first day of Creation and had made itself visible in the Mishkan and the First Temple, returned. This was the light that shone brightly for eight days. The *Shechinah* was manifest. God was among them, His presence once again palpable.

It is interesting that this light was visible only on the first day of Creation. By the second day, the power of argument had appeared:

> Why is "that it was good" not written in connection with the second day? Rabbi Yochanan explained in the name of Rabbi Yosei ben Chalafta: "Because on it Gehinnom was created...." Rabbi Chanina said: "Because on it schism came into the world, [as it is written,] '[And God said, "Let there be a firmament in the midst of the waters, and] let it divide the waters from the waters." ' "
>
> *(Bereishit Rabbah 4:6)*

Argument and discord cause the *Shechinah* to take leave. Perhaps the attempt to introduce Hellenism into Jewish life and the painful struggle which ensued caused the Jews to make a commitment to peace. The Second Temple stood until hatred became the order of the day, when schism and groundless hatred brought the Temple down and caused the *Shechinah* to be exiled. This Divine Light, though, is still available. The passage in the *Zohar* introduced above speaks about a thread of this light which is still accessible:

> Moreover, whenever the Torah is studied by night, a little thread of this hidden light steals down and plays upon those who are absorbed in their study, wherefore it is written: "God commands His lovingkindness in the daytime, and in the night His song is with me" (*Tehillim* 42:9); this has already been expounded. On the day when the Tabernacle was set up on earth, what do we read concerning it? "And Moshe was not able to enter into the Tent of Meeting because the cloud abode on it." What was that cloud? It was a thread from the side of the primordial light, which, issuing forth joyously, entered the *Shechinah* and descended into the Tabernacle below. After the first day of Creation it was never again made fully manifest, but it performs a function, renewing daily the work of Creation.
>
> *(Zohar, Shemot 149a)*

Learning Torah specifically at night, the time when people cry over the destruction of the Temple, is effective in bringing the Light back. Moreover, human behavior can cause more Divine Light to shine, or alternatively can cause the Light's disappearance. One day, though, this light will shine brightly once again:

> "Then the cloud covered the Tent of Meeting" — whereby the *Shechinah* dwelt on the earth, and the unclean spirit, designated "end of all flesh," departed from the world and disappeared into the cavern of the great abyss. The Holy Spirit had thus sole sway over the world, as Scripture says: "Then the cloud covered the Tent of Meeting." It is further written: "And Moshe was not able to enter into the Tent of Meeting, because the cloud abode on it." In other words, because the Holy Spirit hovered over the world and the unclean spirit departed.

The wicked, however, draw him again into the world, and if not for them he would completely disappear. But in the days to come the Holy One, blessed be He, will cause him to depart completely from the world, as Scripture says: "He will swallow up death forever, and the Lord God will wipe away tears from off all faces; and the reproach of His people will He take away from off all the earth, for God has spoken it" (*Yeshayah* 25:8); also, "And [I will cause] the unclean spirit to depart from the land" (*Zecharyah* 13:2).

Blessed be God forevermore. Amen and Amen. "God will reign forever" (*Tehillim* 146:10).

(Zohar, Shemot 269a)

Chanukah

Catch the Bull by the Horn

While the story of Chanukah is well known, Rabbinic sources relating to these events are terse and obscure. Other holidays are biblically based and mandated; hence they are far richer in terms of primary sources. Even Purim, which is also created by Rabbinic decree, has both a megillah and a tractate in Mishnah and Talmud. Chanukah remains the most mysterious of the holidays. Much of the information we have comes from historians, religious and secular, who have had to base themselves on unwritten tradition and extracanonical sources.

We know that the Greeks subjected the Jews to various oppressive decrees, the most familiar to us revolving around the violation of the Temple. Tradition tells us that what was built as a place of worship to God became violated and impure. Some sources suggest that the Temple became a place of depravity and licentiousness.

> What is [the reason for] Chanukah? For our Rabbis taught: On the twenty-fifth of Kislev [commence] the days of Chanukah, which are eight, on which lamentation for the dead and fasting are forbidden. For when the Greeks entered the Temple, they defiled all the oils therein, and when the Hasmonean dynasty prevailed against and defeated them, they searched and found only one cruse of oil which lay with the seal of the high

priest. It only contained enough for one day's lighting but a miracle was done with it and they lit [the lamp] from it for eight days. The following year these [days] were appointed a festival with [the recital of] Hallel and thanksgiving.

(Shabbat 21b)

Tradition speaks of other aspects of the persecution — not only against the Temple but decrees against other forms of Jewish practice. The Greeks prohibited circumcision, keeping the Shabbat, and declaring the new moon.[1]

Yet despite the public humiliation of the Temple and the attack against our most basic institutions, the persecution of the Greeks against the Jews became associated in Rabbinic literature with one particular, strange phrase:

"And darkness" symbolizes Greece, which darkened the eyes of Israel with its decrees, ordering Israel, "Write on the horn of an ox that you have no portion in the God of Israel."

(Bereishit Rabbah 2:4)[2]

While it is clear that the Greeks had rejected the Jewish idea of God and of monotheism, this particular phrase seems strange: What is the relationship between Greek anti-Semitism and the horn of an ox?

The other decrees are more easily understood: The Greeks rejected the idea of Creation, thus the idea of Shabbat was an absurdity to their way of thinking. Similarly, the idea of a "new month" was foreign: For Jews, the new month indicates renewal and a testimony to Creation. The Greeks clearly rejected this notion. Moreover, the Torah teaches us this process of renewal and the testimony it bears are within the domain of the Jew: The new moon

---

1   See *Megillat Antiochus* in *Otzar Midrashim*, p. 186. There is a source which describes similar decrees: "For the government had once issued a decree that [Jews] might not keep the Sabbath, nor circumcise their children, and that they should have intercourse with menstruant women" (*Meilah* 17a). However, this source describes the Roman period.

2   Also found in *Bereishit Rabbah* 16:4 and 44:17, *Shemot Rabbah* 15:16, *Vayikra Rabbah* 13:5 and15:9, *Pesikta Rabbati* 33, *Yerushalmi Chagigah* 77d, *and Tanchuma, Vayechi* 13.

occurs only when declared by the Rabbinic court, indicating that the so-called forces of nature are placed under our control.

This tenet of Jewish philosophy is encapsulated in the *midrash* in which the angels ask God when the new moon is and God responds, "Ask the Jews" (*Devarim Rabbah* 2:14). God, as it were, is seen to have abdicated the right to declare the new moon, which is a physical reality, and given it over to the courts, making it a religious act. This idea must have been particularly offensive to the Greeks, for whom natural phenomena were sacrosanct, not influenced or dictated by man, and certainly not by the Jews.[1]

The Greeks worshiped nature as perfection; the Jewish idea that even the human body required circumcision to perfect or complete it was repulsive to them. Testimony from the Greek period reveals to what extent the Greek worship of the human form made inroads in the Jewish community: We are told of Jews who underwent dangerous and painful surgery to "reverse" at least the aesthetic aspects of circumcision, indicating the extent to which some Jews were swayed by Greek values.

These three decrees have a common theme: the Jews believe that there is something beyond the physical, that there is a metaphysical reality — God. The Greeks focused exclusively on the physical. The fact that Chanukah is eight days, equal to the days leading to circumcision, is no accident. Both Chanukah and milah point to metaphysical reality — the very point of contention between the Jews and the Greeks. For Jews, circumcision represents man's ability to control the physical, to transcend physical urges by connecting to God, the ultimate metaphysical Being. Judaism sees man as a complex combination of the physical and the metaphysical; Creation is the moment when the physical form is imbued with a dash of the metaphysical — a soul. The very number eight points to something which exists beyond the seven days of the week.

We now understand the Greek objections to Shabbat, milah, and the observance of the New Moon. But why did they insist that

---

1   See *Sefat Emet, Chanukah* 5636.

Jews write on the horn of an ox that we have no portion in the God of Israel? The decree is obscure, and countless commentaries have offered explanations. Perhaps the most basic explanation is that this was a "walking advertisement," a means of putting the Jews' rejection of God on parade. If so, the central mitzvah of Chanukah, lighting candles in order to publicize the miracle, may be seen as counteracting the "negative publicity."

The specificity of the decree, that the public heresy of the Jews be carried on the horn of an ox, may have a deeper meaning. The most famous ox in Judaism was the golden calf, which symbolized mass rejection of God, the nadir of the Jewish community. The Maharal (*Ner Mitzvah*, p. 14) explains that the Greek decree was a conscious effort to sway the Jews to reject God once again; the choice of an ox horn as the vehicle reflected this goal. The weakness with this approach is the choice of an ox and not a calf, and the insistence that they write specifically on the horn, a detail not singled out in any tradition describing that earlier monumental sin.

There is a second association that may relate to Chanukah: When Yaakov blesses Yosef he uses the term *alei shur* (*Bereishit* 49:22). Some would translate this phrase "arise, ox," but the Midrash explains the actual meaning in the context of the verse: "the daughters [or branches] run over the wall."[1]

> "The daughters run over the wall" — You find that when Yosef went forth to rule over Egypt, daughters of kings used to look at him through the lattices and throw bracelets, necklaces, earrings, and rings to him, so that he might lift up his eyes and look at them; yet he did not look at them.
>
> *(Bereishit Rabbah 98:18)*

However, when Moshe blesses the tribes he refers to both an ox and horns in reference to Yosef:

> The firstborn of his herd, grandeur is his, and his horns are like

---

1   There is a tradition that the term *"alei shur"* relating to Yosef actually caused the golden calf. See *Rashi, Shemot* 32:4.

the horns of a wild ox; with them he shall push the people to-gether to the ends of the earth.

(Devarim 33:17)

We see that "ox" certainly refers to Yosef, but what connection does this have with the story of Chanukah?

When one looks at Jewish history from the perspective of the Hellenized Jews, Yosef represents a fascinating precedent: Here was a biblical figure who acculturated. From their perspective, Yosef had joined the Egyptian royal court and left his family traditions behind. Moreover, as we saw from the blessing of Yaakov and the alternative meaning of *"alei shur,"* Yosef was incredibly good look-ing. The Torah attests to his physical beauty:

And Yosef was handsome and good-looking.

(Bereishit 39:6)

When we recall that the Greeks placed such a premium on aes-thetics and the physical form, Yosef may have seemed an even more attractive role model: He had looks, he joined the Egyptians, and he had cultural and political stature in the foreign culture into which he assimilated. The Greeks may have been tipped off by as-similated Jews that using Yosef as a role model would convince more traditional Jews to leave Jewish practice. Use of the horn of an ox would have been a trigger for them, a code or symbol to guide them along the path of assimilation, used to remind them of Yosef, the symbol of the "modern Jew."

Yet Yosef, despite the Hellenists' propaganda to the contrary, re-mained steadfast in his traditions. Despite temptation, Yosef never cut corners or lost sight of his identity. In fact, Yosef is often re-ferred to as the one who "guarded his covenant [brit]."[1]

While the Hellenized Jews were performing surgery to cancel the brit, Yosef was guarding his.

The Hellenized Jews, then, misused Yosef as an example. How-ever, examining Yosef as a role model may deepen our understand-

---

1   Shelah HaKadosh uses this term in *Torah Or, Vayeishev* 2,7. Many later books also utilize the term, including Rav Tzadok HaKohein and the Sefat Emet.

ing of the issues in question. While the Greek worldview put a premium on aesthetics, the Jewish worldview did not reject it. The Torah does not ignore Yosef's physical beauty, dismiss it, belittle it. Rather, Judaism considers that beauty; as with all physical things, physical beauty must be imbued with spirituality and thus elevated. The beauty referred to in the Torah was misconstrued by the Hellenists, for in all cases, the Torah's understanding of beauty is far different from that of Greek philosophy. A case in point is the Jewish tradition that the most beautiful place on earth was Yerushalayim, with the Temple standing at its epicenter:

> Ten portions of beauty descended to the world: nine were taken by Yerushalayim and one by the rest of the world.
>
> *(Kiddushin 49b)*

Perhaps this is what infuriated the Greeks: the obligation to elevate the physical — to seek the metaphysical and not simply enjoy the physical on its own terms.

The conflict between these two opposing philosophies, indeed between the Greek and Jewish cultures in general, is actually rooted in a much earlier episode and a more basic relationship.[1]

> The Lord shall grant beauty to Yefet, and He shall live in the tents of Shem.
>
> *(Bereishit 9:27)*

Shem and Yefet were brothers; Shem is the father of all the Semitic peoples, and Yefet is the ancestor of Greece. The name *Yefet* indicates beauty, but the Torah speaks of the beauty of Yefet manifesting itself in the tents of Shem. Moreover, the term used is *veyishkon*, to dwell: the root of this word is shared with *Mishkan*

---

1   See also *Megillah* 9b: "Rabbi Shimon ben Gamliel says that books of the Scripture also are permitted to be written only in Greek... Rabbi Yochanan further said: 'What is the reason of Rabbi Shimon ben Gamliel? Scripture says, "God shall grant beauty to Yefet, and He shall dwell in the tents of Shem"; [this means] that the words of Yefet shall be in the tents of Shem. But why not say [the words of] Gomer and Magog?' Rabbi Chiya ben Abba replied: 'The real reason is because it is written, "Let God grant beauty to [*yaft*] Yefet": implying, let the chief beauty [*yafyut*] of Yefet be in the tents of Shem.' "

and, or more importantly, *Shechinah*. The beauty of Yefet is to be manifest in the Temple of Shem, but only with the presence of God manifest, only when the *Shechinah* is felt. The Greeks and the Hellenized Jews rejected the holy, rejected the God of Israel, and desired only the physical beauty. They sought the beauty of Yefet without the metaphysical awareness of Shem. Judaism sought a marriage of the physical and the spiritual.[1]

This may lead us to a deeper understanding of the horn on which the Jews were commanded to write.[2] Many commentators note that the term *horn* is written in the singular. The image is of a unicorn, with one horn in the center of its head. Rav Nachman of Breslov suggested that the unicorn represents a man wearing tefillin.[3] Tefillin, with one on the head to represent the mind and the other on the arm to represent man's strength, is the symbol of the merger of physical and spiritual. The Greeks, in decreeing that Israel be led away from God by inscribing on the unicorn's horn, aimed to defile this symbol of purity of mind, to reinterpret and refocus the image of tefillin, by giving the horn a new message. This, according to Rav Nachman, is the meaning of the "horn of the ox."

The idea of the unicorn may allow us to go one step further. According to the Sages, when Adam sinned he brought a unicorn as an atonement offering:[4]

When Adam, on the day of his creation, saw the setting of the

---

1   The Talmud (*Zevachim* 54b) describes the Temple as a place of beauty: "What is meant by the verse, '[And he asked and said: "Where are Samuel and David?"] And one said: "Behold, they are at Nayot in Ramah"' (*Shmuel* I, ch. 19). What connection then has Nayot with Ramah? It means, however, that they sat at Ramah and were engaged with the glory [beauty] of the world. Said they, 'It is written, "Then you shall arise, and ascend to the place [which God, your Lord, shall choose]": this teaches that the Temple was higher than the whole of Eretz Yisrael, while Eretz Yisrael is higher than all other countries.' "

2   It is interesting that they were forced to write. As we noted at the outset, the period when the struggle with the Greeks took place was a time after the biblical canon was complete, religious creativity was now centered in the oral Torah and not the written Torah.

3   *Likutei Maharan, Mahadurah Kamma* 38:6.

4   See comments of Kli Yakar to *Vayikra* 1:1.

sun he said, "Alas, it is because I have sinned that the world around me is becoming dark; the universe will now become again void and without form — this then is the death to which I have been sentenced from Heaven!"

So he sat up all night fasting and weeping and Chavah was weeping opposite him. When, however, dawn broke, he said, "This is the usual course of the world." He then arose and offered up a bullock whose horns were developed before its hoofs, as it is said, "And it [my thanksgiving] shall please God, better than a bullock that is horned and hoofed" (*Tehillim* 69:32).

Rabbi Yehudah said in the name of Shmuel: "The bullock which Adam offered had only one horn in its forehead, as the verse says, 'And it shall please God better than a bullock that is horned and hoofed." But does not "horned" imply two horns? Said Rabbi Nachman ben Yitzchak: "Horned is here spelled [defectively]."

(Avodah Zarah 8a)

The Talmud on the same page mentions another holiday from antiquity which was celebrated by Adam for eight days in the winter:

When Adam HaRishon saw the day getting gradually shorter, he said, "Woe is me, perhaps because I have sinned, the world around me is being darkened and returning to its state of chaos and confusion; this then is the kind of death to which I have been sentenced from Heaven!"

So he began keeping an eight-day fast. But as he observed the winter equinox and noted the day getting increasingly longer, he said, "This is the usual course of the world. "He then established an eight-day festival. In the following year he appointed both as festivals. He fixed them for the sake of Heaven, but the [heathens] appointed them for the sake of idolatry.

While the pagan holiday celebrates a purely physical, astronomical phenomenon, devoid of any spiritual content, the holiday of Chanukah, celebrated at the same time of year, points out the Divine hand in our lives and celebrates the victory of light over darkness, purity over impurity, the miracle of a small flask which lasted for eight days; in a word, the metaphysical.

When Adam sinned, the world changed. On the one hand, Adam became diminished, losing some of his luster, his beauty. On the other hand, the necessity arose for a place where man and God could rekindle their relationship; hence the Temple. After his sin, Adam brought a pleasing offering to God in attempt to rekindle the relationship between them. Greek philosophy rejects the very notion of a God with whom man can communicate; in rejecting God, they rejected the Jewish idea of the Temple and of offerings.

> For Yaakov inherited the beauty of Adam; hence those garments found in him their rightful owner and thus gave off their proper aroma. Said Rabbi Yosei: "Can it really be so, that Yaakov's beauty equaled that of Adam, seeing that, according to tradition, the fleshy part of Adam's heel outshone the orb of the sun? Would you, then, say the same of Yaakov?" Said Rabbi Eliezer in reply: "Assuredly Adam's beauty was as tradition says, but only at first before he sinned, when no creature could endure to gaze at his beauty; after he sinned, however, his beauty was diminished."
>
> *(Zohar, Bereshit 142b)*

Furthermore we are told that Yosef inherited the beauty of Yaakov.

> "These are the generations [*toldot*, lit. offspring] of Yaakov: Yosef" (*Bereishit* 37:2) — Or, again, we may take the words to signify that whoever looked at Yosef thought he was looking at Yaakov.
>
> *(Zohar, Bereshit 180a)*

But this beauty is not about pure aesthetics; it is another mode designed to relate to God.

> Observe further that Adam's beauty is a symbol with which the true faith is closely bound up. This is hinted at in the passage: "And let the graciousness of God, our Lord, be upon us" (*Tehillim* 90:17), as well as in the expression, "to behold the graciousness of God" (ibid. 27:4). And Yaakov assuredly participated of that beauty.
>
> *(Zohar, Bereishit 142b)*

This is what the Greeks never understood. They saw beauty as an ends in and of itself and not as a conduit toward the spiritual and metaphysical.

> Thus says God, the King of Israel and its redeemer, the God of Hosts: "I am the first, and I am the last; and beside Me there is no God. And who is like Me? Let him declare it and set it in order for Me, since I appointed the eternal people. And the things that are coming, and shall come, let them relate to themselves.... The carpenter stretches out his rule, he marks it out with a pencil, he fits it with chisels, and he marks it out with the compass, and makes it after the figure of a man [Adam], according to the beauty of man, that it may remain in the house.
>
> *(Yeshayah 44:6–13)*

The beauty of man can be found in the house — the beauty of Adam, which is his image of God, can be found in the Temple. The Greeks, who did not understand holiness — the connection with the metaphysical, with God — settled for beauty, aesthetics. The Maccabees redeemed the Temple — in order to once again show the world the real beauty diminished ever since the sin of Adam.

Adar

Amalek: A Question of Race?

This week we read the portion of the Torah that recounts the commandment to obliterate Amalek. Because this is arguably the most important Torah reading of the year, understanding the substance of the command is of supreme importance. The commandment appears quite simple: We are told that we must make this world "Amalek-free." There are those who perceive in this precept a racist doctrine; after all, not only are those guilty of perpetrating wickedness to be killed, but also their children. Clearly, the charge is racially linked and motivated. All who possess Amalekian blood must perish.

The moral argument against genocide is certainly compelling, especially for a nation who heard the commandment "You shall not murder" from the mouth of God at Sinai. Therefore, many Jews sense a difficulty with the commandment to destroy Amalek. I have heard Rav Aharon Lichtenstein (the *rosh yeshivah* of Yeshivat Har Etzion) quoted on this paradox: The Torah is the benchmark for moral behavior. The Torah taught the world the concept of value of human life and the prohibition of murder. If this same document teaches that murder is abhorrent and genocide evil, yet the killing of Amalek is allowed, the situation would be one in which the exception proves the rule. The Torah had to command us to wipe out Amalek, who are identified with the epitome of evil, because in other circumstances the Torah prohibits the taking of life.

There may, however, be a more direct approach to this paradox. Killing Amalek may ultimately have little to do with race. The litmus test would be the case of a person who changes his "racial status" but not his genetic makeup: What is the proper treatment of an Amalekite who converts to Judaism? Is he, because of his birth, still slated for annihilation, or is his new identity the deciding factor? Is the issue a purely racial question, or are other factors equally or even more important?

Can an Amalekite lose the status of "Amalek," together with all "rights and privileges"? More generally, how can someone change his status, his identity? The simplest model would be via conversion. Judaism recognizes the possibility that an individual born to a different faith may join the children of Avraham, Yitzchak, and Yaakov. The prototypical example is Rut, who was born a Moavite, yet changed her national identity and became a Jew. Is conversion an option for an Amalekite? The *Mechilta* which discusses this question seems direct and unequivocal:

> God swore by His throne of glory, "If converts come from any nation they will be accepted, but from the progeny of Amalek and his household they will not be accepted."
> *(Mechilta, end of Beshalach)*[1]

The option of conversion is open for all nations and peoples, with the exception of Amalek, who can never join the Jewish people. On the other hand, the Gemara in a number of places relates that descendants of Haman, who was a prominent member of the Amalek family, did in fact join the Jewish people.

Naaman was a resident alien; Nevuzaradan was a righteous proselyte; descendants of Haman learned Torah in B'nei Brak;

---

1   See *Midrash Tanchuma, Ki Teitzei* 11, and *Pesikta D'Rav Kahana* 3.

descendants of Sisera taught children in Yerushalayim; [and] descendants of Sancheirev gave public expositions of the Torah.

(Gittin 57b; Sanhedrin 96b)

If a descendant of Amalek cannot convert, how can the Gemara declare that they learned Torah, in a way which indicates their having joined the Jewish people?

A careful reading of the Rambam in the *Mishneh Torah* indicates that his opinion was that a person from Amalek may, in fact, convert to Judaism. Apparently, the Rambam preferred the tradition recorded in the *Bavli* to the explicit dictum in the *Mechilta*. The Rambam writes:

All non-Jews when they convert and accept all the commandments...are like Jews for all matters...except the four nations exclusively (who cannot convert) and they are Amon, Moav, Egypt, and Edom. These nations, when they convert, are Jews for all matters with the exception of joining the community [in marriage].

(Hilchot Issurei Bi'ah 12:17)

The inference seems quite clear: the option of conversion is open to the erstwhile Amalekite. Furthermore, the Rambam mentions a second possibility for an Amalekite to lose the status of Amalek without entering the fold of Judaism:

The Rambam (*Hilchot Melachim* 6:4) describes the etiquette of war and says that prior to battle the opposing side should be offered the possibility to accept the commandments and subjugation. This offer is also extended to Amalek. Apparently, when Amalek accepts the seven Noachide laws, they lose the status of Amalek and no longer must be obliterated. In other words, there are three possibilities for an individual born of Amalekian blood: maintaining his initial status of Amalekite and thus being slated for obliteration; accepting the seven Noachide laws, at which point his status becomes that of a righteous gentile; and full-fledged conversion.

It is important to consider the other side of this coin: Can a person become an "Amalekite"? According to Rav Chaim Soloveitchik's understanding of the Rambam,[1] the answer is affirmative: When describing the obligation to eradicate the seven nations who occupied the Land of Israel at the time of Yehoshua's conquest, the Rambam writes that they have already assimilated among the nations, and therefore this commandment cannot be fulfilled. The source for this teaching is a tradition cited in the Talmud:

> Do Amon and Moav still reside in their original homes? Sancheirev, King of Assyria, long ago went up and mixed up all the nations, as it says, "I have removed the bounds of the peoples and have robbed their treasures and have brought down as one mighty their inhabitants" (*Yeshayah* 10:13), and whatever strays [from a group] is assumed to belong to the larger section of the group.
>
> *(Berachot 28a)*

On the other hand, in the very next law, the Rambam writes of the obligation to destroy Amalek. Here the Rambam leaves out this important caveat. For some reason the Rambam believes that the identities of the seven nations have disappeared due to the policy of massive population transfers employed by Sancheirev, yet Amalek lives as a distinct, identifiable entity! Reb Chaim explained that Amalek is therefore a conceptual category and not merely an historical reality: One who behaves as an Amalekite can achieve the status of Amalek. Reb Chaim's grandson, Rav Yosef Dov Soloveitchik, applied this teaching to the Nazis, who adopted an Amalekian worldview, unfortunately with more success than the historical Amalekites.

What we have, then, is a more complex formula than was originally assumed: Someone born an Amalekite can, through his actions, lose his Amalekian status, and someone born to any other

---

1   See *Divrei Hashkafa* (Jerusalem: Elinor Publications, 1992), p. 217, and *Fate and Destiny* (Haboken, N.J.: Ktav Publications, 1990), p. 65, 92–95.

nation — perhaps even Jewish — can achieve the status of Amalek. The original "racist" complexion of the law seems to have dissipated upon analysis. The only Amalekite who is to be killed is the individual who adheres to the teachings of his ancestors (even the presumption that an Amalekite remains true to the Amalekite belief system suffices to warrant execution). Upon acceptance of at least the Noachide laws, this status changes.

The tradition that former Amalekites studied Torah in B'nei Brak has a fascinating postscript. Who is referred to in this passage? The Ein Yaakov cites a tradition that the person referred to was Rav Shmuel bar Shilat. Other sources identify the descendant with B'nei Brak's most famous citizen, none other than Rabbi Akiva! We know that Rabbi Akiva lived in B'nei Brak from a celebrated passage in the Haggadah of Pesach. The Talmud also tells us that B'nei Brak was the home of Rabbi Akiva:

> "Justice, justice shall you pursue" (*Shoftim* 16:20) — This means, follow the scholars to their academies; e.g., Rabbi Eliezer to Lod, Rabbi Yochanan ben Zakkai to Beror Chayil, Rabbi Yehoshua to Peki'in, Rabban Gamliel [II] to Yavneh, Rabbi Akiva to B'nei Brak.
>
> *(Sanhedrin 32b)*

We also know that Rabbi Akiva was either himself a convert or a child of converts:

> We can hardly appoint Rabbi Akiva because perhaps Rabban Gamliel will bring a curse on him because he has no ancestral merit.
>
> *(Berachot 27b; see comments of Rav Nissim Gaon)*[1]

Based on the combination of these sources, there are those[2] that understand that the descendant of Haman who learned and taught Torah in B'nei Brak was, in fact, Rabbi Akiva.

There is a certain poetic justice in members of Amalek casting

---

1   See *Yerushalmi, Berachot* 32b.
2   See Rav Mordechai Cohen, *Ishim U'Tekufot* (Israel: Yad Rama, 1977), p. 84–91.

their lot with the Jewish people, converting and following the word of God. The Talmud describes the origin of the tribe of Amalek in a conversion that didn't happen:

> What is the purpose of [writing], "And Lotan's sister was Timna" (*Bereishit* 36:22)? Timna was a royal princess, as it is written, "*alluf* [duke] Lotan, *alluf* [duke] Timna"; and by "*alluf*" an uncrowned ruler is meant. Desiring to become a proselyte, she went to Avraham, Yitzchak, and Yaakov, but they did not accept her. So she went and became a concubine to Elifaz the son of Esav, saying, "I would rather be a servant to this people than a mistress of another nation." From her descended Amalek who afflicted Israel. Why so? Because they should not have rejected her.
>
> *(Sanhedrin 99b)*

Timna was an aristocratic woman who wished to join the Jewish people. Avraham, Yitzchak, and Yaakov rejected her. She chose what seemed to her the next best thing and joined Esav, reasoning that Esav was from the same family. Timna's union with Esav is thus reminiscent of the Midrashic accounts of Hagar's relationship with Avraham: She, too, was a descendant of royalty. Evidently, the "*beit din*" of our forefathers felt that Timna should not be accepted into the fold; perhaps they sensed that Amalek would emerge from her. The Talmud, though, concludes that had they accepted her, Amalek would never have emerged.

Our observations began with the stipulation that the Torah portion regarding Amalek is one of the most important of the yearly cycle, and that we are enjoined from generation to generation to wipe out the nefarious memory of our archenemy. At this point, we have come to appreciate another option the Torah offers for "wiping out the memory of Amalek": Teach them Torah and correct the mistake and injustice perpetrated against Timna long ago.

Jews have forged a covenant with the Almighty to rid the world of evil. Amalek symbolizes and represents the manifestation of evil. These insidious forces at times take form in people, and horrific actions are perpetrated. At times these forces possess the hearts of good men. At times we need to go on "search and destroy missions" to rid the world of evil. At times we need to look into our own hearts. There is, however, another path to rid the world of evil; it can be eradicated by replacing it with good. In the words of Rav Avraham Yitzchak Kook:

> Pure tzaddikim don't complain about evil; rather, they increase righteousness. They don't complain about heresy; rather, they increase belief. They don't complain about ignorance; rather, they increase wisdom.
>
> *(Orpelei Tohar, p. 39)*

Purim

The Heroism of Esther

The role of Esther, the undisputed heroine of the story of Purim, is somewhat troubling. We are told of a beauty contest run by pagans and heathen; how was it that Mordechai allowed Esther's participation? Surely Esther was taken against her will, as the verses indicate and the Talmud stresses. Nonetheless, why did Esther not choose martyrdom over life in the palace or harem? This question takes on more poignancy when we recall the Talmudic teaching that the First Temple was destroyed due to lack of adherence to basic Jewish doctrine: The three cardinal sins that Judaism was to eradicate— murder, idolatry, and sexual immorality — were rampant.

> By a majority vote, it was resolved in the upper chambers of the house of Nit'zah in Lod that in every [other] law of the Torah, if a man is commanded: "Transgress and you will not suffer death" he may transgress and not suffer death, excepting idolatry, incest [which includes adultery], and murder.
>
> *(Sanhedrin 74a)*

> Why was the first Sanctuary destroyed? Because of three [evil] things which prevailed there: idolatry, immorality, and bloodshed.
>
> *(Yoma 9b)*

Esther might have made the argument that had she given up her life, refusing to succumb to the sexual immorality of the "beauty contest," perhaps she could have brought about some type of rectification for the fallen Temple. Nevertheless, upon the advice of Mordechai, she was encouraged to participate as a passive victim. The only advice that he gave her was not to reveal her national identity.

> So it came to pass, when the king's command and his decree were heard, and when many girls were gathered together in Shushan the capital, to the custody of Heigai, that Esther was brought also to the king's palace, to the custody of Heigai, guardian of the women. And the girl pleased him, and she won his favor; and he quickly gave her her ointments and her appointed portions, and seven maids, chosen to be to given her, from the king's palace; and he advanced her and her maids to the best place in the harem. Esther had not declared her people nor her country; for Mordechai had charged her that she should not tell.
>
> *(Esther 2:8–10)*

From a legalistic Jewish perspective we can understand Mordechai's instructions: Jewish law recognizes that a rape victim is not expected to give up her life, as she is considered a passive victim who unwillingly transgresses one of the three cardinal laws (*Sanhedrin* 74b). On the other hand, any desecration, even of a more minor offense, if publicly known, becomes a desecration of God's name and therefore would also require martyrdom. This would explain Mordechai's insistence that Esther conceal her heritage, not just from the king, but from the Jewish community as well.

The argument in favor of martyrdom is compelling on a psychological level as well: The martyr is assured respect by coreligionists in this world and an exalted status in the next. This, coupled with an act of defiance against the enemy, seems like a combination too good to turn down. Yet Mordechai does not allow Esther to take this course of action. Later in the megillah, when the nefarious plans of Haman become known, Mordechai instructs Esther to go in to see the king. This uninvited entrance to the throne room of a paranoid despot could result in her death, and indeed Esther hesitates. However, perhaps we can understand her hesitation on a different level. If she enters the throne room willingly, thus initiating contact with Achashveirosh, she is no longer passive. Her halachic status would be transformed from that of victim to participant, and she would be then be required to offer her life.

On the other hand, the existence of the entire Jewish community hangs in the balance. She must go. The Talmud describes the pathos of the situation, and the implications for Esther's erstwhile marriage to Mordechai:

> "Go, gather together all the Jews...which is not according to the custom" (*Esther* 4:16) — Rabba said: "[She said], 'It will not be according to the custom of every other day. Till now [I have associated with Achashveirosh] under compulsion, but now I will do so of my own will. And if I perish, I perish. As I am lost to my father's house, so I shall be lost to you.' "
>
> *(Megillah 15a)*

After consensual contact with Achashveirosh, Esther will no longer have any possibility to remain Mordechai's wife. Rav Tzadok HaKohen (*Takanat HaShavin*, p. 17) sees another aspect of Esther's hesitation: If Esther seduces the king, she will forfeit her share in the World to Come! Her response to Mordechai's directions, "As I am lost, I am lost" (*Esther* 4:16), refers to her halachic situation: Just as she may lose her life in this world, she risks losing her share in the next one.

Rav Tzadok stresses that a person must be willing to "love God with all their heart and all their soul," even if it means giving up one's soul. This is true love of God. How ironic! Had Esther given her life rather than spend even one night in the palace, she would have been a martyr deserving an exalted share in the World to Come; now, having given up her body, she faces the possibility of her soul being wiped out.

The more we think about Esther the more we appreciate the sadness of her life. Orphaned as a child, she was married, but torn away from her husband, forced to live a life of secrecy, and distanced from her people. In the Talmud, Esther is compared to *ayelet hashachar*, the first ray of light in the morning (*Yoma* 29a). The psalm of *Ayelet HaShachar*, Psalm 22, is dedicated to her:

> My God, my God, why have You forsaken me? Why are You so far from helping me, despite my cries? My Lord, I cry in the daytime, but You do not respond, and in the night I have no rest. But You are holy, enthroned by the praises of Israel.
>
> *(Tehillim 22:2–4)*

The Midrash expands on this idea:

> "My God, my God, why have You forsaken me?" — My Lord at the [splitting of] the sea, my Lord at Sinai, why have you forsaken me? Why has the order of the world changed concerning me? The order of the mothers? With regard to our mother Sarah, she was held captive by Pharaoh one night and he and his whole household were struck with a plague...but I have been placed in the bosom of this wicked man all these years, and for me You do no miracles. "My God, my God, why have You forsaken me?"
>
> *(Midrash Tehillim, Buber edition, 22:16)*

In the time of Esther, some "rules" had changed. The Divine grace which had been felt since God spoke to Avraham had disappeared. It was a time when God was "hidden." Esther is not saved by a miracle or a plague. Esther is left alone. She realizes what she must do for her people, and her response is telling: She instructs Mordechai to gather the nation to pray and fast for her. Her identity will thereby become known in the Jewish community, but by this point that is no longer an issue. If she is to become a willing participant, it no longer matters if the people know who she is. Forfeiting her "passive victim" status wipes out her hope for a share in the World to Come, regardless of the public or private nature of her transgressions. In fact, her plan cannot succeed if it is carried out secretly: for the plan to be successful, the Jewish community must join together.

Mordechai is somewhat taken aback by her suggestion to institute a fast, as the Midrash explains:

> "And fast for me for three days" (*Esther* 4:16) — the thirteenth, fourteenth, and fifteenth of Nissan.
>
> Mordechai said to her, "But the third day is Pesach!"
>
> She said to him, "Tzaddik of Israel, if there is no Israel, why do we need Pesach?"
>
> ...And Mordechai went and abolished [for that year] the first day of Pesach and made it into a fast.
>
> *(Otzar Midrashim, Eisenstein edition, p. 51)*

Esther insisted that the people fast for three days prior to her entering the chamber of the king. Pesach would not be celebrated that year, as if to say that when the Jewish world hangs in the balance and she herself is about to lose her portion in the World to Come, there is no place for a festive celebration of freedom. This source highlights the antinomian aspect of Esther's plight and destiny. A full understanding of her actions can reveal the depth of the message of megillah.

Esther's behavior was motivated by pure love — of God, and of her fellow Jews. Despite her tragic circumstances, she did not lose faith or hope. The Midrash tells us that while turning to God, Esther stresses:

> Master of the universe, you have given me three commandments — *niddah*, challah, and candles. Even though I am in the house of this evil man, I have not broken one of them.
>
> *(Midrash Tehillim, Buber edition, 22:16)*

Imagine the heroism of Esther: she would prepare for the systematic rape perpetrated on her body by going to the *mikveh*. Her body was taken, but her soul was intact and pure. Now she makes the decision that she must blemish that soul for the sake of God and her people. Rav Tzadok concludes that Esther did not lose her share in the World to Come because her action was a "sin for the sake of Heaven." The Talmud teaches that a sin performed for the sake of Heaven is greater than a mitzvah performed with wrong intention.

> Ulla said: "Both Tamar and Zimri committed adultery. Tamar committed adultery and gave birth to kings and prophets. Zimri committed adultery and on his account many tens of thousands of Israel perished." Rabbi Nachman ben Yitzchak said: "A transgression performed with good intention is better than a precept performed with evil intention."
>
> *(Nazir 23b)*

The Talmud teaches that *teshuvah* motivated by love of God is so profound that it can transform a sin into a mitzvah. Perhaps a "sin performed for the sake of Heaven" is another expression of the same idea.

Obviously this concept of justified sin is dangerous territory. All sorts of people justify their sins without going so far as to convince themselves that in actuality they are performing a mitzvah. According to our Sages, the conditions needed to qualify as a sin performed for the sake of Heaven are twofold: Number one, the intention must be to save the entire Jewish people. Number two, no personal gain or enjoyment should be involved. Esther's actions fulfilled both conditions. (Other commentaries[1] add a third condition: a rabbi, *beit din*, or prophet must have given the order to perform that particular sin, as in the case of Esther and Mordechai.)

When she decided on her course of action, Esther did not know how things would turn out. She performed an incredible act of *chesed*, "with all her heart and soul." Perhaps this fits in with the theme articulated by the prophet:

---

1   See Rav Yechezkel Landau, *Responsa Noda BeYehudah*, first edition, section 161.

It was your *chesed* I desired, and not your offerings.

(Hoshea 6:6)

Had Esther chosen the path of martyrdom, it would have taught the wrong lesson. God neither wants nor needs our sacrifices. Instead, Esther teaches a different lesson, the idea that *chesed* is more important than sacrifice, and that a pure mind is at the core of the service of God. Esther's pure mind, coupled with her love of God, saved the Jewish people from annihilation. Perhaps the Fast of Esther, commemorated annually on the day before Purim rather than at its original time, on Pesach, is meant to remind us of the sadness of Esther's plight, of the sacrifices she made to teach us this lesson.

The *Zohar* teaches that Yom Kippur is "a day like Purim," from the play on words where Yom Kippur is called "Yom Kippurim." The association seems obscure, these days seeming so different both in external practice and internal mood. Kabbalistic sources connect Yom Kippur and Purim to the two aspects of *teshuvah*. Yom Kippur is permeated by fear of God, a type of *teshuvah* which, while quite effective, is not the highest level of religious experience. Love of God outshines fear of God, and Purim represents the joy born of love of God, *teshuvah* motivated by love. The basis of this teaching comes from Esther, whose love was so profound that she was prepared to sacrifice all. This is the joy we seek on Purim.

In a sense, Yom Kippur offers us an easier way of reaching God: Fear of God is relatively simple to achieve. But the *avodah* of Purim — reaching out to God via love — is real *avodah*, service of God. Only after Esther taught us how to love, taught us how to perform *chesed* for others, could the Temple be rebuilt. Now we understand why the Second Temple, built on a foundation of the *chesed* of Esther, could not exist in a time of groundless hatred. Mordechai and Esther attempted to teach the Jewish people love, *chesed*, and brotherhood, by establishing Purim's mitzvot of giving gifts, "*mishloach manot ish l're'ehu*" and "*matanot l'evyonim.*" The Talmudic teaching that in the future, when all other holidays are forgotten, Purim will remain, takes on new importance in light of its message of love. Purim is the holiday which reveals the hidden, the essence of Judaism: love of God and love of man.

Subject Index

acts of kindness, 229

Adam, 224; and Chavah, 150; Adam's beauty, 286

Adler, Rav Natan, 217

akeidah, 212f

Alon, Gedalyahu, 28

am ha'aretz, 199

Amalek, 113, 127, 164, 301

Amidah, 78, 80

angels, 63, 218

Arizal, 221, 264

atchalta d'geulah, 76

avot, 219

ba'al teshuvah, 240

Bar Kochva, 28, 87ff, 178

Bar Koziba, 88

bat kol, 143

beauty, 291f

beinoni, 225

Beit HaMikdash, 114

Beitusi, 253

belief in one God, 147

binding of Yitzchak. *See akeidah*

birkat hachamah, 74

birth of Messiah, 181, 189

blood, 31, 33

blood libels, 85

B'nei Brak, 305

boils, 34

Book of Death, 222

Book of Life, 222, 234

burning bush, 279

cattle, 34

Chafetz Chaim, 5, 237

Chanukah, 15, 279, 288f

Chavah, 150

Chavel, notes on Ramban, 216

chesed, 64, 67, 69, 77, 228, 314

Chevron, 161

Chizkuni, 34

circumcision, 289

coat of many colors, 5, 179

coincidence, 128

cosmology, 7

Creation, thought of, 208ff

cup of Eliyahu, 49

custom, 168

darkness, 35, 65f

David, 69
Davidic dynasty, 112
Days of Awe, 185
death, 219; of firstborn, 35; of Moshe, 267
Defano, Rav Menachem Azarya, 168
dew, 219
divine cloud, 280
Divine Name, 232
divinity, 141f
doorposts, 65, 67

Eden, 102, 150, 218, 256, 258
Egyptian immorality, 42, 57
Eliyahu, 16, 102, 107
Elokim, 209
Elon, Rav Mordechai, 200
Emek Berachah, 224f
erev Shabbat, 113
Esav, 131f
eschatological, 73, 186
Ethiopians, 139
eved Hashem, 225
evil, 9
evil inclination, 134
exile, 150
Exodus, 62

fear of God, 214
first fruits, 136
First Temple, 194
firstborn, 45
forbidden relations, 171

forty-nine levels of impurity, 69
fratricide, 150
free will, 32, 36
frogs, 33

Garden of Eden. *See* Eden
gate of the city, 62
Gehinnom, 103
gevurah, 77, 216
Givat Ze'ev, 115
Givon, 115
glory of God, 280
golden calf, 36, 46, 152, 254, 279, 291
golden calves, 175
Greek, 284
Greeks, 288f, 290, 292
groundless hatred, 5, 91, 314

haftarah, 140
Haggadah, 22, 24, 305
Hai Gaon, Rav, 72
hail, 34
HaYerushalmi KiPhshuto, 24
Hell, 103
hester panim, 123, 189f
Hevel, 179
Hoffman, Rav Dovid Tzvi, 24
Holocaust, 189
Holy of Holies, 249

idolatry, 36, 148, 152
Imrei Emet, 138
ingathering of the exiles, 191

intellect, 210

jealousy, 175
Jewish calendar, 147
Judeo-Christian, 27ff
judges, 62
judgment, 210
justice, 73

Kahn, Rav Yair, 257, 279
Kararites, 251
Kasher, Rav Menachem, 24, 49
Kayin, 150, 179
ketoret, 250
Kever Shmuel HaNavi, 110, 115
kohein gadol, 249ff
Kook, Rav Avraham Yitzchak, 138, 307
korban Pesach, 17, 27, 67
Kotzker Rebbe, 104

Lag BaOmer, 97ff, 110
lashon hara, 5
lice, 33
Lichtenstein, Rav Aharon, 301
light, 9
locusts, 35
love, 159
luchot, 154
Luria, Rav Dovid, 24
Luria, Rav Shlomo, 15

ma'apilim, 165f
Maharshal, 15

marriage, 159
martyrdom, 308
matan Torah, 139
Mechilta, 23ff
mercy, 73, 209f
Merkavah, 140
Messiah, 11f, 21, 28, 47, 71, 87ff, 177f, 192, 234
Messiah, son of Yosef 177
Messianic Age, 15f, 57, 69, 233
metaphysical, 290
mikveh, 312
minhag, 168
mitzvah, 223ff
Moabites, 70
monotheism, 147f
moon, 6ff, 289
Moreh HaNevuchim, 4, 210, 231
Mount Sinai, 219, 279
mussaf, 6
mysteries of creation, 208

nations of the world, 259
ne'ilah, 258
new moon, 289
Nile, 31
Nine Days, 147
Ninth of Av. *See* Tishah B'Av
Nitzavim, 185
Noach, 220
Noachide laws, 62, 303

Omer, 83
oral Torah, 250

original sin, 150

Parashat Devarim, 147
Parashat Ha'azinu, 194
Parashat Va'Etchanan, 147
Passover. *See* Pesach
Pe'or, 149
Pesach, 22ff, 61, 312
Pharisees, 250
Pharaoh, 31ff, 38ff
physical realm, 263
plague of darkness. *See* darkness
primogeniture, 43
primordial light, 281
Promised Land, 266
prophecy, 36
punishment, 239
Purim, 15,123ff
purkan, 15

Rabbeinu Yonah, 226, 229f
Rabbi Akiva's students, 178
Racanati, 213
rain, 263
Rambam, 32, 223, 231, 235, 254
Ramchal, 237
Redemption, 21, 80, 193, 228, 231
Resurrection, 73, 77ff, 219
Revelation, 36, 119, 139, 143, 151, 212, 257
Rosh Chodesh, 3
Rosh HaShanah, 19, 185, 207,
224, 222, 227
Ruth, 69
Sadducees, 250
Salanter, Rav Yisrael, 223
Samaritans, 139
second Tablets of the Law, 170
Second Temple, 194, 279, 284
Sefer HaYashar, 195
serpent, 45, 131, 150
seventeenth of Tammuz, 154
sexual misbehavior, 151
Sha'arei Tzedek, 7
shaatnez, 179
Shabbat, 18, 113, 289
Shabbat HaGadol, 15
Shavuot, 83, 126, 134f
Shechinah, 10, 94, 154, 167, 189, 231, 279, 281, 284ff, 293
Shema, 147, 202
Shmuel HaNavi, 110
Shmuelevitz, Rav Chaim, 223f
Shneerson, Rabbi Menachem M., 91
shofar, 215, 258
Simchat Beit HaSho'eivah, 262
sin, 233; of Adam, 297; offering, 3ff
Sinai, 221, 257, 270
sinat chinam, 5, 91, 314
Sokoloff, 247
Soloveitchik, Rav Chaim, 304
Soloveitchik, Rabbi Yosef Dov (the Beit HaLevi), 124

Soloveitchik, Rabbi Yosef Dov (twentieth century), 15, 45, 48, 56, 89, 123, 158, 160, 188, 236f, 240, 272, 284, 304

souls, new, used, 189

Sperber, Rabbi Professor Daniel, 110

spiritual realm, 263

spy, 156

suffering, 229f

Tablets of the Law, 169

Tabori, Joseph, 137, 139, 252

Temple, 126, 169

Ten Tribes, 186

tenth of Nissan, 18

teshuvah, 185, 192, 223ff, 229f, 236ff, 239, 248; from fear, 314; from love, 314

Tishah B'Av, 156ff, 172f

thought of Creation, 208

Torah readings, 147

Tree of Knowledge of Good and Evil, 131, 218f, 254

tree of life, 231

Tzadok HaKohein of Lublin, Rav, 3, 19, 131, 168, 181, 292, 310

tzedakah, 228ff, 231f

tzelem Elokim, 210

tzidduk hadin, 194

unicorn, 294

Vilna Gaon, 9, 18, 179

Wasserman, Rav Elchanan, 237f

wild animals, 34

World to Come, 310

Yaakov, 131f; Yaakov's beauty, 296

Yerushalayim, 109, 126, 262

Yom Kippur, 19, 168, 171, 203, 222, 224, 227f, 249ff, 314

Yosef, 5, 49f, 291f, 296

Zeman Matan Torateinu, 137ff

Source Index

Mishnah
Rosh Hashanah 1:1, 207
Sukkah: 2:6, 235; 5:1, 262
Ta'anit 4:1, 109, 153f, 168f,
    174, 257
Sanhedrin 10:3, 156
Avot 1:1, 270
Eduyot 2:9, 85

Talmud
Berachot: 6b, 180; 7a, 239; 21b,
    141; 27b, 305; 28a, 304; 29a,
    252; 32b, 275; 35b, 102;
    47b, 273; 59a, 108; 60b, 201;
    61b, 202, 255
Shabbat: 21b, 284, 288f; 33b,
    101ff; 80b, 141; 86b, 83,
    137; 87a, 138; 87b, 16, 112;
    88a, 120, 122; 88b, 78, 219,
    257; 118b, 21; 127b, 196ff;
    146a, 219
Eiruvin: 54a, 153; 54b, 270f
Pesachim: 36a, 71; 49b, 93, 199;
    68b, 136
Rosh HaShanah: 16a, 262; 25a,

10; 26a, 255; 29a, 164;
10b–11a, 73, 208; 11a, 16,
60; 16a, 215; 16b, 222; 17a,
224; 32b, 222
Yoma: 4b, 281; 9a, 91, 176, 252;
9b, 150, 283, 308; 18a, 251;
18b, 251f; 19b, 253f; 28b,
61; 29a, 311; 68b, 170; 69b,
37; 70b, 170; 86b, 191, 228
Sukkah: 28a, 104; 45b, 100; 52a,
177f; 52b, 12; 55b, 260
Ta'anit: 9a, 244; 16a, 217; 25b,
232f; 26a, 257; 26b, 109,
153f, 168f, 174; 30b, 169;
30b–31a, 171f
Megillah: 9b, 293; 15a, 310; 16b,
176; 17b, 76; 24b, 141; 25a,
141; 29a, 190; 30b–31a, 139;
31a, 72
Moed Katan 22b, 267
Chagigah: 9b, 235; 11b, 141,
208; 12b, 78; 16a, 108
Yevamot: 22b, 235; 62b, 84, 97;
63b, 189; 72b, 246; 76b, 70
Ketubot: 62b, 199; 77b, 100;
84b, 246; 104a, 245

Nedarim 40a, 87f, 245
Nazir 23b, 313
Sotah: 33a, 252; 34b, 161f; 47a–b, 252
Gittin: 47a, 240f; 57b, 302f
Kiddushin: 39b, 239; 40a, 211; 40b, 238; 49b, 293; 82a, 61
Bava Kama: 117a, 245
Bava Metzia: 58b, 245; 84a, 242ff; 85b, 248
Bava Batra: 17a, 134; 75a, 267; 134a, 141
Sanhedrin: 7a, 152; 17a, 163; 32b, 305; 38b, 150; 58b, 248; 68a, 268; 74a, 149, 308f; 93b, 87; 96b, 302f; 97b, 74f, 100; 98b, 189; 99a, 90; 99b, 306; 102a, 180
Makkot: 10b, 246; 24a–b, 202
Shevuot 9a, 6
Avodah Zarah: 3a, 259; 3b, 265; 8a, 294f; 18a, 194
Zevachim 54b, 112f, 294
Menachot: 65a, 253; 68b, 88; 93b, 245
Chullin: 5a, 21; 60b, 7; 92a, 100; 125a, 243
Bechorot 58a, 92
Temurah 16a, 268
Me'ilah 17a , 289

Talmud Yerushalmi
Berachot 5:2, 79
Bikurim 3:3, 171

Terumot 8:4, 247
Rosh HaShanah 1:3, 225
Pesachim: 10:1, 49; 10:4, 23, 25f
Ta'anit: 1:1, 75; 4:5, 87f
Chagigah 2:2, 289
Sanhedrin 1:2, 105

Tosefta
Yoma 1:8, 253
Shavuot 3:6, 154
Arachin 1:4, 137
Menachot: 13:22, 90f; 13:23, 90
Avot D'Rabbi Natan ch. 6, 93

Midrash Halachah
Mechilta D'Rabbi Yishmael Bo, Mesechta DePischa 13, 42
Mechilta Mesechta D'Amalek 2, 302
Sifra Acharei Mot 8, 57

Midrash Aggadah
Bereishit Rabbah: 1:1, 127; 1:4, 187; 2:4, 289; 4:6, 285; 12:15, 209; 16:4, 289; 35:2, 99, 100; 41:6, 65; 42:8, 64; 44:17, 289; 48:14, 270; 50:11, 69; 51:6, 67; 55:7, 217; 56:1, 214; 56:1–2, 213; 56:3, 221; 56:4, 221; 56:8, 218; 61:3, 84; 66:4, 260; 84:14, 162; 85:1, 69; 89:3, 54; 98:18, 291

Shemot Rabbah: 5:7, 35, 38, 45; 11:3, 34; 13:3, 32f; 15:12, 61; 15:15, 45; 15:16, 289; 15:27, 41; 16:2, 18; 16:3, 17; 18:5, 41; 19:7, 47; 27:6, 130; 41:7, 152f

Vayikra Rabbah: 13:5, 289; 14:1, 70; 15:9, 289; 23:7, 58

Bemidbar Rabbah: 1:8, 217; 3:1, 100; 4:8, 46f; 10:1, 236; 14:3, 108; 14:5, 4; 16:2, 156; 16:1, 269; 17:3, 166f; 21:14, 272

Devarim Rabbah: 2:14, 19, 290; 11:10, 194; Lieberman edition, *Parashat Ha'azinu*, 223

Shir HaShirim Rabbah: 7:8, 37; 7:16, 90

Kohelet Rabbah: 3:12, 246; 11, 84

Eichah Rabbah: Prologue 33, 172f; 2:4, 87, 89; Buber edition, 88

Aggadat Bereishit 68, 181

Midrash Tanchuma: Chayei Sarah 8, 88; *Toldot* 19, 79; *Vayechi* 13, 289; *Ancient Tanchuma Bo* 18, 44; *Tetzaveh* 9, 113; *Ki Teitzei* 10, 130; *Ki Teitzei* 11, 302

Midrash Tehillim: Buber 22:16, 311f; 68:9, 217f; 136:6, 16, 44

Otzar Midrashim Eisenstein: p. 51, 312; p. 146, 77; p. 162, 217; p. 186, 289

Pirkei D'Rabbi Eliezer: 3–7, 208; 33, 79; 42, 241f; 51, 113; 30 or 31, 216, 218f

Pesikta D'Rav Kahana: 3, 302; 26, 227

Pesikta Rabbati 14, 93f; 33, 289; *Ish Shalom* 40, 224

Seder Olam 5, 112

Tanna D'Vei Eliyahu Zuta 22, 84

Yalkut Shimoni: Yehoshua 10:22, 113; *Chavakuk* 3:564, 113; *Mishlei* 929, 5; *Kohelet* 989, 84

Zohar

Bereishit: 20b, 9; 28b, 189; 36b, 47b, 15; 71b, 108; 104a, 232; 130b, 79; 134b, 187; 142b, 296f; 180a, 296; 192b, 11; *HaShmatot* 205, 105f; *HaShmatot* 252, 7

Shemot: 28b, 79; 45b, 44; 65a, 129; 135a, 179; 149a, 281f 286; 269a, 287; 204a, 15

Vayikra: 15a, 106; 34b, 187; 70a, 187; 70a, 58; 113b, 232

Devarim: 297b, 195

Tikunei Zohar: 40b, 15; 100

Gaonim and *Rishonim*

Iggeret Rav Sherira Gaon, Sephardic recencion, 85

Krakowsky, Rabbi Menachem,
  Avodat HaMelech, 237
Lechem Mishneh, Hilchot
  Teshuvah 3:3, 223
Machzor Vitri: 259, 15; 424, 92
Or Zarua, 200
Otzar HaGeonim: Megillah, p. 64,
  72; *Yevamot* 62b, p. 141, 85
Ra'avad, *Hichot Melachim* 11:3,
  87
Rabbeinu Chananel, *Rosh*
  Hashanah 17a, 225
Rabbeinu Tam: *Bava Metzia* 84a,
  240; *Ketubot* 62b, 240
Rabbeinu Yonah, *Sha'arei*
  Teshuvah 1:47, 229
Rambam: Commentary to *Pirkei*
  Avot 1:3, 250; *Haggadah*, 24;
  Hilchot Chanukah 3:3, 284;
  Hilchot Issurei Bi'ah 12:17,
  303; 21:8, 57; *Hilchot*
  Matanot Aniyim 10:1, 228,
  233; *Hilchot Melachim* 11:1,
  192; 6:4, 303; 9:14, 62; 11:3,
  87, 91f, 95; *Hilchot Teshuvah*
  1:1, 237; 1:4, 229; 2:2, 222ff;
  3:3, 238; 3:4, 227; 7:5, 192,
  227; 7:6, 235; Introduction
  to *Mishneh Torah*, 271;
  Moreh HaNevuchim 3:8, 210;
  3:46, 4; 3:53, 231; *Sefer*
  HaGeulah, 75
Ran, *Nedarim* 40a, 245
Rashbam, *Pesachim* 112a, 92

Rashi: *Avot* 1:1, 268; *Bava*
  Metzia 84a, 241, 243; *Chullin*
  5a, 21; *Sanhedrin* 36a, 266;
  96a, 245; *Shevuot* 9a, 6;
  Sukkah 55b, 260; *Ta'anit*
  26b, 171, 179, 257
Rav Nissim Gaon, *Berachot* 27b,
  305
Ritva, *Kiddushin* 66a, 252
Sheiltot of Rav Achai Gaon,
  Parashat Shemot 40, 198
Tosafot: *Bava Batra* 113a, 92;
  Bechorot 58a, 92; *Eiruvin*
  65b, 240; *Ketubot* 62b, 240;
  Kiddushin 39b, 224;
  Menachot 30a, 267; *Pesachim*
  112a, 92; *Rosh HaShanah*
  27a, 73, 208; *Shabbat* 87b,
  16; 88a, 121; *Ta'anit* 16a,
  217; *Yevamot* 57a, 240

Halachic Works

Aruch HaShulchan, 85, 245
Birkei Yosef 493:10, 85
Biur Halachah, Orach Chaim
  430, 18
Chatam Sofer, Responsa Yoreh
  Dei'ah, 138, 217
Chok Yaakov, Orach Chaim:
  493:3, 85; 494, 138
Daat Kohen, Responsa Yoreh
  Dei'ah 80, 138
Hegyonei Halachah, 223
Iggrot Moshe, Choshen Mishpat,

vol. 2, section 74, 245
Magen Avraham, Orach Chaim,
    18, 137
*Mateh Moshe,*15
Minchat Chinuch, mitzvah 364,
    237
Minchat Yitzchak: 3:38, 88;
    10:10, 109
Mishnah Berurah: 229:7, 74;
    292:6–8, 267; 551:2, 147;
    625:1, 263
Noda BeYehudah, 313
Piskei Teshuvah 551:2, 174
Radbaz 2:608, 110
Rama, *Orach Chaim* 430:1, 18
Sheiltot, Ha'Amek Sh'eilah, 198
Shulchan Aruch, Orach Chaim:
    229:2, 74; 292:2, 267; 493:1,
    84; 493:2, 111; 551:1, 147;
    580, 110
Taz, Orach Chaim, 18
Tur, Orach Chaim, 72
Tzitz Eliezer 15:4, 110
Yabia Omer, 15, 85
Yechaveh Daat, 171

Torah Commentary
Beit HaLevi, Shemot 19:5, 124;
    24:7, 124
Berlin, Rabbi Naftali Tzvi
    Yehudah (*Ha'Amek Davar*),
    Bemidbar 15:39, 239; Intro-
    duction of *Bereishit,* 195f;
    Shemot 15:1, 43

Chizkuni, Bemidbar 28:15, 4
Gur Aryeh, Shemot 19:17, 123
Hirsch, Rav Shimshon Rafael,
    Vayikra 23:21, 138
Ibn Ezra: *Bereishit* 6:11, 151;
    Devarim 33:5, 266; 4:41, 148;
    Shemot 34:19, 39; *Tehillim*
    135:8, 39
Kli Yakar, Vayikra 1:1, 294
Meshech Chochmah, Vayikra
    8:36, 5; 16:30, 5
Or HaChaim, Shemot 19:5, 123
Rabbeinu Bechaya: *Shemot*
    23:19; *Vayikra* 16:2, 256
Ramban: *Bereishit* 15:13, 40;
    Devarim 4:41, 148; Introduc-
    tion to *Shemot,* 257, 279;
    Shemot 7:3, 31, 36; *Shemot*
    19:13, 216
Rashi
    Bereishit: 1:1, 127; 13:14, 67;
        19:17, 67; 33:9–11, 133;
        36:3, 171; 45:14, 176
    Shemot: 4:23, 39; 9:14, 39;
        32:4, 291; 32:6, 153; 33:11,
        171
    Vayikra: 16:2, 249, 257; 16:4,
        255; 20:17, 69
    Bemidbar: 7:22, 4; 11:28, 163;
        13:2, 156
    Devarim: 9:18, 171; 11:19,
        142; 25:18, 113, 128; 26:16,
        131, 143; 33:5, 266
    Yeshayah 11:13, 178

Zecharyah 14:16, 261
Seforno: *Devarim* 7:9, 239;
    Shemot 4:21, 36
Tiferet Yehonatan, 190f
Torah Sheleimah, 104
Torah Temimah, 171

Sifrei Machshavah

Arizal, *Sefer HaLikuttim,* 221
Avodat HaKodesh 4:8, 8
Bnei Yissachar, Purim, 254
Chokrei HaZemanim, Rav Alter
    Hilovitz, 49, 91
Explorations: Creation, 209;
    "leap of faith," 212; *Parashat
    Noach,* 108; *Parashat
    Vayakhel,* 21; *Parashat
    Beha'alotcha,* 163; *Parashat
    Bo,* 95; *Parashat Vayigash,*
    176; *tzelem Elokim,* 210
Ha'Avot VeHashevatim,
    Avraham Korman, 217
Ishim U'Tekufot, Rav Mordechai
    Cohen, 305
Kedushat HaLevi on *Shemot,* 123f
Kochvei Or, Rav Yitzchak Blazer,
    223
Kovetz Maamarim, 238f
Maamar HaChochmah, 218
Mabit, *Beit Elokim,* 230
Maharal: *Ner Mitzvah,* 291;
    Tiferet Yisrael, 15; *Netivot
    Olam,* 235
Margoliot, Rav Reuven, Intro-
duction to *She'eilot
    U'Teshuvot Min HaShamayim,*
    200
Mesillat Yesharim, 237
Michtav Me'Eliyahu, Rav Eliyahu
    Dessler, 189
Nachman of Breslov, Rav:
    Likutei Maharan, 131, 294;
    Sichot Maharan, 142
Or Gedalyahu, Rav Gedalya
    Shor, 209
Orpelei Tohar, Rav Avraham
    Yitzchak Kook, 307
Pachad Yitzchak, Rav Yitzchak
    Hutner: Pesach, 239; Purim,
    226; Rosh HaShanah, 223,
    225, 238
Sefat Emet: 104; Chanukah, 290;
    Ki Tavo, 131; Shabbat
    HaGadol, 20
Shelah HaKadosh (Rabbi
    Yeshayah Horowitz), *Torah
    Or,* 292
Sichot for *Sefer Shemot,* Rav
    Avigdor Nebenzahl, 113
Sichot Mussar, Rav Chaim
    Shmuelevitz, 223
Sifrei HaPardes, Rav Yechiel Ep-
    stein, 21
Siftei Chaim, Rav Chaim
    Freidlander, 218
Soloveitchik, Rav Yosef Dov:
    Divrei Hashkafa 304; *Fate and
    Destiny,* 304; *Halakhik Man,*

248; *Harerei Kedem*, 236; *On Repentance*, 237; *Y'mei Zikaron*, 231
Tzadok HaKohen of Lublin, Rav: *Pri Tzaddik*, 19; *Resisei Lailah*, 131; *Takanat Hashavin*, 310; *Yisrael Kedoshim*, 168